THE
DA VINCI
FRAUD

Robert M. Price

THE
DA VINCI
FRAUD

Why the Truth Is Stranger Than Fiction

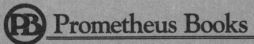

Prometheus Books

59 John Glenn Drive
Amherst, New York 14228-2197

Published 2005 by Prometheus Books

Inquiries should be addressed to
Prometheus Books
59 John Glenn Drive
Amherst, New York 14228–2197
VOICE: 716–691–0133, ext. 207
FAX: 716–564–2711
WWW.PROMETHEUSBOOKS.COM

09 08 07 06 05   5 4 3 2 1

Library of Congress Cataloging-in-Publication Data

Price, Robert M., 1954–.
    The Da Vinci fraud : why the truth is stranger than fiction / Robert M. Price.
        p. cm.
    Includes bibliographical references and index.
    ISBN 1–59102–348–3 (pbk. : alk. paper)
    1. Brown, Dan, 1964– Da Vinci code. 2. Mary Magdalene, Saint—
in literature. 3. Christian saints in literature. 4. Jesus Christ—in literature.
5. Christianity in literature. I. Title.

PS3552.R685434D3367 2005
813'.54—dc22

                                                                2005014004

Printed in the United States of America on acid-free paper

To Bob Funk and Char Majetovsky,
for a thousand kindnesses,
including suggesting I write this book!

CONTENTS

CONTENTS

Introduction
NOVEL IDEA

Those of us who teach and practice scientific biblical criticism often find ourselves engaged in an uphill battle against the misconceptions of popular, TV-preacher-driven fundamentalism. But we have our work cut out for us in another direction, too. For there exists a surprisingly large public who has notions about Jesus and the Bible that are every bit as ill founded and erroneous as those of the fundamentalists—only these people believe themselves to be, like us, scientific critics of scripture. They are avid readers of books that claim to "blow the lid off Christianity" by means of new discoveries, real or imagined. Don't get me wrong: In many ways, the work of biblical critics has threatened to blow the lid off traditional faith, or so our critics claim. But such is not our goal. Our aim is only to pursue the facts wherever they seem to lead. By contrast, much of the popular radical criticism is based squarely on fiction. This is not on purpose, mind you. It is just that these people, despite their admirable intellectual curiosity, just do not know how to separate fact from fiction. And in recent days their imaginations have been much stirred up by the best-selling novel *The Da Vinci Code* by Dan Brown. It is a fictional narrative, but its author claims it is based on fact. That, too, alas, is part of the fiction.

The novel begins with the murder of a curator at the Louvre. His body is discovered in a odd position, aping that of Leonardo's famous "Vitruvian Man" diagram, depicting a spread-eagled male form with double limbs, almost seeming to move like hands around a clock face. He has written a cryptic clue in his own blood. Eventually a pair of investigators plumb the mystery. They are Sophie, eventually revealed as the dead man's estranged granddaughter, and Robert Langdon, a symbolism expert from Harvard. Framed for the murder, they flee into France, seeking safe haven with Langdon's friend and colleague Professor Lee Teabing, a crippled savant steeped in the lore of the Holy Grail. He explains to them, and to the reader, that the grail was a coded symbol revealing (to insiders) and concealing (from outsiders) the fact of the royal bloodline of the Merovingian kings of France, who happen to be descendants of Jesus Christ and Mary Magdalene! This is important to the story because it develops that the slain curator, Sophie's grandfather, was one of the elite guardians of this secret, the latest Grand Master of the Priory of Sion, a secret society reaching all the way back to the Crusader-era Knights Templar. He must have been killed by zealous Catholics who wanted to prevent the secret from ever coming to public notice, as the news of a married, hence human, Jesus would explode the Church dogma of Jesus as a superhuman god, not a man. Teabing leads the pair out of France, a step ahead of the authorities, back to England, where the trio drops into one grail-related site after another, looking for clues. Shockingly, it turns out that the much-maligned Catholics, particularly the ultra-conservative Opus Dei group, had nothing to do with the killing or the intrigue. Instead, the whole affair has been engineered by none other than the learned Professor Teabing for ambitious reasons of his own! He has dedicated himself to finding the true grail (the mummified body of Mary Magdalene, as well as reams of secret gospel scrolls buried with her) at all costs. But he fails in his Promethean efforts, at the cost of his life. Langdon and Sophie, the latter now revealed as the current heir of Jesus Christ, live happily ever after, Langdon back in his cushy job at Harvard, Sophie with her long-lost grandmother in Scotland at her family's ancestral seat. They had first imagined the Magdalene trove to lie there, but instead Langdon discovers it lies concealed in the Louvre, where the whole adventure started out.

Every time a book like Dan Brown's *The Da Vinci Code* makes waves in the religious public, one can be sure it will call forth a raft of books trying to refute it. This is one of them. But most of these books tend to be rejoinders in behalf of the oppressive orthodoxy that Brown's novel attacks. They are defenses of the party line, cranked out by spin doctors for Mother Church. This book, however, is decidedly not one of *those*. No, though I myself am a loyal Episcopalian and a regular church-goer, my primary identity is that of a New Testament historian, and so my first duty is to the facts as far as I can discern them. Thus, I had my work cut out for me when I began to examine *The Da Vinci Code*, taking upon myself the task of clearing up the many serious errors Brown foists upon the reader as gospel truth (if you and he will forgive the expression).

I have tried to be as even-handed as possible, defending and explaining orthodox tradition where Brown has caricatured and vilified it, seconding him where he is right about its shortcomings, and frequently showing how the facts and possibilities may be much more extravagant than even he would lead readers to believe. This leads me to invoke the overcited old saw that the truth (in our case, the truth about Christian origins) is not only stranger than we think, but probably even stranger than we are capable of imagining. Dan Brown has not told you the half of it! I think I have.

STYLE IF NOT SUBSTANCE

The Da Vinci Code is certainly a page turner. Its brisk narrative is full of twists and turns, and the reader's perseverance is frequently rewarded with deft turns of phrase, sparkling metaphors, and resonating observations, the stock in trade of an author who can show us not only what we did *not* know but also what we *did* know but were not *aware* of knowing. There is a real wisdom in such art. And yet the book has certain major shortcomings. This is worth mentioning, it seems to me, since some advocates of the book seem to regard it as such a masterpiece of fiction that all the gaffes and historical errors are worthwhile, needful grist for the mill. But the book does not deserve such exemption.

First, there is no real protagonist. The ostensible hero, Robert Langdon, also stars in Brown's previous novel, *Angels and Demons*. He is a Harvard professor of symbology. (Is there such a thing?) But that appears to be a pretty sedentary job. No Indiana Jones, our man Langdon seems merely an intranarrative incarnation of the reader. He is purely passive, figuring out occasional puzzles simply because the narrative requires them to be solved at this or that juncture before the action can get any further. The dutiful appearance of such solutions in the text at the appropriate point is often conveyed merely by means of italics and an exclamation mark, as if author Brown is cuing the reader, in the manner of a sitcom laugh track, to feel astonishment and a sense of (illusory) discovery.

Second, much of the resolution of the plot depends on a series of arbitrary mechanical reversals, with this or that character suddenly revealing unsuspected good or evil dimensions or hitherto-unhinted connections with other characters. Too much of it comes off as mere fiat on the part of the omnipotent author, who feels he has the right to jerk the reader around as he sees fit. By contrast, one expects of a more polished mystery that one shall have the opportunity to shift already-extant factors into different possible configurations (like a Rubik's Cube), so as to disclose an implicit thread of logic. The greater the number of surprises needed to make the plot work, the less organic, the less plausible, the story will seem. Like the "hero," the reader is reduced to near passivity.

Third, Brown trips over himself when he tries to supply a background of plausibility for the great secret that forms the prize that all the characters seek: the fanciful speculation that Jesus Christ and Mary Magdalene married and gave rise to the Merovingian dynasty of France with present-day heirs. Surely the whole premise of the book is that this supposed knowledge is a carefully guarded secret, in fact the secret of the ages. And yet we shortly discover that, thanks to books like Michael Baigent, Richard Leigh, and Henry Lincoln's *Holy Blood, Holy Grail*, this "secret" is well known among scholars! Apparently it is only the definitive proof (in the form of a trove of first-century documents salvaged from the ruins of the Jerusalem Temple) of the secret bloodline of Jesus and Mary that awaits disclosure. But all this comes across as confusing back-pedaling. What exactly is the secret? The truth or the proof? Brown seems to shift from one foot to the other and back again.

FRIENDLY INQUISITION

That said, my strictly literary criticism of Dan Brown's novel is done. The rest of the present book is dedicated to sifting the scholarly and pseudoscholarly assertions that pepper the text of *The Da Vinci Code*. Let it be clear from the outset that this book is not intended as a defense of what Dan Brown attacks. He aims a number of barbed harpoons at the beached whale of traditional, so-called orthodox Christianity. Some of the most astonishing contentions in the book are well founded, and here I distance my project from more orthodox attempts to refute Brown. My concern is just to scrub away the encrustation of bad research and misunderstanding that plagues *The Da Vinci Code*. To this end, my presentation distills a list of major topics addressed in Brown's novel and seeks to set forth a fresh statement of the case, criticizing Brown or seconding his motion as either may seem appropriate. It may well be that, in some cases, the truth is even stranger than Brown's fiction.

I will begin by surveying the context of Dan Brown's book, the shelf of research materials he seems to have used. ("'The royal bloodline of Jesus Christ has been chronicled in exhaustive detail by scores of historians.' He ran a finger down a row of several dozen books. Sophie tilted her head and scanned the list of titles."[1]) In a number of cases, his point is much better understood once one realizes where it came from and just what particular ax the original author was grinding. Sometimes Brown is not grinding the same one. Many of these books are interested in putting down ancient roots for a modern organization, the Freemasons, and they do it by tracing back their antecedents, in an imaginative way, to the medieval order of the Knights Templar. Often these authors find Jesus a helpful link for casting speculative lines back even further through the time stream. And more often than not, it is a married messiah that helps the most. This is where Mary Magdalene comes in. So I will spend a little time guiding the reader through the initiatory labyrinth of some of these fascinating books, pausing to indicate where *The Da Vinci Code* has drawn upon them. And this will give me the chance to take the first of a few looks, from different vantage points, at the central contention that Jesus and the Magdalene were husband and wife. This, too, is the stage of the game where the Da Vinci link becomes relevant, and it will be easy to show there is rather less on that score than meets the eye. Contra frequent claims, there is no real reason to suppose that a holy man like Jesus would have, or must have, been married. Beyond this, there is certainly no real evidence that he was married to Mary Magdalene or anyone else. Moreover, the Gnostic gospels often cited to make the point do not change that verdict.

INTRODUCTION

Dan Brown follows several of the same authors in viewing the enigmatic symbol of the Holy Grail as the tip of an iceberg of ancient conspiracy, concealing (or revealing, if you're one of the in-crowd) the secret bloodline of Jesus and Mary. To evaluate this claim, we will have to dig a little into the fascinating history of the grail romances. If mention of the grail triggers visions of the mothballs of literature, then put this book down and go rent the DVD of John Boorman's great 1981 film, *Excalibur*, and believe me, you will warm to the task! In any case, what we do know about the origin and evolution of the grail legend may make acceptance of the "Holy Blood, Holy Grail" theory no mere matter of faith. There are, it happens, facts to be checked. And we will see that the grail legend did not and cannot have originated as a blind for the secret of Jesus's bloodline for the simple reason that the grail of the legends was originally a celtic myth, the magical cauldron of Bran the Blessed that served up whatever delicacy one might wish. Subsequently this legend was superficially Christianized; only in later versions does the horn of plenty become the chalice of the Last Supper.

A number of Brown's predecessors have revived the ancient and perennially controversial theory that Jesus cheated death on the cross, taken down alive. Usually dubbed the Swoon Theory, this view is held today by all kinds of adherents, including members of the Ahmadiyya offshoot of Islam, writers of sensationalist pseudoscholarly books like Donovon Joyce's *The Jesus Scroll*, and serious biblical critics like Barbara Thiering and J. Duncan M. Derrett. Can there be something to this view, so shocking to some? I will try to show why the theory continues to fascinate and to command attention. To sneak a peak at my conclusion, I will try to show how the gospels do in fact

16

seem to betray traces of an earlier version of the passion story according to which Jesus escaped the cross still alive. Whether this is what actually happened to the historical Jesus is quite a different matter, as we can never really know his fate at all.

The Da Vinci Code and its predecessors are filled with (mostly confused) references to something called "Gnosticism," usually misleading the reader by making one think the word refers to any sort of minority freethinking variety of Christianity. The facts are otherwise, though considerably more astonishing. So I want to provide a brief account of what Gnosticism as an ancient religious philosophy was all about. But I also take seriously the wider reference people give the word today, and I will show how it is only once we understand what Gnosticism really was that we can see how very relevant it is to the modern religious outlook many of us share—much more than Dan Brown hints.

Constantine the Great, the first Christian emperor of Rome, comes in for quite the drubbing in Dan Brown's novel. Brown, as we will see, is just handing on the slander from the bad company he hangs with. Like sex education, church history is probably better learned in school than on the street from one's half-educated pals. So I hope you'll excuse a few of the facts in the case. Constantine, like many great historical figures, continues to provoke division and to arouse ire after he is gone. I'll admit he is no favorite of mine. On the other hand, fair is fair, and I find myself obliged to try to set the facts straight here, too. The story of Constantine's dramatic conversion at the Milvian Bridge, his beholding a cruciform vision in the sky, is no doubt a piece of propaganda, as Brown says. But this does not mean the emperor was a sneaky pagan. No, just the reverse: The legend masks the fact that he was, in all likelihood, born and raised a Christian! As such he had a lively interest in the theological debates of his day, and he blundered into them like a bull in a china shop, with historic results. But this is far from the silly caricature Brown promotes. And Constantine never had anything to do with determining the contents of the Bible.

Dan Brown's smearing of Constantine reaches over, like the mark of a tar brush, onto the history of Christology, the theological study of Jesus Christ. Was he God or man, or neither, or a bit of both, or something else? It is admittedly quite a subject, but not unmanageable or even boring, if one has the right guide (namely, me). And I'm afraid you are obliged in good conscience to hear someone set the record straight after reading Brown's hopelessly messed-up version of events and ideas. Do you think he is revealing the unknown truth under his literary microscope? You ain't seen nuthin' yet! The truth is much, much more colorful. Only the intellectually lazy will shun it. The official line on Jesus grew and developed, in its early stages, via widespread, popular, and informal debate. Once Christianity achieved an official status, the discussion was carried on through a series of ecumenical councils of bishops, starting with Nicea in 325 CE. And the resulting creeds, whether one accepts or rejects them, were certainly the product of careful and serious theological debate, not of conniving conspiracy by a cabal of ancient marketing executives, as Brown would have us believe.

Similarly, Brown's hack job on the selection of writings that make up the Bible is just fantasy. And why resort to fabrication, when the truth is so much more interesting? But he does, God bless him, raise an excellent question, one that millions of believers somehow never ask or are afraid to ask. But when it comes to the answer, Brown is like a student with a hangover, trying to bluff his way through an exam he hasn't studied for. Don't worry: You'll find the crib sheet here. You'll end up knowing how the whole process worked and what decisions were made (well or badly) by whom. You won't be able to take for granted the Bible's table of contents any more, even if you still agree with it. You will know what scholars have pretty much always known: that the canon was the product of a gradual and anonymous process of selection, made "official" by two local North African synods of bishops in the late fourth century. Their criteria were rather arbitrary and, to us, probably unconvincing.

One of Brown's throwaway comments that sent me running into far left field with the sun in my eyes is his claim that the early ecclesiastical censors waded through some eighty gospels before they weeded out seventy-six of them, like contestants on *American Idol*, for inclusion in the New Testament. In fact, there were very many gospels that failed to make the cut. All we have left of many is their bare titles, mentioned in this or that old treatise. But we do have a few whole texts of some, as well as substantial fragments of others. For a guide to these writings, as well as vibrant translations of every snippet of them, you couldn't do better than the brilliant Robert J. Miller's recent collection *The Complete Gospels*. But I feel I must provide a foretaste here, in the form of my own take on some of the most interesting pieces. So you'll find liner notes for some thirty of these rejected gospels. Make your own choice.

I will return to the character and history of Mary Magdalene in a big way for a couple of chapters. One will explore the theory, central to *The Da Vinci Code*, that she was an apostle in her own right, the fountainhead of secret teaching in underground Christianity. I am going to trace this tradition to its source in the Gospel of Matthew, where the women disciples meet the Risen Jesus. Since this appearance scene is Matthew's creation, based on a rewriting of Mark's gospel, I conclude that the tradition of the Apostle Mary is largely fictitious, a verdict disappointing to me and a reversal of my own previously published theories. My other Magdalene chapter will consider the question of whether Mary is perhaps a Christian version of the goddess common to many ancient religions, Israelite religion included. Here I think a pretty strong case may be made, but then such a Mary Magdalene character turns out to be more of a myth than a historical figure. This result may not be pleasing or theologically useful, but that should not deter us.

In all of this, I would like to play the role of the Bunko Squad, warning the uninformed and misinformed reader when he or she is being sold a bill of goods. But on the other hand, I have no vested interest in any institutional party line either, and I will be setting forth some notions that no readers should ascribe to biblical critics as a whole. Each of us thinks for ourselves, and I hope you, dear reader, will, too. As ever, my aim is a Socratic one. I seek not to make converts to any pet theories of my own. Rather, my goal, the goal of this book, is to provoke and to assist every reader to think things through and arrive at his or her own conclusion. Let a hundred flowers bloom!

NOTE

1. Dan Brown, *The Da Vinci Code* (New York: Doubleday, 2003), p. 253.

Chapter 1

CONSPIRACY OF DUNCES

Brown and the Pseudo-Templar Tradition

In view of the manifest shortcomings of *The Da Vinci Code* as a piece of narrative art, the book has achieved a remarkable degree of popularity. We may hope the reason for this is a suspicion on the part of many that there is a deeper truth to Christian origins than their churches have taught them and that people are hungry to know the inside story. Too bad they aren't getting it in *The Da Vinci Code*. The trouble is, the author assures them that they are. He thinks so because he has read many books based on the same notions, and in them he thinks he has found adequate documentation. But no such luck. His version of Chartres Cathedral, so full of enticing and profound mysteries, turns out to be a flimsy house of (Tarot) cards, a tissue of mistakes, hoaxes, and arbitrary speculations.

A PRIORI SION

Right up front Brown promises the reader: "The Priory of Sion—a European secret society founded in 1099—is a real organization. In 1975 Paris's Bibliotheque Nationale discovered parchments known as *Les Dossiers Secrets*, identifying numerous members of the Priory of Sion, including Sir Isaac Newton, Botticelli, Victor Hugo, and Leonardo da Vinci."[1] None of this is quite true.

The fact is that, while there was indeed a medieval monastic order called the Priory of Sion (Zion), it long ago died out, absorbed by the Jesuits in 1617. The name was revived and appropriated in 1956 by a far-right French political faction, previously called Alpha Galates and led by Pierre Plantard, an anti-Semite Vichy sympathizer who fancied himself the rightful Merovingian heir to the throne of France. Plantard's group claimed connection to the original Priory for the same reason the Masonic Lodges claim (spuriously) to be descended from the Knights Templar.[2] It is no surprise that the Priory of Sion also claims descent from the Templars and, again like the Masons, to have received from them secret knowledge. But this is like Ralph Kramden's Raccoon Lodge claiming the ancient secrets of Solomon. And as for the Secret Dossier, also known as the Priory Documents, these have been exposed as modern fakes perpetrated by the same political sect as part of the attempt to fabricate a venerable pedigree.[3] Once these facts are known, the whole sand castle washes away.

The Priory of Sion hoax (to which Dan Brown appears to be a victim, not an accomplice) was made popular twenty years ago through a long and tedious pseudodocumentary tome called *Holy Blood, Holy Grail* by Michael Baigent, Richard Leigh, and Henry Lincoln. (Brown's scholarly character Lee Teabing is a scrambled version of the names of Baigent and Leigh.) These gents argued that the Templar Knights were sent by the ultrasecret Priory of Sion on a top-secret mission to retrieve the legendary treasure of Solomon's Temple or Herod's Temple (which the authors, like the Knights, seem to regard as the same thing). They succeeded beyond their wildest dreams, discovering also a cache of documents telling the real story of the Holy Grail, that is, the royal bloodline of Jesus. Possession of these moneys and of the highly volatile secret of Jesus and his queen Mary Magdalene enabled the Templars and Priory of Sion to bribe and blackmail their way to unchallenged prominence for centuries, all the while protecting the descendants of Jesus and Mary among the Merovingian dynasty. In turn, the Merovingian heirs, notably Crusader Godfrey de Bouillon, mindful of the messianic destiny implied in their very DNA, sought to regain their lost glory, finally establishing the short-lived Crusader Kingdom of Jerusalem. This much is absolutely fundamental to *The Da Vinci Code*. It really forms the whole premise. Without this, there is no secret, nothing for the rival international conspiracies to fight and to kill over.

Despite their indefatigable research, motivated no doubt by true scholarly zeal, these authors seem unacquainted with inductive historical method. They proceed instead, as they themselves recount the evolution of their hypothesis, more in a novelistic fashion, just like their recent disciple Dan Brown. That is, Baigent, Leigh, and Lincoln constantly connect the dots of data provided by medieval chronicles and such, linking them with the cheap Scotch tape of one speculation after another: "What if A were really B?" "What if B were really C?" "It is not impossible that. . . ." "If so-and-so were the case, this would certainly explain this and that." These are the flashes of imaginative inspiration that allow fiction writers like Dan Brown to trace out intriguing plots. It is essentially a creative enterprise, not one of historical reconstruction. It seems the authors of *Holy Blood, Holy Grail* concocted more than anything else a novel much like *The Da Vinci Code*, and, like Dan Brown, they managed to convince themselves that it was really true. (In fact, I think this explains why the authors of the numerous faux-documentary volumes we will consider do not simply set forth their evidence and arguments but instead narrate the whole adventure of their research, their frustration at hitting temporary dead-ends, their excitement when making discoveries, etc. They are really engaged in writing a kind of historical fiction adventure novel starring themselves.)

Admittedly, had the Templars discovered proof that Jesus and the Magdalene were husband and wife, messianic king and queen, and had they threatened to reveal it, this *might* account for their considerable clout. But what are the chances that this is the explanation? It is a shot in the dark, seeking to explain one unknown by a bigger one. We are familiar with this logic from tabloid theories that space aliens built the pyramids. Or that we may explain the big bang by positing that God lit the fuse.

THE KNIGHTS WHO SAY . . .

Who were the Templar Knights? They were a monastic order, the Poor Knights of the Temple of Solomon, founded some time between 1110 and 1120. Their sworn duty was to protect

Christian pilgrims on their way to and from Jerusalem. For a long time, there were only nine of them, which may not seem enough to do the job, but they weren't the only ones assigned the task. The Templars worked with the older Order of Knights Hospitallers. Over the years, as ascetic and admired religious groups tend to do, they acquired considerable fortunes and clout, eventually founding the practice of modern banking, as they used their vast funds to bail out the crowned heads of Europe. Finally, in 1308, Philip the Fair, king of France, subjected the Templars to a ruthless inquisition, stripping them of their moneys, the real object of his covetous lust. They were accused of the most abominable heresies and blasphemies, and on this basis, many of their latter-day admirers (including Dan Brown) have insisted that they *were* heretics, and more power *to* them! But the evidence of their signed confessions is worthless, precisely as in the case of the so-called witches persecuted in Europe. Tortured wretches eagerly signed any crazy-sounding confession shoved in front of them. As the witches owned up to having had sex with the devil himself, describing the great size and unnatural coldness of his Satanic majesty's phallus, so did the beleaguered Templar Knights confess to blasphemies that included the worship of a goat-headed demon statue called Baphomet and kissing its anus, as well as ritual homosexuality, trampling the cross, and eliciting oracles from a still-living severed head! Actually, "Baphomet" is, contra Baigent and company, almost surely an Old French spelling of "Mahomet" or "Muhammad."[4] This, in turn, means the accusations against the Templars reflect not actual Gnosticism or even diabolism but garbled French beliefs about Islam. In just the same way, the medieval *Song of Roland* (verses 2580–91) imagines Muslims as worshiping idols and devils, including Muhammad, Termagant, and Apollo.[5]

The Templars became lionized in folklore and in esotericist belief as adepts who guarded heterodox secret doctrines that they had discovered, perhaps in the form of ancient manuscripts, while resident in Jerusalem. Wolfram von Eschenbach, in his spiritual allegory of the Holy Grail, *Parzifal*, so depicts the Templars. Followed by *The Da Vinci Code*, Baigent, Leigh, and Lincoln link the Templars with the French Cathars (or Albigensians) wiped out in the Albigensian Crusade, another Catholic-backed persecution, in 1209. These Cathars were late-medieval sectarians who had rediscovered or reinvented something like ancient Manichean Gnosticism.[6] But any link between the Cathars and the Templars is, again, part of the latter-day syncretism of modern occultists trying to cobble together an appearance of antiquity for their own inventions. There is no basis in fact or evidence. Only dots to be connected.

Brown and his sources want to take as much of this material as possible as factual in nature. But their "historiography" too often amounts to the reasoning of protagonists in horror movies: "But *every* legend has a basis in fact!" Not this one. It is rather simply part and parcel with the spurious lore of the Masons. And yet it is absolutely integral to the "Teabing hypothesis," if we may call it that, using the name of Brown's scholarly character to stand for Brown's recycling of the fanciful pseudoscholarship of his mentors. And this means their Templar castle is built on sinking sand.

The Teabing hypothesis posits an underground stream of esoteric knowledge passed on, ultimately, from the ancient Gnostics and the monastic Jewish sect of the Essenes. And it has always been irresistible to speculate whether Jesus and/or John the Baptist may have been connected with the Essenes and/or Dead Sea Scrolls community. Another advocate of the Templar Jesus scenario, Laurence Gardner, cleverly appropriates the work of Dr. Barbara Thiering in order to gain new plausibility for this connection.[7] Dr. Thiering has advanced a controversial theory about Jesus that does happen to parallel two cardinal features of the Teabing hypothesis. The first of these is that Jesus, a messiah-designate of the Qumran Essenes, did marry Mary Magdalene and beget an heir, also born to royal pretensions. The second is that Jesus survived crucifixion thanks to Essene allies. Neither notion is absurd, despite the unwillingness of mainstream scholars to entertain them seriously. Dr. Thiering is well aware of the need to buttress such claims with evidence, and she has provided it in the form of a complex body of work that subjects the gospels to the same sort of "pesher" (decoding) exegesis used by the Qumran scribes on their own scriptures. Her unique mastery of the textual, hermeneutical, and calendrical lore involved has left her a voice crying in the wilderness, as none of her critics so far seems to be in a position to evaluate her theories competently, either positively or negatively. Suffice it to say that Dr. Thiering's reconstruction of the cult-political connections of Jesus would come in very handy for the Teabing hypothesis. But Dr. Thiering vociferously repudiates the connection, pointing out in some detail how Gardner selectively misrepresents her work, then gratuitously extends it.[8] If Gardner even understands why Thiering says what she does, he does not attempt to explain where he derives the rest of his "insights" on the connections between Jesus, Magdalene, and the Essenes.

BRIDE OF KONG

As I say, there is nothing historically implausible about Jesus having been married (and later I will try to show how the idea should not be theologically embarrassing either), but that by itself does not make it probable. Short of going the whole way with Professor Thiering's decoding method (too large a topic to pursue here), one must ask what early (i.e., gospel or gospel-era) evidence there might be on either side of the question. A number of scholars have argued in an a priori fashion that, lacking specific statements on the issue in the gospels, the best the historian can do is to look at the *kind* of figure Jesus would have been in the religious and social categories of his time to see whether that would imply anything re his marital status. The next step is to note that ancient Judaism considered it incumbent upon every capable man to get busy being fruitful and multiplying, propagating the House of Israel. If he didn't, he was suspected of being a homosexual or a gigolo. Rabbis, in particular, we are told, were nearly always married. Thus, since marriage was the norm, it is a man's being married, not his being single, that would be taken for granted in a biographical account of him. If he had been single, this must have been an anomaly, even if for a good reason, that would require explanation. If Jesus, or any other man, had been single, we would surely hear of it. And his being some kind of rabbi clinches it—at least in the minds of some. But this is a silly argument.

First, one can never deduce a historical fact about an individual from general historical or social factors, since all such are generalizations, never universals. Otherwise we could argue that, since most Jews in the first century were not crucified, Jesus probably wasn't either! By the same homogenizing logic, one could argue that Jesus had nothing distinctive to say, since most contemporary Jewish teachers did not say things like "Turn the other cheek" or "Sell your possessions and give to the poor." We cannot simply assume that any individual member of a group shares all the characteristics of that group. That is known as the Division Fallacy: "Since Matilda is a member of a very smart family, she must get straight A's." Well, maybe she does; maybe she doesn't. We'll have to look at her report card to tell, and perhaps she will be reluctant to show us if she is the black sheep of the family. So, even if most Jewish men, and rabbis in particular, were married, this tells us absolutely nothing about Jesus's marital status.

Second, Jesus is being compared to the wrong template in this argument. Our biographical data about the Jewish rabbis comes mostly from the late first through the third centuries. It is gratuitous, in this matter as in so many others, to ascribe to first-century Jewish thinking what we only know to have been true generations later. Were Jews really so enamored of universal matrimony in Jesus's day? Or could it be that the decimating Jewish wars against Rome (67–73, 116, and 132–136 CE) might have provided new reasons not existing in Jesus's day for second-century Jews to encourage men to father children?

On the other hand, we do know of a first-century Jewish group where celibacy was highly prized, namely, the Essenes. Josephus tells us that many Essenes foreswore marriage, not because they thought it morally wrong, but just because domestic duties were incompatible with the sort of hundred-per-center religious devotion they required. We find the same idea in 1 Corinthians 7:32–34a: "I just want you to be free of worries.

The unmarried man is preoccupied with the Lord's business, how he may win his Lord's approval. But the married man is perforce preoccupied with mundane matters, with pleasing his wife, and his focus is divided." Oh, the irony that many of the same authors who want to link Jesus with the Essenes appeal to the precedent of "family man" rabbis to argue that Jesus couldn't have been celibate! Now, we don't know that he *was* an Essene. But he sure does appear, like John the Baptist, to have moved more in a sectarian orbit than that of the later rabbis.

Third, Jesus is actually portrayed in Matthew 19:12 as advocating celibacy! "Some men are born eunuchs. Others have been castrated. Still others have made themselves eunuchs for the sake of the Kingdom of God. Whoever is up to the challenge, let him accept it!" Of course, it is a devilishly tricky business determining which among the gospel sayings may actually go back to Jesus. I have devoted a whole book (*The Incredible Shrinking Son of Man*) to the task, and the collaborative work of the Jesus Seminar on the question is on display in the marvelous compendium *The Five Gospels*.[9] Jesus may or may not have advocated celibacy and for who knows what reason. But the good possibility that he said it, or even that someone felt it not incongruous to ascribe such a sentiment to him, implies that the ancients need not have taken it for granted that Jesus was married. Nor can we, no matter what hay it might make for our pet theories.

TEMPLARS REVEALED—OR EXPOSED

One of the books Dan Brown shows on Professor Teabing's bookshelf is the 1996 work by Lynn Picknett and Clive Prince,

The Templar Revelation: Secret Guardians of the True Identity of Christ. Obviously, Brown is tipping his hat to one of his major sources by mentioning it in this way.

Since the publication of *Holy Blood, Holy Grail*, the builders, so to speak, have rejected their prized cornerstone, the Priory Documents or Secret Dossier. These papers have been utterly debunked by the confession of the forger himself, a member of the far-right sect of Pierre Plantard. But authors Picknett and Prince remain largely undaunted. In the manner of all polemicists boxing with one arm tied behind them, they plead that bad evidence might as well be treated as good anyway. They argue cleverly, if not convincingly, that the Priory of Sion must be up to *something* to go to all the trouble of faking those documents! The Priory claims to have some sort of shocking information that could blow the lid off Christianity. So maybe they do! So there *is* a secret to hunt down after all! And so *what* if the Priory of Sion that exists today is not the same as the one that was connected to the Templars many centuries ago? There might still be some sort of underground connection . . . or something.

The next step in the argument is to try and forge a link between the Templars and the Cathars. The authors invoke interests apparently held in common by the two movements, including, paramountly, an interest in John the Baptist and Mary Magdalene. They start spreading out the pushpins across the map and come to the conclusion that there was a significant overlap in France between Templar-related sites, centers of devotion to Mary Magdalene in local village churches, and the presence of the Black Madonna statues, which some scholars hypothesize may have originally represented Isis or some such pagan goddess. They will soon be drawing the net closed, with the conclusion that the Templars worshiped Mary Magdalene as Isis. And as if that gratuitous leap were not daring enough, Picknett and Prince focus briefly on the Alchemists, interpreting them as Tantric-style sex mystics who preserved the rites of *hieros gamos*, the archaic intercourse ritual performed by the pagan faithful. The pagan pious (including Old Testament Baal worshipers) would ritually play the roles of the god and goddess, their sexual intercourse aping and magically stimulating Baal's fertilizing the womb of Anath (Mother Earth) with good crops. This precarious argument is the basis for the ceremonial sex orgies central to the plot of *The Da Vinci Code*. Remember how Sophie had fled from her grandpa when she chanced upon him having sex amid a torch-lit ceremony in a secret cave? She thought they were just having fun, but it was all on the up-and-up! It was a kind of Gnostic Mass, a la Aleister Crowley. As if this weren't plenty nutty enough, right? Would poor Sophie have calmed down had her priapic gramps sat her down and explained it? My guess is, she'd have run all the faster! I know I would have!

A deep dive into the Time Tunnel takes Picknett and Prince back into the first century and Christian origins. Here they make clever use of more mainstream scholars like Burton L. Mack and C. H. Dodd (whom they persistently misspell as "Dodds," unlike whoever compiled their bibliography), employing them as hammers to chip loose the New Testament from traditional Christian conceptions. They try to soften up the reader with the ideas that Galilee may not have been strictly Jewish and that Jesus may not have been a Jew, and neither was John the Baptist for that matter. Picknett and Prince invoke the Gnostic Nag Hammadi texts, discovered in Egypt in

1945, to show that early Christianity was much more diverse than scholars had traditionally supposed (a valid enough observation) and that it was likely Gnostic.

Our authors maintain that Mary Magdalene corresponds to the Egyptian Isis in so many respects that Mary pretty much becomes the Christian version of Isis, with Jesus as her consort Osiris. The mythological parallels here are numerous and significant. Much of the discussion is derived from Barbara G. Walker's endlessly fascinating tome, *The Woman's Encyclopedia of Myths and Secrets*. Though no longer taken seriously by mainstream scholars, even critical ones, the identification of Jesus with Osiris and of Mary Magdalene with Isis is, I think, a strong and finally even a persuasive theory. (See chapter 9, "A Christian Goddess?") Most who have advocated it, like Walker, understand that the natural implication is that Jesus as a dying-and-rising god, raised by his divine consort, is *nonhistorical*. If there was a historical Jesus, this myth was soon applied to him. That would be Rudolf Bultmann's view, for instance. Jesus himself, on this understanding, would never have had such a thought.

Of course, with Walker, Gilbert Murray, and others, we might go the whole way and understand Jesus and the Magdalene simply as a local variant of the old myth that was eventually historicized into the (fictitious) Jesus and Mary of the gospels. But this Picknett and Prince do not do. They insist on historicizing the myth. They believe that the historical Jesus and Mary Magdalene actually suffered under the delusion of regarding themselves as somehow being the incarnations of Osiris and Isis. This seems to me a fundamental misstep. Not only does it yield a reconstruction of the intentions of Jesus that is grotesque in its extravagance, but it fundamentally misses a crucial feature of myths as Rene Girard explains them. Girard knows that, for example, the Oedipus myth does not record a genuine historical case of scapegoating but that it is a sacred story embodying and presupposing the *kind* of thing that used to happen in the ancient world.[10] Picknett and Prince are historicizing the myth of Jesus and Mary as Osiris and Isis in much the same way Plutarch insisted that Osiris and Isis must have been real people in remote Egyptian history.

Their historical Jesus is composed of equal parts of Hugh J. Schonfield's Jesus as "scheming messiah" and Morton Smith's "Jesus the magician." From Schonfield's *The Passover Plot* they have learned that "Jesus the Nazorean" denoted not "Jesus from the town of Nazareth" but rather "Jesus of the Nazorean sect" and that "Nazorean" meant "Keepers of the Secrets," related to today's Mandaeans. (Both are valid insights.) This gives us a sectarian and Gnostic Jesus. From Schonfield they also derive the notion that Jesus did believe himself to be the messiah, or at least planned to be accepted as such, orchestrating even his own crucifixion, which he planned to survive. From Smith's *Jesus the Magician*, our authors borrow the notion that Jesus must have been a sorcerer. Not only is he depicted as driving out demons and healing with spit, mud, and imitative gestures—the stock in trade of magicians as described in Hellenistic Egyptian magic handbooks—but also he received his powers and divine sonship by the descent of a familiar spirit in the form of a bird, as the Egyptians did. Some early Christians, as well as Jewish and Gentile critics of Christianity, regarded Jesus as a magician, and so Smith judges that he was.

What was Jesus's own personal mission? Picknett and Prince

take seriously what the Talmud said about Jesus being crucified for attempting to introduce alien gods (a familiar charge leveled at Socrates, too). They believe Jesus was essentially an initiated priest of the Isis religion who had experienced orgasmic deification in a ritual union with Mary Magdalene, a temple "prostitute" (what I like to call a "priestitute"). He felt it incumbent upon him to restore to Israel its original gods, the Egyptian pantheon, particularly the worship of Isis, whose local avatar, Anath, had long been worshiped in the temple. To gain public support he had to prove himself (or pretend to be—the authors are not sure) the Davidic Messiah, a notion more familiar to Jews. Then, once in a position of power and respect, he would lead them to believe in himself as Osiris and in Mary as Isis.

Dan Brown, without explaining all of this in detail, assumes a good bit of it with his vague statements that the Priory of Sion worships Mary Magdalene as the goddess and that Mary's marriage to Jesus was this mystical union of goddess with god. So now we know what he is referring to!

In a revealing admission, Picknett and Prince confess that there is a millennium-long gap between the ancient sects of Jesus and John and the (apparently interchangeable) Templars, Masons, Cathars, Leonardo, and Priory of Sion. But their guess, obviously, is that all these groups learned and passed down the secret that the authors think they have pieced together. As for the great gap, which is to say, the lack of any evidence of a historical transmission or dissemination of these ideas, can we offer a better explanation than *The Da Vinci Code* and *The Templar Revelation*? As it happens, we can. Ioan P. Couliano, in his book *The Tree of Gnosis*, observes that the human brain is much the same from generation to generation, from century to century, and that whenever it is faced with similar challenges and similar data, the brain of whatever century will produce the same range of solutions.[11] Thus Gnosticism as a theodicy (a theory of how evil came to infest the world even though God is good) can be expected to resurface, independently, again and again through the ages. We don't need to picture some cleric discovering some dusty old parchments and reading some blasphemous gospel, which then acts as a match to spark a rediscovery of Gnosticism. No, we can just count on the inventive human mind to put the pieces together in similar ways again and again. If the world is infested with evil, and if God is good, how can he have created this world? Faced with this difficulty, some minds will always come to posit: "Perhaps it wasn't God who *made* the world! Maybe some disobedient subordinates did it!"

The same is true when it comes to certain tantalizing biblical puzzles. Was something going on between Jesus and Mary Magdalene? You don't have to read the Gospel of Philip to suspect that there was! Martin Luther thought so. So did Garner Ted Armstrong and numerous others, who apparently all came up with the idea from their own reading of the scriptures. Likewise, Pentecostal healer William Marrion Branham and the Rev. Sun Myung Moon both came up with the theory that Eve was sexually seduced and impregnated by the Serpent in Eden.[12] Neither knew of the other's interpretation or that some of the ancient rabbis thought the same thing. No, it is just that "inquiring minds want to know," and, given the same set of data, some of the answers are going to come up again and again. So if the Cathars had doctrines similar to the Nag Hammadi texts, that hardly means they must have read them there.

It certainly looks as if much of the material we read in *The Da Vinci Code* concerning the alleged occult connections and convictions of Leonardo—as well as the highly doubtful speculations about his depictions of John the Baptist, Jesus, and Mary Magdalene, filled with esoteric symbolism *amounting to a "code"*—have been transferred almost bodily from *The Templar Revelation*. Reading first either one, then the other, certainly brings with it a pronounced sense of déjà vu. All the business about the difference between the two versions of the *Virgin on the Rocks* triptych panel, the bit about the disciple next to Jesus in the Last Supper scene looking like a woman, the characters seeming to form an "M"? It was all in *The Templar Revelation* years before it appeared in *The Da Vinci Code*. And keep in mind it is no simple matter of common art history information. No, it is a specific and highly speculative interpretation that appears in both books. None of this means Brown is a plagiarist. Certainly not. It is rather a case of what H. P. Lovecraft called "second-hand erudition."[13]

SKELETON KEY

Another source of *The Da Vinci Code*'s Templar Jesus myth is *The Hiram Key: Pharaohs, Freemasons and the Discovery of the Secret Scrolls of Jesus* by two Freemasons, Christopher Knight (which ought to be a pen name if it isn't!) and Robert Lomas.[14] Knight and Lomas, as Masons and as inquisitive fellows, found that, no matter how superficial Freemasonry may appear (even to its members), there may yet be more to it than meets the eye. Where did the Masonic names and stories come from? How far back did their traditions go? So they embarked on a grail quest of their own. The trouble with the result is that, assuming there would be something substantial to find, they at length cooked up something substantial and claim to have found it! The subtitle of the book, promising rediscovered Nasorean scrolls containing the Q document and so forth, is a perfect cameo of the whole. It is only a tease; our authors merely surmise that such a trove of texts resides within the vault of Roselyn Chapel in Scotland. Exactly as Geraldo Rivera was so sure he had located the lost treasure of Al Capone in what turned out to be an empty concrete bunker.

In this exercise in Mason apologetics, the authors go back to ancient Egypt. In the Egyptian concept of *Maat*, which Knight and Lomas understand as denoting something like, let's say, "a sure foundation of virtues balanced in an architectonic manner," they cannot help but see the central insight of today's Masonic moral catechism clothed in Home Depot terminology. This is nearly enough, our authors imagine, to demonstrate direct succession by the Masons from the mysteries of the Egyptian pharaohs. And this is a tendency observable throughout their work. They discover "amazing" parallels to this or that piece of Masonic symbolism and jump to the conclusion that the Masons got it from ancient, arcane sources—when it was readily available in the Bible all the time! A good example of this methodological overkill is their quest for the true identity of Hiram Abif, the martyr hero of Masonic lore. They identify him with a minor pharaoh, a client king of the interloping Hyksos dynasty, one Seqenenre Tao. They disdain the obvious and much simpler solution that Hiram "Abif," pious architect of Solomon's temple, must have been intended as King Hiram of Tyre, period. Hiram supplied the materials and plans for the temple according to the Bible (1 Kings, chapter 5), but Masonic ritual splits him into two Hirams so as to be able to kill one of them off as a Masonic martyr. Hiram of Tyre did not so die, so they had to make up a second Hiram. "Hiram Abif" is like "Judas not Iscariot" (John 14:22), an artificial attempt to distance one version of the same character from another.[15]

According to the text of a Masonic ritual, a delver in Solomon's temple during Zerubbabel's restoration spelunks his way into a cavernous pillared chamber where he discovers a lost scroll of the Law of Moses, the Ten Commandments. This seems most likely to be simply a garbled (or artfully rewritten) version of the "discovery" of the Book of the Covenant by the priest Hilkiah during a renovation of the temple in 2 Kings 22:8–10. But in order to get their theory home, Knight and Lomas make the Masonic story refer instead to a hypothetical Templar discovery of early Christian (Nasorean) scrolls beneath the ruins of Herod's temple. And they feel sure this document trove must include the Q document, even though they do not know what that is. They think Q underlies all four gospels in the manner of the old Nazarene Gospel theory of Robert Graves.[16] Now, according to some evidence, the Templars may indeed have excavated beneath the Dome of the Rock to get to the treasures, including hidden gold, of Solomon's ruined temple.[17] It is sheer surmise, though certainly not absurd, to suppose that they found such wealth. But it is wild speculation to dogmatize that they discovered a library of early Christian scrolls there, too! And with this we have found the origin of Dan Brown's description of "the Purist

Documents" written by Jesus's first followers and buried with the Magdalene. Not exactly an impeachable historical source!

Knight and Lomas also slander the Emperor Constantine, reducing him pretty much to the level of a clever Mafia thug. According to them, Constantine never sincerely embraced the Christian faith, being instead an adherent of Sol the Invincible Sun. I will deal with this portrait of Constantine in more detail later (chapter 5, "Constantine's Christ"). For the moment, suffice it to note that this seems to be the origin of Dan Brown's grossly confused account of Constantine and his influence on formative Christianity. Knight and Lomas make him a cynical advertising executive. They blame Constantine and the Greek Christians for paganizing Christianity.

AND WE HAVE KILLED HIM!

The Da Vinci Code lifts another extensive complex of spurious data relating to ancient Templar discoveries and the mystery of Rennes-le-Château from yet another pair of authors, Richard Andrews and Paul Schellenberger.[18] Like most others in this genre, The Tomb of God concerns itself with the mystery of a nineteenth-century village priest named Bergier *Sauniere* (used as the name of Dan Brown's murdered museum curator), who is said to have discovered four (or five) parchments within an old pillar while his church was being renovated. He eventually took these documents to Paris and had their cryptic Latin translated. Hitherto poor as a church mouse, the Abbé Sauniere returned home a very wealthy man. The speculations offered in most of these books is that the priest had found a treasure map and decoded it, unearthing a fabulous trove of golden treasure brought back from Jerusalem by the Knights Templar—or else he discovered documentation of some shocking truth he was able to use in order to blackmail the Roman Catholic Church. One of the first things he did with his newfound funds was to spruce up his church in hideous bad taste, including some possibly heretical, Rosicrucian-tilting decorations. Our various authors see in this detail a sure sign of the priest's occult sympathies. All this is familiar from *The Da Vinci Code*.

Another of the priest's purchases was of copies of three paintings, traced down by Andrews and Schellenberger, which, as their painstaking analysis demonstrates, embody complex Platonic-Pythagorean geometric forms. Andrews and Schellenberger next turn their attention to the parchments discovered by Sauniere. There is no pretense or claim that these Latin texts represent ancient scriptures or the like. No, they are of admittedly recent vintage and convey, to the knowing eye, a set of geometric and verbal puzzles referring back to the three paintings. Someone had cracked a code, and it turned out that all these enigmatic charts and hints were pieces of a map of the Languedoc area. Scrutiny of a fourteenth-century Templar map of Jerusalem disclosed the use of the same underlying geometric cipher. This discovery led our researchers to the conclusion that the three eighteenth-century painters, some of whom are known to have had Hermetic or occultist connections anyway (such things were then quite chic), were in touch with an ancient geometric code. It may have been one of many bits of classical learning rediscovered among the Arabs by the Templar Knights on their tour of duty in Jerusalem and its environs. None of this is unreasonable.

Nonspecialists (like me!) are in no position to evaluate the geometrical and art-historical claims made in these pages. Robert A. diCurcio vouches for both the existence of the Platonic geometrical code and the widespread, centuries-spanning use of it in both ancient paintings not discussed in *The Tomb of God* and in canvasses by Vermeer, disclosing hidden maps of Jerusalem and southern France.[19] The question for us, however, is what any of this has to do with the contention of Andrews and Schellenberger later on that the treasure to which these enigmatic clues lead is *the tomb containing the earthly remains of Jesus!* Andrews and Schellenberger guess (hypothesize is too restrained a word) that either Jesus survived crucifixion and fled Palestine for less-hostile territory, where he carried on his ministry. Or, equally as likely as far as they are concerned, the Templars, in the course of their excavations beneath the ruins of Herod's temple, discovered the burial place of Jesus and decided to bring the holy relics back home to France. From this we see that the possible, even plausible, existence of a "Da Vinci code" hidden in his paintings (or the canvasses of others) is one thing. What it points to is quite another.

Perhaps the most fascinating hint they produce concerns the decipherment of a motto appearing in one of the relevant paintings, Nicolas Poussin's *Les Bergers d'Arcadie* ("Shepherds of Arcadia"), where we see, chiseled into the lintel of a tomb, the words *ET IN ARCADIA EGO*. The phrase, which figures significantly in Dan Brown's novel, is usually rendered something like, "I am present in Arcadia, too." In this case, the sentiment is Kierkegaardian, a chill whiff of a reminder that even in Paradise death intrudes. Actually, even this reading would comport with Andrews's and Schellenberger's theory, if one were to take the phrase as the words of Jesus, meaning, "Though risen in heaven, I am also buried in Arcadia." But they are still more imaginative. If one reads the line as an anagram, it comes out ARCAM DEI TANGO: "I touch the tomb of God." This would leave four letters left over: E, I, S, U, reshuffled to form "Iesu," or Jesus!

One must take care never to dismiss a radical theory simply *because* it is radical and would require a realignment of belief and assumption if accepted. Sounding outlandish is no argument against a theory. The real problem with the theological blackmail scenario posited by *The Da Vinci Code; The Tomb of God;* and *Holy Blood, Holy Grail* and the rest is this ill-founded assumption that the Templars, or the Masons, or whoever, could have sat on their secret, holding it in store as a trump card to disprove the doctrine of the resurrection of Jesus Christ. It is easy for a modern writer to imagine such a thing, for it rings true as a piece of a good mystery novel. But if one actually thinks out the implications of any attempt to cash in on this, to spill the beans and topple the Catholic Church, it immediately becomes apparent that the whole endeavor would be wasted effort. Who would believe such an announcement? Whoever made it would be considered insane. And, again, what hope could the keepers of the body have had of corroborating their claim?

Dan Brown borrows from Andrews and Schellenberger a groundwork of religious history and theological warfare that would make sense of some Templar grave-robbing scheme. Our authors seem to know they must make it sound reasonable that Christians, even heretical ones, would have thought it a *good idea* to announce the discovery of the corpse of Jesus!

In their view, possession of the dead body of Jesus would be the vindicating token of a suppressed kind of Christianity for which Jesus Christ was a simple human being, albeit a great one, whose teachings have been lost behind the stained-glass curtain of his divinity, a later and artificial corruption of the historical truth by the Roman Church. Notions like Jesus's inherent divinity, his incarnation, virgin birth, and resurrection they dismiss as inventions by Paul (already a Catholic?) intended to lift Jesus and his achievements beyond the capacity of mere human beings. The point was to reduce people to passive servitude to the institutional church, which could declare them "original sinners" and forgive them at the price of fealty and quiescence. If we were to excavate the site where Jesus's bones lie buried and expose his lack of resurrection, our authors claim with hushed tones, maybe it would not be too late to restore to our generation the sort of freethinking self-help faith that the real Jesus preached.

But this is all hopeless confusion. It has been clear to critical New Testament scholars ever since Ferdinand Christian Baur in the nineteenth century that, far from being the charter of Catholic orthodoxy, the Pauline Epistles are among the most important roots of Gnosticism![20] By contrast, the Catholic Church represents a dilution of the Pauline faith with the Torah piety of Judaism. Catholicism is seen by many as a declension from Paulinism, while genuine Pauline emphases continued on primarily in the forms of Gnosticism and Marcionism.[21] And while Gnosticism did encourage spiritual self-liberation and innovation, it certainly was not friendly to the simple humanity or mortality of Jesus! For Gnostics the human Jesus, if he even existed and was not some sort of a holographic phantom, was merely the unimportant channeler for the Christ spirit, who spoke through him. What Brown and his literary-theological mentors are really interested in, it sounds like, is the victory of Liberal Protestantism or Unitarianism, a vaguely religious philosophy that will happily quote the maxims of a human Jesus and will rejoice equally to be rid of dogmas that make him an oppressive theological abstraction. The irony is: What a subtle and tortuous path one must trace, over geometrical chasms and around historical mountains, to obtain the key to this supposedly commonsensical piety! Whose is the simple faith here?

CODE AND CODEX

Finally, some have alleged an unwarranted degree of borrowing by Dan Brown in *The Da Vinci Code* from a 1983 novel by Lewis Perdue, revised for 2004 republication as *The Da Vinci Legacy*. As one compares the two novels, it does start to look as if Brown may have picked up some ideas from the earlier work, but there is nothing wrong with that, nor is there any question of plagiarism. We would be considerably poorer without various literary works that were conceived when their authors read other people's work and reflected, "That was a good idea, but the author might have done better with it! Well, there's nothing stopping *me!*"

What are the points of similarity? Well, for one thing, the phrase "the Da Vinci Codex" appears a few times in Perdue's book, referring to a newly discovered notebook of Da Vinci containing designs for a dangerous superweapon. But the similarity between "code" and "codex" is as unimportant as any casual pun. Brown's interest in Da Vinci focuses on his painting and the esoteric knowledge supposedly hinted in it, while Perdue concentrates instead on the artist's famous prescience, hatching the basic designs of later inventions such as the airplane, the submarine, and the bicycle. Both mystery plots involve the early murder of three experts who had enjoyed privileged access to the coveted Da Vinci information, as well as their murder by a fanatic who appears to be carrying out orders from a secret cabal within the Catholic Church. In both books, it turns out that the Catholic schemers had nothing to do with the deaths. Perdue made up his arch-conservative Catholics, the Elect Brothers of St. Peter (whose founders included the literal bastard son of the apostle!). Brown's, on the other hand, are the very real Catholic renewal group Opus Dei ("the work of God"). As one reads Brown, one is first inclined to accuse him of Catholic-bashing, but, as any reader of Brown knows, by the end of the book we discover that Opus Dei is innocent, off the hook. There was instead a single, hidden mastermind.

Lewis Perdue even has the element of a secret involving holy relics that, if disclosed, would threaten to turn the Catholic Church upside down. But, unlike many of the pseudo-scholarly tomes already reviewed, the body in question is not that of Jesus, nor even that of Mary Magdalene, but rather that of Simon Peter. It seems that the Elect Brothers long ago spirited away the Petrine carcass from its resting place beneath Saint Peter's Basilica and substituted some unremarkable non-apostolic bones. However, it is more than doubtful whether such news would disturb anyone a fraction as much as the Vatican II reforms did! As if sensing this, Perdue no sooner mentions the theft among the other fiendish pranks of the Elect Brotherhood than he drops it to move on to far more nefarious things—like whisking Adolf Hitler away from his flaming bunker and hosting him in their monastery till his *real* death in 1957 (a year earlier than the movie *Hellboy* has him die!).

At most, as in the case of the other books surveyed here, we may posit that Dan Brown was influenced by Lewis Perdue's book. But there's nothing untoward about that. The public is too quick to think, in these litigious times, of charges like those made against Stephen Spielberg, that he read some nonentity's idea for a movie, said "no thanks," and then went on to steal the idea and cheat the true creator out of her due rewards. This is hardly the same sort of thing. Both books were published; both authors made money. And Brown has not plagiarized from Perdue. Besides, the common ideas are neither very distinctive nor even central to the plots.

In this chapter, I have tried to do what Dan Brown's Professor Teabing does for his guests in *The Da Vinci Code*, providing the reader a quick introduction to that body of scholarship underlying the Teabing hypothesis. None of it is original to Brown, just as his mouthpiece Teabing freely admits none of it is original with him. But I have taken the liberty of providing a bit more detailed introduction to the shelf of pseudoscholarly works in question in order to show just how arbitrary, ill-informed, and distorted the whole business is. Please note that I have never once discounted an idea because it is unorthodox or unsettling in some way, as if these things counted against a theory. (As for some people they do!) All I ask is some evidence and some idea of what can feasibly be done with it. Where shocking notions in these books do have an evidential basis, I am not reluctant to say so, and in the next chapters I will further examine some of these, and not at all negatively.

NOTES

1. Dan Brown, *The Da Vinci Code* (New York: Doubleday, 2003), p. 1.

2. Robert Richardson, "The Priory of Sion Hoax," *Alpheus: Site for Esoteric History* [online], http://www.alpheus.org/html/articles/esoteric_history/richardson1.html.

3. As such, they are only the most recent in a long chain of Templar-related forgeries. See Peter Partner, *The Murdered Magicians: The Templars and Their Myth* (New York: Oxford University Press, 1982), pp. 103, 135, 140, 146, 161–63.

4. Ibid., p. 138.

5. Robert Harrison, trans., *The Song of Roland* (New York: New American Library, 1970), pp. 129–30.

6. Steven Runciman, *The Medieval Manichee: A Study of the Christian Dualist Heresy* (New York: Viking Press, 1961), pp. 116–70.

7. Laurence Gardner, *Bloodline of the Holy Grail: The Hidden Lineage of Jesus Revealed* (Rockport, MA: Element, 1996); Barbara Thiering, *Jesus the Man: A New Interpretation from the Dead Sea Scrolls* (London: Corgi, 1993).

8. Barbara Thiering, "The Date and Unity of the Gospel of Philip," *Journal of Higher Criticism* 2, no. 1 (Spring 1995): 102–11.

9. Robert M. Price, *The Incredible Shrinking Son of Man* (Amherst, NY: Prometheus Books, 2003); Robert W. Funk, Roy W. Hoover, and the Jesus Seminar, eds., *The Five Gospels: The Search for the Authentic Words of Jesus* (New York: Macmillan, 1993).

10. Rene Girard, *The Scapegoat*, trans. Yvonne Freccero (Baltimore: Johns Hopkins University Press, 1989), pp. 24–44.

11. Ioan P. Couliano, *The Tree of Gnosis: Gnostic Mythology from Early Christianity to Modern Nihilism* (San Francisco: HarperSanFrancisco, 1992).

12. William Marrion Branham, *An Exposition of the Seven Church Ages* (Jefferson, IN: William Marrion Branham, n.d.), pp. 98–99; *Divine Principle* (New York: Holy Spirit Association for the Unification of World Christianity, 1973), pp. 72–73.

13. H. P. Lovecraft to E. Hoffmann Price, 24 March 1933, MS in the John Hay Library, Brown University. Thanks to David C. Schultz for tracking down the reference.

14. Christopher Knight and Robert Lomas, *The Hiram Key: Pharaohs, Freemasons and the Discovery of the Secret Scrolls of Jesus* (Rockport, MA: Element, 1997).

15. Jacques Maccoby, *The Albigensian Crusade: An Historical Essay*, trans. Barbara Wall (New York: Fordham University Press, 1967), p. 127.

16. Robert Graves, *The Nazarene Gospel Restored* (Garden City, NY: Doubleday, 1954); Edgar Johnson Goodspeed, *Famous Biblical Hoaxes: Originally Entitled, Modern Apocrypha*, Twin Brooks Series (Grand Rapids, MI: Baker Book House, 1956).

17. Karen Ralls, *The Templars and the Grail: Knights of the Quest* (Wheaton, IL: Theosophical Publishing House/Quest Books, 2003), p. 145.

18. Richard Andrews and Paul Schellenberger, *The Tomb of God: The Body of Jesus and the Solution to a 2,000-Year-Old Mystery* (London: Little, Brown, 1996).

19. Robert A. diCurcio, *Vermeer's Riddle Revealed: The Sphinx, the Jester, and the Grail Geometry: Robert A. diCurcio's Analysis of Vermeer's Pictorial Compositions* (Nantucket, MA: Aeternium, 2002).

20. Ferdinand Christian Baur, *Paul the Apostle of Jesus Christ: His Life and Works, His Epistles and Teachings*, 2 vols. in 1, trans. A. Menzies (Peabody: Hendrickson, 2003).

21. Ernst Käsemann, "Paul and Early Catholicism," in Käsemann, *New Testament Questions of Today*, trans. W. J. Montague (Philadelphia: Fortress, 1979), pp. 236–51.

Chapter 2

THE HOLY GRAIL
Whom Does It Serve?

A bsolutely central to *The Da Vinci Code* is the legend of the Holy Grail. Brown uses it as a metaphor for the remains of Mary Magdalene and the documents buried with her, but he also uses it in a more general, overarching way to stand for the quest theme of the novel as a whole. As everyone knows, the term *grail* or *Holy Grail* denotes whatever it is that someone desires most and seeks most fervently. The Holy Grail of physicists is the Unified Field Theory. The Holy Grail of a book collector might be a rare first edition of his favorite author's work. And so on. We get this figure of speech from the numerous sagas and romances of the grail connected to the King Arthur legend cycle. In them, various knights, notably Lancelot, Galahad, Gawain, and Perceval, seek to find the grail against all odds, enduring every trial and temptation. And precisely what is it they are looking for with such indefatigable devotion? This, as we will see, is the great question, and to fail to ask it is to fail in the quest itself.

GRADUALLY, THE GRAIL

The word, originally *graal*, comes from the Old French *gra(d)al*, from the medieval Latin *gradalis*, referring to some kind of dish. We usually think of the Holy Grail as the cup from which the disciples drank at the Last Supper. According to some forms of the legend, the risen Jesus appeared to Joseph of Arimathea, imprisoned as a disciple of the executed ringleader, and entrusted the cup to him. In other versions, Joseph had earlier gained possession of the vessel and used it to collect the shed blood of Jesus from the wound in his side (heart?) once Jesus's side was pierced. At any rate, Joseph is said to have taken the cup and made his way to Brittany with his companions, where they established the second table for the grail's repose, the first having been the table of the Last Supper. From there the grail is taken to Britain, where King Arthur prepares the famous Round Table to be the third table of the grail.

The question of the grail is very fascinating in its own right and for its own sake. It is a powerful spiritual symbol, perhaps more so than it is usually credited for. But our discussion here is of course prompted by the claims made by Michael Baigent, Henry Lincoln, and Richard Leigh (*Holy Blood, Holy Grail*) and followed by numerous other recent writers, including Dan Brown. The favorite theory of all these writers is that the Holy Grail (*San Greal*) always functioned as code for the continuing royal bloodline (*Sang Real*) of Jesus, eventuating in the Merovingian dynasty of France. I want to take a closer look at the origin and evolution of the grail concept to see whether the data lends itself naturally to their theory, or to what I like to call the Teabing hypothesis.

CANONICAL CUP

One cannot simply presuppose some idea as to what the grail was supposed to be and then measure individual grail texts against it like paper edges against a yardstick. Rather, one must first examine the sources that tell us anything about the grail and then decide, if we can, whether a given grail concept arises naturally from these texts or rather has been forced upon them. The earliest grail texts (though that word does not appear in them) are the New Testament accounts of the Last Supper: 1 Corinthians 11:23-26, Mark 14:22-25, Matthew 26:26-29, and Luke 22:17-20. (John's gospel contains a Last Supper sequence, chapters 13-17, but there is no reference in it to the bread and the cup, though Eucharistic material about the body and blood of Christ does appear in a different setting in chapter 6). You will recall that *The Da Vinci Code* lays great store by Leonardo's classic depiction of this gospel scene, so it deserves our attention. The specific mentions of the cup are as follows:

> In the same way also the cup after supper, saying, "This cup is the new covenant in my blood. Do this, as often as you drink it, in remembrance of me." (1 Cor. 11:25)

> And he took a cup, and, when he had given thanks, he gave it to them, and they all drank of it. And he said to them, "This is my blood of the [new] covenant, which is poured out for many." (Mark 14:23-24)

> And he took a cup, and, when he had given thanks, he gave it to them, saying, "Drink of it, all of you; for this is my blood of the [new] covenant, which is poured out for many for the forgiveness of sins." (Matt. 26:27-28)

> And he took a cup, and, when he had given thanks, he said,
> "Take this, and divide it among yourselves." (Luke 22:15)

Why do the texts differ in detail? For example, why does the 1 Corinthians version mandate that readers repeat the eating and drinking? It is no doubt making explicit what is implicit in the others. Why does only Matthew have the element of "forgiveness of sins"? He is probably trying to explain to the reader the point of the "covenant" embodied in the bread and cup. The point is the same as in Acts 13:38–39: "Let it be known to you therefore, brothers, that through this man forgiveness of sins is proclaimed to you, and by him everyone that believes is justified from everything from which you could not be justified through the Law of Moses."

Why is the word *new* in brackets in the Matthew and Mark versions? Because some ancient manuscripts of each gospel lack the word, which then begins to look like someone's gloss (explanatory comment). Or maybe some scribes were trying to make it look more like the wording in the 1 Corinthians version. Who knows? But the major point we have to infer is that all of these versions are not primarily historical reports. They may contain an element of reporting, but as we read them, they are surely liturgical texts. They were part of the early Christian Holy Communion service. If you have ever taken the trouble to visit other churches than your usual congregation on a Communion Sunday, you may have noticed how the wording differs from one denomination to the next. Roman Catholics add "new *and eternal* covenant," for example. Scholars surmise that this process of local customizing had already begun by the time the various gospels were written.

That means that each gospel writer (and the author of 1 Corinthians 11) is passing on the particular version of the Communion liturgy he was familiar with.[1]

THE SHAPE OF THE CUP

What sort of cup is presupposed in this scene? Artistic representations often take the license of making it a beautiful and elaborate vessel, something one might see in an art museum. What has happened here is that the artist is externalizing the theological significance of the cup, intimating the redemptive blood of Christ by transfiguring its container's appearance to match. A good example from a text that does this would be *The Dolorous Passion of Our Lord Jesus Christ* by the visionary nun Anna Katharina Emmerich, a collection of pious fever dreams that forms the basis of Mel Gibson's epic film *The Passion of the Christ*.[2] In the book, the cup is described as an elaborate piece somewhere between a silver samovar and a punch bowl with attached cups. But we are probably closer to the truth in the depiction of the cup in *Indiana Jones and the Last Crusade*; the intrepid archaeologist finds himself amid a gallery of chalices, each more bejeweled and spectacular than the one before it. One of them is the fabled cup of the Last Supper. His life depends upon choosing the right one. How is he to decide? He asks himself, "Which one is the cup of a carpenter?" And sure enough, there is one, and only one, made of glazed clay.

Why do the gospel versions (and 1 Cor. 11) not do what Anna Katharina Emmerich did, especially if, like hers, theirs are documents more of faith than of history? Simply because they are in essence liturgical directions intended to provide a script for the reader, and when they say "he took *a* cup," what they are saying is, "Use *any* cup." Who among the early Christian communities would have been able to afford elaborate chalices? It will be interesting to see how the conception of the cup transforms in later grail literature.

The Da Vinci Code and *The Hiram Key* profess to see great significance in the fact that in his great painting of the Last Supper Leonardo neglected to depict any cup at all. This is supposed to mean that he understood the cup, or the grail, to refer to something symbolic, something that would not have been visible to the physical eye, perhaps the holy seed of the Christ. But isn't there another explanation ready to hand? What if he is just painting *John's* version of the supper? That one has no reference to the Eucharistic cup and bread, as we have already observed. In fact, we can be sure this is what he was doing because of the depiction of the youthful (supposedly effeminate) disciple John sitting next to him, an arrangement peculiar to John's gospel (13:23, 25). So much for that.

CHALICE OF CHIVALRY

As everyone knows, the grail forms an important part of the King Arthur mythos. The legends of the grail serve a purpose analogous to that of the Book of Mormon, which extends the biblical tradition to a latter-day Christian community far removed from either the time or the place of the Bible. What the Book of Mormon does for American Latter-day Saints the grail sagas do for Western Europeans: They tie them into the salvation history of the Bible. But, as we shall see in a bit more detail, the grail legends teem with elements that do not naturally fit into such a framework and cannot be explained easily within it. Basically, what happens in the grail legend is that, after an ethereal apparition of the grail in midair above the Round Table, King Arthur resolves to locate the holy relic and to provide a fitting setting for it. So he sends forth his knights to find and retrieve it. In the end, only the purest is able to procure the grail, and only after a series of arduous labors.

Presently we must survey the principal sagas and ballads, that is, written literary texts, from which this rough summary has been distilled. But first let us note that, like the New Testament gospels, these documents constitute a writing down or compilation of oral traditions. The materials from which they have been composed are the songs and prose stories told at the fireside or at the feasting board by a class of wandering raconteurs who sang for their supper before moving on to their next venue. They were much like the performing troupes of the medieval miracle and mystery plays as depicted in Ingmar Bergman's *The Seventh Seal*.

They were also much like the itinerant charismatic prophets and apostles who made the rounds of the earliest churches, repeating, expounding, and sometimes coining sayings and stories of Jesus. After much repetition and redaction, these stories came to rest in our gospels, the work of editors who, like the Brothers Grimm, decided to collect the precious material before it should vanish, replaced by the dry abstractions of institutional preaching. As Roger Sherman Loomis, in *The Grail: From Celtic Myth to Christian Symbol*, says, "Nothing better explains, then, some of the typical features of Arthurian romance in its early stages—its episodic, loose structure, its glaring inconsistencies—than the fact that it was based on the numberless short *contes* which formed the stock-in-trade of wandering *conteurs*."[3] Loomis might as well be describing the synoptic gospels (Matthew, Mark, and Luke).

The oral origin and character of the grail romances already throw into serious question the Teabing hypothesis, namely, that the grail was an esoteric cipher invented to communicate to a chosen few the secret of the bloodline of Jesus. How strange, if this were so, that those who transmitted, who had even, so far as we know, *created* the legend, should have been oblivious of the "true" meaning of it, since they themselves give nary a hint of it.

Now, theoretically, it is always possible that the transmitters of the grail cycles were unaware of a prior, deeper significance of stories that they and their hearers appreciated simply for their entertainment value. But then we would need to have some proof, at least some evidence, that there had been an earlier stage in which the stories were designed and circulated as a vehicle for the supposed esoteric message. And there is none.

By contrast, in his masterpiece *Love in the Western World*, Denis de Rougemont makes an impressive case that the soap-operatic ballads of the fourteenth-century troubadours of southern France, the songs of courtly love, were dumbed-down versions of paeans of mystical devotion addressed by Cathar mystics and Sufis to Dame Wisdom, the heavenly Sophia. These singers had sought to unite their spirits with her in an exercise of Platonic Eros. These Gnostic psalmists were forced by the rigors of the Albigensian Crusade to go underground. Their celestial love lyrics had to be put into the adjacent idiom of secular, romantic, albeit chaste, male-female love between mortals. This would be a case closely analogous to that demanded by the Teabing hypothesis, in that we would have an initially esoteric allegorical myth forced subsequently to don the garb of secular entertainment and thus doomed to be perpetuated in ignorance by the uninitiated. The fatal difference is that de Rougemont is able to point to ample evidence of the earlier esoteric stage of interpretation, later lost, whereas Baigent, Leigh, Lincoln, and Brown cannot. Theirs is a circular argument.

THE GRAIL CANON

There are ten major grail texts, or groups of texts, all written in the first half of the thirteenth century. Again we may spot analogies to the New Testament gospels in that some of these grail gospels are interdependent, while others embody rival or variant underlying traditions. The first, written about 1180, is the *Conte del Graal* or *Perceval* by Chrétien de Troyes, which he wrote up from some older book in the possession of his patron, Count Philip of Flanders. He did not finish the tale, dropping the pen before the grail knight, having missed an earlier opportunity, redeems himself by finding the grail again and asking the proper questions. Just as Matthew and Luke, like various later copyists, found Mark's ending too abrupt and added their own continuations, so did at least four writers continue Chrétien's work only twenty years later, namely, Manessier (writing between 1214 and 1227), Gerbert de Montreuil (ca. 1230), and two anonymous writers (before 1200). These four constitute the second version.

The third version of the grail saga is the famous *Parsifal* of Wolfram von Eschenbach, a knight of Bavaria, written between 1200 and 1210. The fourth is the Welsh romance *Peredur*, which forms part of the collection of Welsh tales the *Mabinogion*. Fifth is a French version that scholars have denominated the *Didot Perceval* in honor of the former owner of the sole extant manuscript. Sixth is *The High History of the Holy Grail*, or *Perlesvaus*, stemming from Belgium or the north of France. Seventh is a portion of the Vulgate cycle, the *Prose Lancelot*. The eighth is the next chapter of the Vulgate cycle, the *Queste del Saint Graal*. The ninth source is Robert de Boron's *Joseph d'Arimathie*, penned in Burgundia. Tenth is the *Estoire del Saint Graal*, the first segment of the Vulgate cycle but written later than the other two listed here. The fourth through tenth are of uncertain date, but all of them appear to have been completed by 1230.

And only the ninth and tenth feature the prehistory of the grail, Joseph of Arimathea, and so forth. The other accounts do not presuppose it. This is important because it suggests the connection to Jesus and his alleged relatives (Joseph of Arimathea) is not an integral part of the tale but rather a later addition. That does not look good for the Teabing hypothesis, for which the bloodline connection is the whole raison d'être of the grail story.

EXPANDING EPIC

Chrétien's version lacks any epiphany of the grail and has Perceval simply happen upon the ailing Fisher King, who suffers a loss of virility due to a wound in the thigh (a euphemism, as sometimes in the Bible, for penis). Sitting with the king in the palace, he observes a strange procession. One maiden carries aloft a steely lance, unaccountably bleeding from its tip. Another carries "a grail," a large, moderately deep serving pan, into a closed-off chamber (apparently where *another* lame king, the father of the first one, eats in seclusion). Perceval thinks of asking the meaning of all this: "What is the significance of that grail? Whom does one serve with it?" But he thinks it better to remain tactfully silent, not to speak out of turn. His better judgment causes him to lose his golden opportunity: Everyone was waiting for him to ask these questions, for (as he discovers on the morrow) only when a visitor should ask them would the Fisher King be restored to soundness.

Next morning, Perceval awakens to discover himself alone and abandoned in the castle. Not far off he meets a beautiful maiden, his long-lost cousin, who knows what has transpired and tells him of his error and of the dire consequences it must bring. Much later, back in Arthur's palace, a hideous old crone appears and repeats the same tidings. Reproaching himself heartily, Perceval vows to find the grail again, and then he will ask the requisite questions. On his quest he suffers amnesia, forgetting both his name and his Christian faith. At length, however, he meets up with his uncle, a pious hermit, who sets him to rights and explains that the grail contained but a single Eucharistic wafer, all the nourishment the hidden king required. But then, prematurely, it is all over. Presumably, Perceval would ultimately have proven his worth and gained the spiritual sensitivity he lacked before. Notice: *Here the grail is not a Last Supper cup*. Not the cup of the blood, and this makes the grail-bloodline link impossible.

PERCEVAL PLUS GAWAIN

The first anonymous continuation of this story is really a separate and roughly parallel account, starring Gawain instead of Perceval. It has been forcibly joined to the original. Sent by Guinevere to apprehend a mysterious knight galloping through Camelot at full tilt, Gawain catches up to him only to witness him being struck down by an unseen assailant. The dying knight, still unknown, bids the hero to undertake his mission, wearing his armor and mounted on his steed. Like Abraham setting out cluelessly from Haran, Gawain accepts the commission and rides through a vast forest. Emerging from it, he reaches the seashore, and stretching away before him he sees a long, tree-lined causeway leading to a great manor house dimly lit by a campfire. Fearing the dark and the wind, he is nonetheless drawn after his frantic horse to the mansion. Soon Gawain beholds a corpse laid out in state, then a funeral service conducted by clergy who vanish when it concludes. Next, a great king welcomes him to a feast, where he beholds a pair of marvels: again the bleeding lance and the grail, which, in this version, magically feeds and serves all present. Then, all the feasters vanish.

The king returns and points to a broken sword lying upon the corpse's breast. Can Gawain reunite the sword? If so, he may avenge the death of the man who lies before them, and the deed will restore all the adjacent territory, the vegetation of which languishes. He tries and fails. The disappointed king begins to answer Gawain's questions about the wonders he has seen, starting with the blood-dripping lance. It is that same lance that pierced the side of the crucified Christ. But before

Gawain can inquire concerning the grail, his long lack of sleep takes its toll and, despite himself, he falls asleep.

When the knight awakens next morning, he is alone. Even the mansion is nowhere to be seen. But as he rides homeward through the wasteland, the peasants assure him that, by asking about the lance, he has caused the parched streams to flow again. But he had stymied full restoration by his failure to ask whom one served with the grail. Note that, while Chrétien's original gave no Christian coloring to the bleeding spear, it did at least have the (unexplained) grail contain a communion host. That does not quite make the vessel the cup of the Last Supper. In the anonymous sequel, the bloody spear becomes the crucifixion spear, but *the grail is a magical horn of plenty with no religious association.*

The second anonymous continuation tries to tie up loose ends left by the first. Perceval arrives at the mansion where Gawain had failed to reunite the sword of the dead hero. He is offered the same challenge and succeeds. We learn that the dead king, whose passing plunged the realm into ruin, was the King of the Waste Land, murdered by a nearby noble, the Red Knight, who may be slain only by him who restores the sword. The king whom Gawain had met and who tells Perceval all this is the Fisher King, the dead king's brother. He, too, is wounded in the thigh, but only due to carelessness in handling the shards of the sword. Perceval manages to avenge the King of the Waste Land, whereupon the Fisher King and the vigor of his realm are renewed. *Nothing is said here about the cup or the blood of Jesus.*

PEREDUR PERDURES

In the Welsh *Peredur*, many of the same elements recur, though in different combinations. Peredur (= Perceval) happens upon a castle belonging to an old man who turns out to be his uncle. He bids Peredur to spar with young men in the court to try his combat skills. He does well, and his uncle offers to train him further. Departing, he reaches another castle, shares supper with another old man, another uncle, who also asks about his fighting skills. The man directs him to strike an iron pillar with a sword. Both shatter. He mends them together again, then repeats the blow and the mending. But after a third blow he fails, signaling that he has not reached his full, destined strength. Two young men pass through the hall carrying between them the bleeding spear, at which all present begin to weep and wail. Peredur is curious but refrains from asking the meaning of the spectacle. Next two young women enter, carrying a large salver with a man's head in a pool of blood! Amid the loud lamentation, Peredur maintains his silence.

He leaves the next day, meets the beautiful young cousin in the woods, and returns to Camelot. There Peredur receives the rebuke of the old hag: Had he asked the meaning of the lance and the head, the Lame King would have regained his health and the land with him. We later learn the Lame King was the second uncle. Later still Peredur learns that the head was that of a cousin killed by the Sorceress of Gloucester, who also maimed the king. And, of course, Peredur is destined to avenge these outrages and to restore plenty to the Waste Land, which he does. The bleeding lance remains an enigma. *In all this there is no Christian reference.* The great platter containing the head fills the space occupied by the grail in other versions, but the head is no sacred relic, such as the head of John the Baptist, as one might expect.

Robert de Boron's *Joseph of Arimathea* represents a whole-sale Christianization of the grail, supplying the famous back story of the grail as the Last Supper chalice and of Joseph as its guardian, and so forth. In it everything is explicit that we have not even been able to trace implicitly in these other versions. The explicitly Eucharistic coloring of any of the remaining versions seems to represent borrowing from Robert de Boron. For instance, *Perlesvaus* makes use of Chrétien and his second continuator, the *Prose Lancelot*, and perhaps Robert de Boron, whence he derived the notion of the grail as the container of the blood of Jesus from the crucifixion. Here is a narrative full of overt, even clumsy, allegorical teaching, but none of the kind posited by *Holy Blood, Holy Grail* or *The Da Vinci Code*. It is all a mass of forced and wearisome parallels between this knight and that virtue, the evil king and the devil, Perceval's liberation of the devil's castle and the Harrowing of Hell. Nothing about a royal bloodline or a messianic marriage.

THE VULGATE CYCLE

We find a more thoroughly Christian version of the grail in the three works combined in the Vulgate cycle, the *Lancelot*, the *Queste del Saint Graal*, and the *Estoire del Saint Graal*. These are also the chief sources for Thomas Malory's *La Morte d'Arthur*. In the *Lancelot*, we find Gawain at the Grail Castle, where he witnesses a holy maiden carrying aloft the "holy vessel" as she passes before those seated in the banqueting hall. It was made "in the semblance of a chalice," and as she passes, each knight, except Gawain, kneels, whereupon the tables become laden with the most sumptuous fare.

Later, in the *Queste del Saint Graal*, we have the famous Pentecost epiphany of the grail at Camelot, the revelation that prompts Galahad's search for the grail. And yet, despite the Christian symbolism, the grail retains the consistent magical feature of feeding all present with whatever food they wish. And indeed when one looks closely at the odd features of any and all versions of the saga, one begins to notice a great many features that appear to have no Christian relevance at all, often making little sense even as features of a coherent plot. It is as if we are viewing a building put together crudely from fragments of older, demolished structures. All manner of oddities protrude to no purpose that nonetheless made sense in the original structure. Where do these features of the grail stories originate?

CELTIC CROCKERY

What would it mean for the Teabing hypothesis if the grail cycle could be shown to be an arbitrary patchwork of mismatched pieces from pre-Christian folklore? It would render utterly superfluous the whole theory of the grail being designed as a cipher for the legacy of Jesus and the Magdalene. Scholars, including Alfred Nutt and Roger Sherman Loomis, have long ago demonstrated that the grail romances are based on materials derived from Celtic myths and legends and that virtually every major and minor puzzle may be solved in this way. To begin with the strange notion of the grail as a miraculous horn of plenty, Loomis shows that the prototype for it was the mythic horn or cauldron of Bran the Blessed, a Celtic god. From it all blessings, all gifts and foods, emerged. The Celtic connection is all the more sure in light of the fact that, in some versions of the grail legend, the maimed Fisher King is named Bron (*Didot Perceval*) or Brons (Robert de Boron). Not only that, but the Celtic divinity Bran is himself the victim of a hobbling wound in the "foot" (another biblical euphemism for penis) or in the thigh.[4] He is the classic case of the nature god, the corn king, whose vitality is identical to that of his realm. Bran is the son of the sea god Lyr, which would seem to account for the doubling of the (implicitly divine) maimed king. The bleeding lance has been taken over from the flaming lance of Lug, the Irish sun god. Both are said to hover upright above a silver bowl.[5]

The fair maiden who carries the grail through the dining hall turns out to be another avatar of the hideous hag who shows up at Camelot to scold Perceval. And this means she was originally a mythic character called the Sovranty of Ireland, a living embodiment, first, of the amazing beauty of Ireland, then of the seasonal rigors of its climate.[6] The crucial questions about the grail and the king who drinks from it (ill-suited to the cup of the Last Supper!) parallel the mystery of the tale of the Irish hero Conn. Like Perceval, he finds himself in a castle, that of Lug the sun god, welcomed to join the king at table, served by a crowned maiden bearing a golden vessel. *She* asks *him*, "To whom shall this cup be given?" In the end, the castle and its occupants vanish, and he is left with the cup of prophecy by which he predicts his successors to the throne.

How did Bran's horn of plenty become the vessel bearing a communion wafer (in Chrétien's version)? As Loomis shows, the transformation must have come about via misunderstanding. The bards and tale-tellers brought their repertoire with them from Britain. French audiences were not familiar with sacred drinking horns common in Britain. The Old French words for "horn" and "body" (as in the sacramental "body of Christ") were identical: *li cors*. When the French heard of a *horn*, or as they thought, a *body*, that brought miraculous bounty, they thought of current ecclesiastical stories of saints and hermits whose sole physical nourishment was the wafer of the mass.[7] And thus the confusion—and Christianization—of the original grail mythos.

A PRETTY EMPTY CUP

What is the relevance of these observations for the Teabing hypothesis? First, the grail legends are Celtic in origin and can therefore have nothing to do with any Merovingian claims to the throne of France. The French loved and retold the grail stories, in their reinterpreted Christian guise, but they came from Britain, where Merovingian claims were moot. This does not mean that the Christian form of the grail legend was innocent of polemics, however. As some have suggested, the (secondary) connection of Joseph of Arimathea with the grail represents a foundation legend for an autonomous Celtic Christianity, resisting the growing domination of Roman Catholicism by claiming an independent apostolic foundation by Joseph of Arimathea.

Second, the late, secondary Christian coloring of the grail

cycle eliminates the possibility that the legends served as the ancient vehicle through which the messianic pedigree of the Merovingians was passed down. In fact, one might say that the Christian appropriation of the pagan Celtic grail material was a co-optation of the earlier tradition in the same spirit of opportunism with which Pierre Plantard and his colleagues in the spurious Priory of Sion have sought to hijack the grail tradition for their own purposes.

Third, the fact that the grail story, in any of its versions, is a late mosaic of legend fragments, originally unrelated to one another, means that the grail legend was never designed to function as a cipher for the dynastic claims of Jesus's heirs or for anything else. It came together almost like single-celled archaeozoa linked fortuitously by cell membranes as they floated haphazardly through the sea of primal ooze. No, what Dan Brown and his mentors see in the grail legend, they brought to it.

NOTES

1. Joachim Jeremias, *The Eucharistic Words of Jesus*, trans. Arnold Ehrhardt (Oxford: Basil Blackwell, 1955), pp. 108–109, 128–29.

2. Anna Katharina Emmerich, *The Dolorous Passion of Our Lord Jesus Christ* (London: Burns, Oates & Washbourne, 1942).

3. Roger Sherman Loomis, *The Grail: From Celtic Myth to Christian Symbol* (New York: Columbia University Press, 1963), p. 13.

4. Ibid., pp. 55–59.

5. Ibid., p. 78.

6. Ibid., pp. 51–53.

7. Ibid., pp. 60–61.

Chapter 3

BEYOND THE CROSS

Did Jesus Survive Crucifixion?

Though *The Da Vinci Code* seems to assume that Jesus died on the cross, in accord with conventional beliefs, many of the writers with whom Dan Brown is allied do not think it happened that way. Michael Baigent, Henry Lincoln, and Richard Leigh; Paul S. Blezard; Laurence Gardner; and others picture Jesus somehow surviving the cross and shaking the dust off his sandals as he left the Holy Land to seek a friendlier clime elsewhere, usually pictured as southern France. Barbara Thiering, though not to be associated with the excesses of the Teabing school, is sometimes cited in the interest of the belief in Jesus cheating death on the cross, as she does argue for it in her books, including *Jesus the Man* (a.k.a. *Jesus and the Secret of the Dead Sea Scrolls*). In so doing, she is reviving the "Essene hypothesis" of the eighteenth- and nineteenth-century Rationalists. Dr. Thiering arrives at her conclusions about Jesus and his postcrucifixion missionary journeys by an esoteric, Qumran-style interpretation of the New Testament. The older Rationalists (Heinrich Eberhard Gottlob Paulus, Karl Friedrich Bahrdt, Karl Heinrich Venturini, even Friedrich Daniel Ernst Schleiermacher), by contrast, were motivated by the dictates of their theology, which now seems quite arbitrary. In short, they juggled two ill-fitting beliefs. First, they believed in the inerrancy of the gospel texts, which meant that if it said Jesus was up on that cross Friday and was seen alive on Sunday, then both must somehow be true. Second, God does not violate the laws of nature; hence there were never any supernatural "miracles." The conclusion they were forced to adopt was that Jesus had indeed been crucified but had somehow survived it. Thus, in both cases, Dr. Thiering's and that of the Rationalists, the belief that Jesus survived crucifixion is a by-product of other considerations. No one will defend the latter today, and to defend the former is beside our point here. What I want to ask is whether there may be anything to be said for the Swoon Theory on the basis of more conventional historical-critical analysis.

Might Jesus have survived crucifixion? Is this not too far-fetched a hypothesis for us to take seriously? Not at all. In fact, it was not unheard of for victims of crucifixion to survive it. After all, the mode of execution was designed to kill the poor wretches slowly, over a period of days. One might be taken down. Josephus the historian, writing at the end of the first century, tells us that the friends or relatives of a crucified man might be able to have him taken down alive.

> When I was sent by Titus Caesar with Cerealius and a thousand horsemen to a certain village called Thecoa, in order to know whether it were a place fit for a camp, as I came back I saw many captives crucified, and remembered three of them

as my former acquaintances. I was very sorry at this in my mind, and went with tears in my eyes to Titus, and told him of them; so he immediately commanded them to be taken down, and to have the greatest care taken of them, in order to their recovery; yet two of them died under the physicians' hands, while the third recovered.[1]

It is surprising that the theory of Jesus surviving crucifixion is not more widely championed. Hugh J. Schonfield is often mentioned as an advocate of the theory, and he very nearly was. In his book *The Passover Plot* (1965), he speculated that Jesus did try to engineer surviving the cross by being fed a drug and taken down early, but the scheme failed when he was stabbed in the side, something he hadn't planned on. Along with Barbara Thiering, the theory's most eloquent and persuasive defender is J. Duncan M. Derrett (*The Anastasis: The Resurrection of Jesus as a Historical Event*, 1982). Most who address it at all hold it up to mockery, and for them it is enough to quote the arch-skeptic David Friedrich Strauss against it: "It is impossible that a being who had stolen half-dead out of the sepulcher, who crept about weak and ill, wanting [i.e., lacking] medical treatment, who required bandaging, strengthening, and indulgence, and who still at last yielded to his sufferings, could have given the disciples the impression that he was a conqueror over death and the grave, the Prince of Life: an impression which lay at the bottom of their future ministry. Such a resuscitation could . . . by no possibility have changed their sorrow into enthusiasm, have elevated their reverence into worship."[2]

But this is not at all clear. Strauss (unusually for him) and the many apologists who quote him are playing the Rationalist game by taking for granted an accurate depiction of the events of Easter and then juggling possible explanations for them. The real issue is whether Jesus might have survived, with his disciples just glad enough to have him back, by the providence of God. All the extravagant preaching of a glorious resurrection, fainting guards at the tomb, angels swooping down in shining robes, would have been the window dressing of subsequent retellings, once the hypothetical original belief in the cheating of death had been transformed into a mythic belief in a resurrection of a dead man.

And yet possibility is not probability. Before going further, however, it must be said that the Swoon Theory, the idea that Jesus survived crucifixion, certainly wins the trophy for probability if the other contestant is the notion of a supernatural resurrection performed by an invisible god. The latter may indeed have happened for all we know, but as poor historians who can do no better than gauge probability on the basis of comparison to what we usually see happening around us, we would have to give the palm to the Swoon Theory every time.

There remains a third alternative, though it is one that will do Baigent, Lincoln, and Leigh no good. It may be that the facts of Jesus's death have been lost, perhaps not having been known or notable, and that the vacuum of this ignorance was filled by imaginative fiction of a kind well known in the period, namely, the romance adventure novel. Books of this sort had entertained mass audiences since the seventh century BCE if not earlier, though their heyday was the second century CE. The composition of the gospels falls well within these limits, and the suggestion offered here is that, at one time, the story of Jesus was told in a novelistic fashion and that the conventions of this genre supplied the source for the crucifixion-resurrection sequence. Only at first it was an escape from death, as in the novels, rather than a resurrection from it.

It is quite striking that in several of the novels, the heroine is falsely thought to have died and is entombed still alive. She awakens in the darkness of the tomb and despairs until fortuitously robbers come to loot the tomb, discovering her alive. Not daring to leave witnesses, they make a fast decision to take her along and sell her as a slave. Soon after, her loved ones visit the tomb to mourn and are startled to find the tomb empty, sometimes with grave clothes or funerary tokens left intact.

In Chariton's *Chaereas and Callirhoe*, Chaereas is falsely incited to rage against his wife, Callirhoe, and delivers a kick that seems to kill her. She is entombed alive. Soon pirates (who are virtually ubiquitous in these novels) arrive to rob the tomb. They discover Callirhoe alive, now having revived in the cool of the mausoleum, and they kidnap her to sell her as a slave. In her captivity, Callirhoe pities her doubly vexed husband in terms strikingly reminiscent of the New Testament empty tomb accounts: "You are mourning for me and repenting and sitting by an empty tomb."[3]

But the resemblance to the gospel accounts only grows stronger a little later when poor Chaereas discovers the empty tomb.

> When he reached the tomb, he found that the stones had been moved and the entrance was open. He was astonished at the sight and overcome by fearful perplexity at what had happened. Rumor—a swift messenger—told the Syracusans this amazing news. They all quickly crowded round the tomb, but no one dared go inside until Hermocrates gave an order to do so. [Compare John 20:4–6.]

The man who went in reported the whole situation accu-
rately. It seemed incredible that even the corpse was not
lying there. Then Chaereas himself determined to go in, in
his desire to see Callirhoe again even dead; but though he
hunted through the tomb, he could find nothing. Many
people could not believe it and went in after him. They were
all seized by helplessness. One of those standing there said,
"The funeral offerings have been carried off [Cartlidge's
translation reads: "The shroud has been stripped off"—cf.
John 20:6–7]—it is tomb robbers who have done that; but
what about the corpse—where is it?" Many different sugges-
tions circulated in the crowd. Chaereas looked towards the
heavens, stretched up his arms, and cried: "Which of the
gods is it, then, who has become my rival in love and carried
off Callirhoe and is now keeping her with him?"[4]

The parallels to the empty tomb accounts, especially to John
20:1–10, are abundant and close. Chaereas even suggests that
Callirhoe has been (like Jesus) translated to heaven. Later,
Callirhoe, reflecting on her misadventures, says, "I have died
and come to life again."[5]

In Miletus Callirhoe comes to believe that Chaereas perished while searching for her. To console her and to lay her
fond memory of his rival to rest, Dionysius, her new husband,
erects a tomb for Chaereas. It lacks his body, but this is not, as
all think, because the corpse is irrecoverable but rather because
he is still alive elsewhere. His tomb is empty because he is still
alive. Why seek the living among the dead?

We meet with the familiar pattern again in the *Ephesian
Tale* of Xenophon. The beautiful Anthia seems to have died
from a dose of poison but has in fact merely been placed in a

deathlike coma. She awakens from it in the tomb: "Meanwhile some pirates had found that a girl had been given a sumptuous burial and that a great store of woman's finery was buried with her, and a great horde of gold and silver. After nightfall they came to the tomb, burst open the doors, came in and took away the finery, and saw that Anthia was still alive. They thought that this too would turn out very profitable for them, raised her up, and wanted to take her."[6]

Equally striking is the recurrent feature of the hero being condemned to the cross, sometimes actually being crucified, but being reprieved or rescued just in time. For instance, Chaereas is condemned to the cross: "Without even seeing them or hearing their defense the master at once ordered the crucifixion of the sixteen men in the hut. They were brought out chained together at foot and neck, each carrying his cross. . . . Now Chaereas said nothing when he was led off with the others, but [his friend] Polycharmus, as he carried his cross, said: 'Callirhoe, it is because of you that we are suffering like this! You are the cause of all our troubles!'"[7] At the last minute Chaereas's sentence is commuted: "Mithridates sent everybody off to reach Chaereas before he died. They found the rest nailed up on their crosses; Chaereas was just ascending his. So the executioner checked his gesture, and Chaereas climbed down from his cross."[8] As he later recalls, "Mithridates at once ordered that I be taken down from the cross—I was practically finished by then."

Here, then, is a hero who went to the cross for his beloved and returned alive. In the same story, a villain is likewise crucified, though, gaining his just deserts, he is not reprieved. This is Theron, the pirate who carried poor Callirhoe into slavery.

"He was crucified in front of Callirhoe's tomb."[9] We find another instance of a crucifixion adjacent to the tomb of the righteous in *The Alexander Romance* when Alexander arrests the assassins of his worthy foe Darius. He commanded them "to be crucified at Darius's grave."[10] We cannot help being reminded of the location of Jesus's burial "in the place where he was crucified" (John 19:41).

In Xenophon's *An Ephesian Tale*, Anthia's beloved Habrocomes goes in search of her and winds up being condemned to death through a series of misadventures too long to recount here. "They set up the cross and attached him to it, tying his hands and feet tight with ropes; that is the way the Egyptians crucify. Then they went away and left him hanging there, thinking that the victim was securely in place." But Habrocomes prays that he may yet be spared such an undeserved death. He is heard for his loud cries and tears. "A sudden gust of wind arose and struck the cross, sweeping away the subsoil on the cliff where it had been fixed. Habrocomes fell into the torrent and was swept away; the water did him no harm; his fetters did not get in his way."[11]

When the hero and heroine, both having brushed death so closely, reunite, each can scarcely believe the other is alive. There is a recognition scene where one insists that he or she is truly alive and no ghost. For example, Habrocomes returns to a temple where, in happier days, he and Anthia had erected images of themselves as an offering to Aphrodite. Still deprived of Anthia and thinking her to be dead, he sits there and weeps. He is discovered by old friends Leucon and Rhode: "They did not recognize him, but wondered who would stay beside someone else's offerings. And so Leucon spoke to him. 'Why are you sitting weeping, young man?' Habrocomes replied, 'I am . . . the unfortunate Habrocomes!' When Leucon and Rhode heard this they were immediately dumbfounded, but gradually recovered and recognized him by his appearance and voice, from what he said, and from his mention of Anthia."[12]

Here we see an unmistakable resemblance to the New Testament empty tomb accounts, where Jesus or an angel accosts a weeping mourner, and a dramatic recognition results. Compare John 20:11–16:

> Mary remained weeping outside the tomb, and as she cried, she bent over to peer into the cavity. There she saw a pair of angels, in white robes, posted where the body of Jesus had been, one at the head, the other at the feet. They inquired of her, "Woman, why are you crying?"
>
> She answered them, "Because someone has moved my Lord, and I have no idea where they put him!" As she spoke, she turned around, only to see Jesus himself standing before her. But she had no inkling that it was Jesus.
>
> Jesus said to her, "Woman, why are you crying? Who is it you are looking for?"
>
> Taking him for the caretaker, she said, "Sir, if you are the one who moved him, tell me where you put him, and I will take him off your hands."
>
> But Jesus said to her, "Mary!"
>
> She looked at him and said to him in Hebrew, "Rabboni!" which means, "My master!"

Here we also have the question "Why are you weeping?" the initial failure of recognition, and the recognition being sparked by the mention of a woman's name. Luke 24:13 ff. is only slightly less close:

That very day, two of them were headed for a village called Emmaus, about seven miles distant from Jerusalem, deep in conversation about everything that had transpired. While they were thus preoccupied, who but Jesus himself should approach, catching up to them. But their eyes could not register his identity. And he asked them, "What on earth so animates this conversation of yours as you walk?" So they stopped in their tracks and fell silent, looking dejected.

Finally, one of them, by the name of Cleopas, replied. "You must be the only pilgrim to Jerusalem unaware of the events of these past few days!"

And he replied, "What events might those be?"

And they answered, "The ruckus over Jesus of Nazareth! Oh, he was a prophet mighty in word and deed! At least God and all the people thought so! But our arch-priests and rulers handed him over to be sentenced to death, and they crucified him. And we had great hopes he would be the one to set Israel free.

"And that's not the end of it! Today is the third day since it all happened. And, to make matters worse, some women of our group threw a scare into us. They went out to the tomb this morning, and found the body was gone! They came back prattling about a vision they'd had, of angels who claimed he was alive! Some of our companions went to check things out: the women were right. But they saw no sign of him."

And he said to them, "You poor fools! Too obtuse to take the word of the prophets! Wasn't it part of the plan that the Christ had to suffer all the things you've described before he could ascend his throne?" So, starting with Genesis, he went through the Prophets explaining which were references to him, and what they meant.

When they finally came near their destination, he pretended he was headed further down the road. But they refused to hear of it and insisted he stay the night with them. "Look, evening draws on apace, and most of the day is gone." So he accepted their invitation and went in. When they were gathered round the table, he picked up the bread, said the blessing, and divided it. All of a sudden, their eyes widened in recognition—then he was gone!

One said to the other: "It makes sense! Didn't you feel that mounting excitement as he deciphered the scriptures for us while we were walking?" Though it was nightfall, they lost no time retracing their steps to Jerusalem. Soon they located the eleven and their companions in a meeting. "What's all this?" they asked, and were told, "What the women said was true! The Lord *is* risen! Simon saw him!" Then the two disciples told what had happened on their journey, and how he revealed himself to them in the breaking of bread.

NOW ACCEPTING IMPLICATIONS

The crucifixion and empty tomb, I suggest, may form not part of the career of the historical Jesus but rather of the novelistic form into which his story was cast. These features may be no more historical than the virgin birth. Many scholars already deem the empty tomb story a legend, but perhaps instead it is fiction, a novelistic embellishment. Perhaps even the survived crucifixion of Jesus is simply a literary convention. (The irony here is choice: Our larger purpose is to scrutinize a novel based on the gospels, and we wind up suggesting that the gospels themselves are in some measure based on ancient novels!)

What are the implications for the historical Jesus question? They are plain. As many scholars now think, Jesus may first have been remembered simply as a great sage like Pythagoras and Apollonius. Eventually his life became novelized in larger-than-life, hero-worshiping terms, as did the "biographies" of Empedocles, Pythagoras, Epimenides, Apollonius, and others. At this stage, the story would have intended not that Jesus actually died and rose from the dead but that he seemed to die and did not, the Swoon Theory. Recognition scenes in which Jesus says, "It is I myself; no spirit has flesh and bones as you see that I have" (Luke 24:39) simply meant he was not dead, had not died, despite all appearances.

In fact, this is certainly the point in a virtually identical scene from the biographical novel *The Life of Apollonius of Tyana* by Philostratus in the third century CE. The sage Apollonius had attracted the unwelcome attention of the cruel Caesar Domitian, who had summoned him to stand trial before him in Rome. Apollonius gladly complied, knowing that Domitian had no power over him. In prison, he told his disciple Damis not to fear, but to go on home. He would be fine. The day came, and he told off the emperor much as Socrates had put the Athenian senate in its place at his own trial. Then he suddenly vanished into thin air! At once he appeared in the midst of his gaping disciples at the other end of the Mediterranean. At first they believed they were seeing a ghost, but he assured them otherwise: "Take hold of me, and if I evade you, then I am indeed a ghost come to you from the realm of Persephone, such as the gods of the under-world reveal to those who are dejected with much mourning. But if I resist your touch, then you shall persuade Damis that I am both alive and that I have not abandoned my body." They were no longer able to disbelieve, but rose up and threw themselves on his neck and kissed him, and asked him about his defence" (8:12).

Again, the otherwise pointless loose end of the fact that Jesus seemed to have died so quickly, to Pilate's surprise (Mark 15:44; John 19:33), is a vestige of the stage when Jesus had simply survived the cross. The quick death, of which nothing further is made in the present gospels, originally would have served as a clue that Jesus had not really died at all. This early release from the cross is what saved his life.

John (or one of his redactors) has interpolated at this point the verses (19:34–37) about the soldier piercing the heart of Jesus. There is a contradiction in that the immediately preceding material says they found him to be dead, but the spear thrust has them make *sure* he's dead, as if they did *not* know him to be dead. Why this redundancy? John wanted to negate the possibility of reading the story as teaching that Jesus only seemed to die, which must be the way some of his contemporaries were reading it.

Similarly John 20:20 has changed the recognition scene from having Jesus display his *solid* hands and *feet* to his gaping disciples, as we still find it in Luke 24:39, to having him display his *wounded* hands and *side*, a redactional change clearly connected with the lance passage. Here he wants to eliminate the reading of the recognition scene as the reunion with a Jesus who escaped the cross. And note that but for this redactional addition, plus the Doubting Thomas story, told to make the same point (John 20:24–29), there is no note in the New Testament that Jesus was affixed to the cross with nails.

Why does Matthew 27:57 specify that Joseph of Arimathea is

wealthy when it says he buried Jesus in his own tomb? Perhaps the evangelist wants to fill out the narrative from Isaiah 53:9a ("And they made his grave with the wicked and with a rich man in his death"), but to invoke this text would actually cause Matthew problems since it makes Joseph a "wicked" man, in contradiction to Matthew's own statement. Nor does he draw attention to it as a prophetic fulfillment. No, rather he simply left a vestige of the original version in which Jesus's burial in a rich man's tomb provided the motive for tomb robbers to open the tomb, whereupon they found Jesus alive inside, precisely as in the novels. Since it is an opulent tomb belonging to a rich man, the rogues naturally expect it to contain funerary tokens worthy of their attentions. Now that it is sealed, they assume Joseph himself has died and is buried within!

In retrospect, it becomes easier to recognize other narrative clues of what was to come. Note that, in the Garden of Gethsemane, Jesus asks his Father to spare him the chore of the crucifixion, a petition in which there is nothing shameful: He can scarcely have been human had escape not crossed his mind. But can we not recognize this as a wink to the reader that Jesus's prayer will be answered, and not in the Pickwickian sense of "Sorry, too bad!"? Though Jesus declares himself ready to die, it will turn out he does not have to! The idea is just like Abraham being called by God to sacrifice his son Isaac. He is willing to carry out the act when God intervenes by an angel and tells him he needn't go through with it. It was only the willingness that God wanted to see, and now that he has seen it, the death is unnecessary. Jews believed that henceforth the sheer willingness of Isaac to *be* sacrificed availed on behalf of Israel so that for Isaac's sake God would forgive his people's sins. Was that the point in the garden, too? By his yielding prayer, did Jesus already accomplish his saving work as he knelt in Gethsemane? And if he did, there would have remained no particular reason for him to die. Take a second look at Hebrews 5:7-8a in this light: "In the days of his flesh, he offered up prayers and supplications, with loud cries and tears, to him who was able to save him from death, and he was heard for his godly fear. And though he was a son, he learned obedience." It is certainly odd to say that God "heard" his prayer for deliverance from the cross—and then let him die the very death he had lamented! Perhaps Hebrews presupposes a different version of the story in which he cheated death on the cross.

Again, consider the infuriating mockery of Jesus's enemies at the cross (borrowed from Psalm 22:6-8): "Save yourself and come down from the cross!" "He saved others, but he can't seem to save himself! Let him descend from the cross right now, so we may see it, and we will believe he is the Christ, the King of Israel!" (Mark 15:30-32a). As Jesus-friendly readers, we are surely intended to want to see these villains forced to eat their words! And how might that happen? Well, it certainly could if Jesus did come down off the cross immediately, still living! The irony was, it happened before their very eyes, and yet they didn't realize it. Prematurely drugged, he was taken down limp in a stupor.

There is even reason to think there had been a sequence in which Jesus left Palestine to teach among the Jewish Diaspora. In John 7:33-35 we read: "Then Jesus said, 'I shall be with you just a little longer before I return to him who sent me. You will look for me and you will not find me; where I am headed, you cannot follow.' The Jewish authorities said to one another,

'Where does this fellow plan on going to be safe from us? Does he mean to journey among the Diaspora among the Greeks and teach the Greeks?'" This is one of the many places where John sets up what he regards as a misunderstanding in order to have Jesus knock it down for the reader's benefit. That implies he might have heard the view that Jesus had indeed left for a teaching ministry among Greek-speaking Jews. So perhaps this is what some people thought.

Our discussion posits that, underlying the present gospel texts, there may still be discerned traces of an earlier version of the story of Jesus according to which he was providentially rescued from death, surviving his crucifixion. The present, canonical, texts of the gospels seem to assume that Jesus really did die, especially John, who even tries to tighten up the tradition on this point. And yet, as John Dominic Crossan has pointed out, it is certainly odd that not one of the gospel crucifixion accounts seems willing to say, bluntly, "Jesus died." All of them retreat behind some euphemism (Matthew and Mark: "He breathed his last"; Luke and John: "He gave up his Spirit"), as if possibly to leave some wiggle room. Who knows? My point is simply to be fair and to show how a theory set forth in many of the Teabing-related books, though fully as outlandish-seeming as those I am refuting, does have certain strengths. If we say we are interested in New Testament history, our agenda must not be to defend any conventional party line, whether that of a church or of "mainstream scholarship." And, again, if we wish to play the role of historians, all we can do is to set forth the probabilities of the case and maintain an open mind. The historian is not in the business of substituting one dogma for another.

NOTES

1. Flavius Josephus, *The Great Roman-Jewish War: A.D. 66–70,* trans. William Whiston, ed. and introd. by William R. Farmer (Gloucester, MA: Peter Smith, 1970).

2. David Friedrich Strauss, *Life of Jesus for the People,* vol. 1. (London: Williams, 1879), qtd. in J. N. D. Anderson, *The Evidence for the Resurrection* (Downers Grove, IL: Inter-Varsity, 1974), p. 17.

3. Translated by B. P. Reardon, in Reardon, ed., *Collected Ancient Greek Novels* (Berkeley: University of California Press, 1989), p. 37.

4. Ibid., p. 53.

5. Ibid., p. 62.

6. Translated by Graham Anderson. In ibid., pp. 151–52.

7. Ibid., p. 67.

8. Ibid., p. 69.

9. Ibid., p. 57.

10. Translated by Ken Dowden. In ibid., p. 703.

11. Ibid., p. 155.

12. Ibid., p. 167.

Chapter 4

THE GNOSTIC CONNECTION

What Was the Secret Tradition?

The Da Vinci Code and many of the books it draws on mention "Gnosticism" frequently. Anyone conversant with the history and doctrines of that fascinating movement will realize quickly that the term *Gnostic* is being used in these books in an inflated sense, pretty much equivalent to "heretic" or "free-thinker." There is a positive point to such a wider usage, and I mean to return to it below, but in order to see what it is, we first need to get straight what historic, dictionary-definition Gnosticism was.

NO SUCH THING?

An irony has emerged recently on the scholarly scene: Some urge us to drop the rubric "Gnosticism" altogether, as if there is nothing for such a definition to denote. These scholars urge upon us the notion that there were certain motifs (which I will explain in more detail just below), such as belief in secret knowledge, in the soul having to evade malevolent angels on its way to heaven after death, in the coming of a redeemer in phantom flesh, in a hierarchical categorizing of human beings according to whether they possess a divine spark, in the creation of the world by angelic beings, and so forth. But since we find these various tenets occurring in different combinations in different ancient religious movements (Valentinians, Basilideans, Phibionites, Sethians, etc.), then it is misleading to lump them all together as "Gnosticism," as if they were a single religion. And to do this, these scholars say, is only to disguise and repeat the ancient Catholic maneuver of labeling these movements as "heresy" as opposed to the shining alternative of *real* Christianity worthy of the name, that is, "Orthodoxy." We will have just replaced "heresy" with a superficially less offensive term, "Gnosticism." So, they say, we ought to drop the term "Gnosticism."

I must respectfully disagree. We simply need to remind ourselves of what we mean by an "ideal type," since the tag "Gnosticism" is one of those. An ideal type is precisely a textbook definition, an abstraction distilled from several actual instances (in this case, several kindred ancient sects) with more in common than separates them. We use the resulting abstraction as a yardstick with which to measure the differences between the specific instances. This way we are able to understand each particular sect (or whatever) in light of what makes it distinctive. Does the Gospel of Mary lack the notion of salvation being for the elect alone? Fascinating! We will understand this gospel better if we start to work asking why it lacks this tenet while possessing so many other pronounced Gnostic traits. Does Mary reject such elitism? Or is it so early that it does not yet possess this feature of more advanced Gnosticism?

Nor is "Gnosticism" a word of denigration and relegation. One need not oppose it to any implied orthodoxy. When we turn our scrutiny to emergent Catholicism, we may have all manner of theories of understanding it other than as the norm from which Gnosticism deviated. In fact, it might be the reverse! I am of the opinion that Catholic orthodoxy represents a combination of a simplified Gnostic understanding of the Godhead and the Redeemer, together with the sacraments of the mystery religions of the dying-and-rising gods.

Finally, if we forswear the use of the word and category "Gnosticism," we must do the same with the similarly vague labels of "Judaism," "Christianity," "Islam," "Hinduism," and "Buddhism," since all of these possess within themselves far more theological and sectarian diversity than the menagerie of movements we have called Gnosticism. I plan on continuing to call them that in what follows.

I KNOW—BUT I WON'T TELL YOU!

Gnosticism was a pessimistic worldview embraced by those who felt themselves to be strangers in a strange land, isolated and superior to the slobs and fools around them.[1] It was also an ingenious answer to the perennial problem of *theodicy*, getting God off the hook for all the evil in the world. How can a world like this have been the creation of a righteous God and be ruled by his justice? Whence all the tragedy and evil? Gnostics chose to resolve the dilemma by positing that the true God, the unknown one, hidden away within the fullness ("Pleroma") of unapproachable light (1 Tim. 6:16), did not create the world. Instead, he emanated from himself a whole series of paired divine beings (*syzygies*, "yolkfellows"). At the end of this process there emerged a single divinity, *Sophia* (Wisdom). She felt alienated from the godhead, from which, of all the divine entities (*Aions*), she was furthest removed. She was also frustrated for having no partner with whom to beget further *Aions*.

But the divine essence was running out by this point, like a tenth-generation videotape, so when Sophia contrived to bear offspring by herself, a virginal conception and birth, the result was a brutish and malign entity called the *Demiurge*, that is, the Creator, Carpenter, or Craftsman. This character was borrowed from Plato, who had posited him as a mythic link between philosophical categories of eternal matter and eternal spirit. The celestial gods, he figured, were too aloof to get involved in creation, leaving it to the Demiurge, whose job it was to ceaselessly impose the likenesses of the eternal Forms (the spiritual prototypes of all things) onto hunks of unstable, shifting matter for as long as they can hold it.

The Gnostics were heavily influenced by the Hellenistic Judaism of Alexandria, with its allegorical method of reading Plato's philosophy into scripture. So they interpreted the Genesis accounts of the creation and the fall in Platonic categories, even as Philo of Alexandria did. But their shocking result was to identify the Demiurge as both evil and as the same as the Hebrew God Yahweh/Jehovah. Religious Modernists have made essentially the same move by saying that the Old Testament writers depicted God according to their limited, primitive conceptions and that the superior, more philosophically abstract concept became clear later. H. Wheeler Robinson comes, it seems to me, amazingly close to a Gnostic position when he says that "the limitations of the Old Testament idea of God . . . may be compared with those which attach to the Carpenter of Nazareth. As the Christian may see the manifestation of the Eternal Son of God within those limitations, so may be seen the manifestation of the Eternal God Himself through the limitations of 'Yahweh of Israel.'"[2] We just speak of different "God-concepts" where the Gnostics spoke of different gods.

CREATION BY COMMITTEE

The Demiurge, imitating the ultimate godhead, of whom he was nonetheless ignorant, declared himself supreme and proceeded to create matter and a series of material creations, a kind of mud-pie substitute for the Pleroma of Light. He also made the Archons ("rulers") to police his creation. (The Archons were based on the fallen Sons of God or fallen angels of Jewish belief found in 1 Enoch, Jubilees, and other apocryphal variations of Gen. 6:1–4). With their help he created a world, but it was inert and chaotic ("without form and void"). To get some action going, he managed to steal some of the spiritual light from the Pleroma. According to whichever Gnostic text you choose, this might have been accomplished by waylaying and dismembering another of the Aions, the Man of Light, Son of Man, or Primal Man. This was a very widespread mythic-theological concept in the ancient world. The Zoroastrians called him Gayomard. In the Hindu *Rig-Veda* he is known as Purusha. He is depicted as "the Man" in 4 Ezra 13:1–4. Or the light may have been taken from the reflected image of Sophia, who had stooped over to look into the dark pool of the newly created abyss of matter. In any case, the Demiurge and his evil lieutenants used these sparks of alien light as something like DNA to program self-replicating order into the otherwise stillborn cosmos of matter.

The trick worked. And just like it says in that old song by the Demiurges, that is, the Carpenters, "On the day that you were born the angels got together and decided to create a dream come true." But they still couldn't get the damn thing to move. This is where some stolen light came in handy. Light stolen from the Heavenly Eve (Eve was already a goddess in Jerusalem, Greece, and Phrygia and among the Hittites long before Genesis demoted her to a primordial Lucy Ricardo) animated the inert Pinocchio. "I've got him up and dancing."[3] The Archons then got the hots for Eve and tried to gang rape her. They did rape her shadowy physical counterpart, the earthly Eve, and then presented her to the now-awake Adam in only slightly used condition. All of this reflects very ancient variants, alternative versions, of the Eden story, which people continued to remember and to pass down in defiance of the official canonical version in Genesis chapters 2 and 3.

LOST AND FOUND

Of the subsequent children of Adam and Eve, the descendants of Seth possessed the divine spark of light inherited from the Heavenly Eve, while the descendants of Cain were the bastard spawn of the Archon rapists. This is at least the version of events put forth by the Sethian sect, who regarded Seth as a messianic revealer and redeemer and later, upon assimilation into Christianity, reinterpreted Seth as a previous incarnation of Christ, or, more to the point, Christ as the second coming of Seth. Others, like the Ophites or Naasenes, rightly understood Adam and Eve to be a local variant of the myth of Attis and Cybele and thus made Jesus a later incarnation of the slain-and-resurrected Attis.

But, whatever name they might use, the various Gnostic sects believed their doctrine, their privileged knowledge (*gnosis*), had come to them from a heavenly revealer who had come to earth, incognito, in human flesh or at least in the likeness thereof, to awaken those possessing the divine spark by explaining to them their true origin and destiny. This would enable them to escape the vicious cycle of reincarnation and to ascend once and for all to the Pleroma, to rejoin the godhead.

As Walter Schmithals speculated, "pure" Gnosticism must have understood the sheer fact of self-knowledge as enough to effect postmortem liberation.[4] But later, more corrupt, superstitious forms of the doctrine pictured Jesus (or Seth or Melchizedek) providing not only self-knowledge but also a set of magical formulae, passwords that would enable the elect soul to slip unnoticed through the cosmic checkpoints in each of the crystal spheres concentrically encasing our world. At each sphere waited its ruling Archon (playing the role of the old Babylonian planetary gods), ready to turn back any escaping soul, like marksmen posted along the old Berlin Wall. And the escaping soul would have to know what answer to give if challenged. "If they say to you, 'Whence did you originate?' say to them, 'We have come from the Light, where the Light has originated from itself. He stood and he revealed himself in their image.' If they say to you, 'Who are you?' say: 'We are his sons and we are the elect of the Living Father.' If they ask you, 'What is the token of the Father's presence in you?' say to them, 'It is both a movement and a rest'" (Thomas, saying 50). Obviously, without such knowledge as the revealer provides, the elect could never even know to seek out their destiny. All they knew was that, as spirits lodged in matter, they felt like strangers in a strange land. Now they knew why.

Often this revealer was himself understood to be an aspect of the Primal Man of Light whose sparks were scattered among the elect. He was on a mission to save himself! Thus he is called the Redeemed Redeemer. The implications of this doctrine are twofold. First, it means that, in awakening the elect, the Redeemer is completing his own salvation, exactly as in Mahayana Buddhism, where it is taught that no one can be saved until everyone is saved. This attitude eliminates any possibility of smug complacence and disdain for others. Second, it means that, once one is awakened, one is united with the Christ as with one's higher self. It was only the illusion of worldly existence that made Christ appear to be other than the Christian and vice versa. Again, for what it may be worth, this is exactly parallel to Mahayana Buddhism, where all possess the Buddha Nature but do not realize it till enlightenment, even though it is the very thing that makes enlightenment possible.

THE BAUER THESIS

Historically, Gnosticism has been like a centrifuge, diversity and pluralism giving birth to a fantastic variety of belief—the "hydra-headed heresy," as the ancients called it. But the Catholic Church has always sought universality by enforcing uniformity by conformity. Both forces were at work in early Christianity. How did the imperialistic, orthodox side gain dominance? Walter Bauer has shed light on this question in his great book *Orthodoxy and Heresy in Earliest Christianity*.[5] Bauer's main project was to refute the traditional model of Christian history as set forth by Constantine's court historian Eusebius, to wit: Jesus the Son of God taught the official, orthodox deposit of faith to the apostles. They, in turn, taught it to their appointed successors, the bishops, who taught it to the next generation of bishops, and so on. So far so good, but as soon as the apostles went on to their reward, Eusebius said, certain base fellows infiltrated the church with no other purpose than to spread the cancer of heresy, that is, unauthorized belief.

To fend off this threat, the bishops ratified the New Testament canon and formulated the great creeds to fortify the walls of truth and to smoke out heretics. Eusebius rewrote history to make it appear that non-Catholic Christianity appeared late in the day and that most of the heretical theologians were each other's disciples, so as to localize and to minimize the existence of heretical Christianity, like the old joke about the small group of laundrymen who stayed in business only by taking in each other's wash.

But Bauer found that the facts were otherwise: There had simply never been a single orthodox mainstream of Christianity. So, as early as we can form any picture of early Christians, there is no one single picture. Instead, the second century presents us with a theological kaleidoscope.

GALLERY OF GOSPELS

In Edessa the first Christianity attested was Marcionism. (More about Marcion in chapter 6, "Loose Canon.") Marcionites were on the scene first and succeeded in claiming the name "Christian." When "orthodoxy" showed up later, it had to be content using the name of the first Roman-leaning bishop Palut, calling themselves "Palutians." In Syria, ascetic and Gnostic Christianity that claimed to stem from Thomas prevailed, giving us the Gospel and Acts of Thomas, plus the Book of Thomas the Contender. In Egypt Gnosticism held sway. In Ephesus and Asia Minor Gnosticism, Docetism (see chapter 5, "Constantine's Christ") and Encratism (the gospel of celibacy) occupied the stage, all tracing themselves to Paul's ministry. In Palestine, Christianity was Jewish, Torah-keeping, and nationalistic, scorning Paul as a heretic and a Gentile, owing allegiance instead to James the Just and the other heirs of Jesus. Everywhere popular Christianity included docetic Christology (Jesus only seemed human) or adoptionism (God adopted Jesus as his Son) and angel Christology (Christ was an angel). As late as the eighth century in Christian Arabia, Christians believed Jesus had escaped crucifixion altogether and introduced that belief into Islam.

Nor was it only emergent Roman orthodoxy that claimed to have been taught by disciples of the apostles. Valentinus claimed to be the successor to Theodas, a disciple of Paul, while Basilides claimed to be the disciple of Glaukias, assistant and secretary to Peter. Some ascribed the so-called Gospel of John to the Gnostic Cerinthus instead. Others claimed Marcion wrote parts of it. Carpocrates claimed to have his teaching from Mary and Martha. Even Tertullian admitted Paul was "the apostle of the heretics." The Gnostics Heracleon and Valentinus wrote the first known commentaries on John and Paul, and it was very likely Marcion who first collected the Pauline letters.

Dan Brown is doing the public a favor when he conveys a dumbed-down version of Bauer's view of the history of Christianity to a wider readership. The danger, as elsewhere in his book, is that he mixes fact with fancy and threatens to make a straw man of the valuable lesson he seeks to teach. (And no one can be so naive as to think he is not trying to teach a lesson, several in fact, in *The Da Vinci Code*.)

TOMBS OF THE PROPHETS

How did this initial Christian diversity give way, and rather soon, to Roman Catholic orthodoxy? Eventually, once Constantine became its patron, the Catholic Church succeeded by means of intimidation and persecution. Before they had the iron fist of state power at their disposal, the bishops had to be content with nonviolent means like propaganda, literary polemics, and co-optation.

Late New Testament works, including the Acts of the Apostles, the Pastoral Epistles (1 and 2 Timothy and Titus), and

1 Peter, try to rewrite history to suggest an early unanimity of faith, with Peter and Paul at one, each the mirror reflection of the other, both repudiating in advance the heresies that would one day appeal to their authority. Other documents were sanitized, censored, and rewritten, including John, Luke, the Pauline letters, and Mark. Still other early documents were fabricated and attributed to early martyrs and legendary bishops, including Polycarp, Ignatius, and Clement. All sought to impose a revisionist history upon the founding events.

Once Catholic Christianity received state backing, Christians formed a canon that included the sanitized editions of certain books and excluding others like the Gospels of Thomas, Peter, Mary Magdalene; the Secret Book of James; the Prayer of the Apostle Paul; the Acts of Paul and Thecla; and so forth. The result was a stacked deck intended precisely to give an "official" version of Christian beginnings. Surprising proof of Bauer's thesis came to light with the 1945 discovery of the Nag Hammadi texts in Chenoboskion, Egypt. These documents had once formed the library of the monks of St. Pachomius. Once the monks received the Easter letter of Athanasius in 367, mandating the exclusive use of the twenty-seven New Testament books we have today, the monks hastened to stash away the others so as not to have them confiscated or burned. (In the same way, the mysterious absence of any New Testament manuscripts before the third century may imply the systematic destruction of these old texts, which may have looked quite different from the "authorized" versions.) And, armed with state power, the Church took to persecuting heretics and pagans with the same ferocity with which the emperors Decius and Diocletian had once persecuted Christians. This much of Brown's repulsive sketch of dominant Constantinian Christianity is sadly true.

THE UNDERGROUND CHURCH

But the major reason it was so easy to supplant non-Catholic Christianities is the fact of their organization—or rather their lack of it.

The Marcionite churches (actually "synagogues") flourished widely and well. Despite their radical belief that celibacy was required for salvation, their appeal was great. Just as in Buddhism, there was a place for those who admired their rigorism but did not feel inclined to embrace it for themselves. "Lord, make me chaste, but not yet!" These weaker brethren might delay baptism till the deathbed, but having supported the saints, they would receive a saint's reward. It was much the same with the Manichean churches. They, too, had public congregations of their own. The Roman Church made war on these and finally destroyed them, but further east, beyond their inquisitorial reach, Marcionites and Manicheans still survived here and there for some centuries thereafter.

With most Gnostics, the situation was very different. The disciples of Valentinus, Basilides, Bardesanes, Satornilus, Simon Magus, and the rest were more like study groups, informal philosophical circles with minimal organization. They were content to exist on the margins of Christian congregations in which they formed a distinct and dubious minority. Many probably met privately during the week without the bishop's knowledge, silently trying to work like leaven within the loaf—much like Charismatic prayer groups within main-stream congregations today. They viewed themselves as Gnostics or *pneumatics* ("spiritual ones"), "stronger brethren," "the perfect," "the mature" in the midst of the merely "natural" or "soulish" churchgoers within the church and the soulless "woodenheads" without. They learned to be circumspect about their advanced beliefs, not to cast pearls before swine. But they succeeded only in getting themselves into trouble. This is surely the situation that led to the remarkable story in Thomas, saying 13:

> Jesus said to his disciples, "Make a comparison: tell me who I am like."
>
> Simon Peter answered him, "You are like a righteous angel."
>
> Matthew said to him, "You are like a philosopher with understanding."
>
> Thomas said to him, "Master, my mouth cannot frame the truth of what you are like!"
>
> Jesus said, "I am not your master, because you have drunk, even become drunk, from the bubbling spring which I have ladeled out." And he took him away from the rest. He said three things to him.
>
> Now when Thomas rejoined his comrades, they pressed him: "What did Jesus say to you?"
>
> Thomas replied, "If I were to tell you even one of the things he told me, you would pick up stones to throw at me! And then fire would erupt from the stones and consume you!"

So when the storm blew up, they hunkered down and kept quiet. Gnostics must have continued to cherish their astonishing beliefs in secret, but they could no longer dare meet together in social entities. So Gnosticism went so far underground as to vanish. But it never really died, for Gnostic mythemes and doctrines continued to pop up again and again on through the Middle Ages. Either the underground river broke to the surface occasionally, or the human mind would ever so often reinvent the Gnostic wheel.

UPON THIS ROCK SHALL I BUILD MY CHURCH?

Was it wise for Marcionites and Manicheans to organize churches? When any movement is popularized, its distinctiveness gets diluted, accommodated to what the evangelistic market will bear. But the two-track system was a clever way of avoiding this, as in Buddhism. In times of peace, the institutionalism was efficient and kept Gnostic teaching available as a public option. But when persecution arose, this institutionalized existence only made their churches sitting ducks.

So was it wiser for the Gnostics to avoid organizing separate churches of their own? Perhaps so, but not from a worldly, practical standpoint. The Gnostics perhaps realized that *gnosis*, illumination, cannot be catechized, cannot be inherited, cannot be routinized, without losing its very essence. The spirit blows where it listeth, and to trap it in an institution is to clip its wings and to suffocate it. The church building too soon becomes a mausoleum for dead truth. Churches become boats that won't rock for fear of sinking, while volatile *gnosis*, with its unpredictable revelations, is more like the dangerous hydra that delights in scuttling boats.

If informal, spiritualistic, freethinking conventicles are not built to make it for the long haul, that is their natural destiny. There is minimal organization for two reasons: First, the people in it are too heavenly minded to be much earthly good at such things, and, second, by leaving organization and administration to pretty much take care of themselves, one is refusing to "reify" the organization, refusing to let it take on a life of its own. Because then it becomes a Frankenstein monster that dwarfs and destroys its creator. And that, of course, is exactly the Gnostic myth. The world is the ill-advised creature of the bungling Demiurge, ruled by fallen Powers, invulnerable to human efforts to overthrow or reform them. It becomes a retarding morass, imprisoning the very souls that built it in the first place.

GNOSTIC IDENTITY

Though they sometimes seem not to know what Gnosticism was, Dan Brown and his colleagues seem to think we would be much better off if we somehow returned to the tenets of that ancient, underground faith. Perhaps they are right. But how would such a sea change be navigated? How would one do it? Would it necessarily entail robed and hooded orgies in torch-lit catacombs, such as Brown portrays his modern Templar Gnostics celebrating? Some may rejoice at the prospect. But ultimately such behavior boils down to childish and grotesque role-playing games—like wearing a Klingon costume to a fan convention. And yet there is a modern Western representation of Gnosticism for serious adults. Gnosticism must be, and has been, demythologized for us. It is the Gnosticism of the critical intellectual.

Today's advocacy of Gnosticism by Elaine Pagels, Karen King, and others, plus the avid interest of their readers, certainly does not stem from any attraction to the specific, literal beliefs of the ancient Gnostic cultists.[6] No, but the ancient Gnostics *are* proof that there was diversity of belief in the ancient church, that so-called Orthodoxy never had a copyright on the term *Christian* and more importantly *does not now*. One appeals to the Valentinians and Marcosians and Simonians and Phibionites not because one actually covets docetic Christology, sexual libertinism, a multiplicity of Aions in the Pleroma, and so on. In fact, who would not rebel just as strongly if *these* elaborate and bizarre beliefs were imposed by an institutional organization? No, it is the right of dissent, of free thought in religious matters, to redefine Christianity in one's own terms, that is appealing to many critical intellectuals today. And yet there is a sense in which the specifically Gnostic name tag still applies. That label does belong on the bottle being sold by Pagels and others. The Gnostics, more than anyone else, have bequeathed us a framework that speaks to the situation of the modern intellectual. We may find ourselves to be Gnostics by analogy, admittedly, but it may be a very strict and close analogy!

THE LAW OF THE CREATOR

The ancient Gnostics believed that the laws of the Torah and the doctrines of the conventional Christianity of the Roman

Empire were impositions of the Demiurge, a self-aggrandizing god who had created the material earth and imprisoned divine souls within it. Once awakened, Gnostics denied any duty to take seriously the established laws and doctrines. They were not revelations of the true God but only fictions fabricated by the god of this world. So outwardly, Gnostics didn't mind going through ordinary Catholic rituals. Why not? But they knew better. They secretly smiled, knowing of a higher truth.

And the intellectual, the historical critic, the philosopher is in precisely the same position, whether or not we have ever heard of Gnosticism. We know too well that every religious doctrine and symbol, every ritual and regulation, has human fingerprints all over it. All alike are fictions, woven by our ancestors, ad hoc arrangements to stem social chaos. We know good and well that Sigmund Freud, Émile Durkheim, Max Weber, and the others were right. What others deem the iron laws, the eternal verities of God, we know for pretentious human creations. That doesn't mean we go out of our way to flout them or destroy them.

As students of Freud, Ludwig Feuerbach, and others, we may have arrived at the conclusion that there is no God, that the biblical deity is no more likely to be real than Zeus, Odin, or any other tribal totem. And we say so because we have been enabled to see the true picture from above. We can look down on the quaint beliefs of churchgoers from a superior perch. If so, we are exactly in the position of the ancient Gnostics, who knew themselves superior to the Demiurge, the biblical deity who was a false deity. Of course, they believed the Demiurge did really exist; we do not. But that is almost beside the point. We understand the conventional God to be a false god, with a greater Truth above him. But, as a belief motivating most of the human race, the Demiurgic god does exist as a force to be reckoned with. We may define our higher truth in whatever way seems best to us. But the structure of our beliefs, and of the manner in which we patronize the childlike literalism of others, is the same.

THE SEMBLANCE OF JESUS CHRIST

The ancient Gnostics tended to believe Jesus Christ had not possessed a physical body of organic flesh. To us such a Christ sounds like some *Star Trek* alien. But is not the point much the same when we arrive at the conclusion that we can know little about any historical Jesus, even that we cannot be sure there was one? And yet we find the hero of the gospels compelling. He *appears* as a figure we would like to emulate. And that has become good enough, with or without any historical basis. Aren't we Docetists?

Do we believe in concentric spheres surrounding the earth, separating it from God? Do we think that the portals of heaven are guarded by evil angels who try to turn back every soul that seeks admittance? That events on earth are caused by these cosmic Powers who rule the world? Unless we are paranoid schizophrenics of an exotic type, we do not. But don't we believe that much of the evil in the world is the result of super-personal, faceless corporate entities that exploit the creation and oppress mere humans? They are multinational corporations, ethnicities, political parties, social conventions, government agencies, television networks, and so forth. And we see that conventional religion, too, is a creature of these forces; thus it is unable to transcend them. So don't we after all reckon with the Principalities and Powers?

FROM THE ROOF OF THE WORLD

The Gnostics believed in a set of fantastically elaborate mythic and philosophical cosmologies. This was the higher truth they knew, the very *gnosis* to which they were enlightened. We dismiss it as, in the words of one Gnosticism scholar, "a queer farrago of nonsense." And yet, do we not share the Olympian conviction that we know the workings of the world as from a superior vantage point? What we have gained from anthropology, psychology, and the sociology of knowledge enables us to penetrate the motives and secret forces of both the individual and society in ways those whom we perceive can never even suspect. "The natural one does not welcome the gifts of the Spirit of God, for they seem foolish to him, nor can he begin to understand them for the simple reason that it takes the Spirit to make sense of them. The spiritual one judges all things but is not susceptible to anyone else's judgment" (1 Cor. 2:14–15).

Once you have read Freud or Peter L. Berger and Thomas Luckmann's *The Social Construction of Reality* or Erving Goffman's *The Presentation of Self in Everyday Life*, you will have passed through the portal of godlike knowledge. This world can never seem the same again. One will see the puppet show from backstage, understanding what makes people tick, why they do what they do (though of course it is always more difficult to see clearly into one's own heart!). You will feel what H. P. Lovecraft's visionary felt:

He waked that morning as an older man,
And nothing since has looked the same to him,
Objects around float nebulous and dim—
False phantom trifles of some vaster plan.
His folk and friends are now an alien throng,
To which he struggles vainly to belong.[7]

GNOSTIC MINISTRY

Perhaps the most striking thing about the present-day vogue for ancient Gnosticism is the desire to enter into it as a form of spiritual life. For many, Gnosticism is no more merely a subject of idle curiosity or armchair study. People are realizing that the Nag Hammadi texts are not a shelf of ancient science fiction novels but rather the scriptures of a once-living religion. These books preserved and fostered the vibrant faith of real human beings. And they can again. One sees liturgies, prayer books, services, and sermons based on these texts. There is the beginning of a new Gnostic ministry, such as must have gone on in the ancient Manichaean congregations.

But our inherited stereotypes of Gnosticism make "Gnostic ministry" sound like an oxymoron. Doesn't "ministry" imply a compassionate outreaching to the least of one's brothers and sisters? And doesn't Gnosticism, on the other hand, imply an elite self-sufficiency, a contemptuous indifference toward the unenlightened? Mustn't a Gnostic, convinced of his or her own possession of godlike knowledge, look upon the masses of sheep without a shepherd and turn away in disgust?

That is how various anti-Gnostic passages and interpolations in the New Testament see it, but they are in the business of theological mudslinging. Paul is made to say, "*Gnosis* puffs up, but loves builds up" (1 Cor. 8:1b). "God has chosen the simpletons to confound the wise" (1 Cor. 1:27). The Church has always inculcated unthinking obedience among its bond slaves. But, in fact, the antithesis between knowledge and love is a false one. *Gnosis* is itself a form of love, as Plato knew. In *The Symposium*, he shows that emotional love is the earthly reflection of the cognitive Eros by which the mind loves the truth or seeks to become one with it by knowing, just as in the Hebrew Bible "to know" often means "to have sexual intimacy with."

Historically, were the Gnostics abusive, arrogant despisers or elitists? Of course not. Marcion and Mani both found ways of incorporating the "weaker brethren" into the life of the church, just as Jesus and the Buddha had. And Valentinus said that, just as the Christ had appeared to reveal to the Gnostics their immortal divinity, so had the human Jesus died as an atonement for the merely "natural" men and women, who lacked divine nature but might yet be saved by "Plan B."

Gnosticism was like Mahayana Buddhism, a wide and capacious raft, accommodating very many more than an elite few. In many other ways, the Gnostic initiate was twin to the Bodhisattva. Like his Buddhist counterpart, he disdained his own private bliss in order to reach down a hand to the mass of weaker brethren who had not and could not make the spiritual ascent on their own. Indeed it was because the Gnostic, like the Bodhisattva, had passed beyond all selfish worldly need and preference that he could embrace all with equal compassion. He had no more enemies. To love one's enemies was to love oneself.

Like Thomas, the Gnostic might hesitate to vouchsafe his higher knowledge to the curious orthodox around him, but he knew that if he did, and they turned on him and stoned him, it was his own fault: He could have known better than to throw holy things before those who could not be expected to do other than turn on him and tear him to pieces.

WHO WOULD BELIEVE OUR REPORT?

In *The Da Vinci Code, The Body of God,* and other such books, we are told that some secret fraternity of Rosicrucians or Masons or Templars or Cathars carefully kept mum about their world-shattering secret. Why would they have done that? It is not that they feared they would destroy the beliefs of most people if they revealed their secret truth, for most people would never believe it. No, they understood that very well, and they knew they would be persecuted for blasphemy if people found out what they believed.

Occasionally Brown; Baigent, Lincoln, and Leigh; and others imply that the Templars blackmailed the pope or that the Priory of Sion may yet blow things wide open by revealing their secrets to the media, but in the real world there is no danger of this. If someone called a news conference and announced they had the bones of Jesus and the certificate to prove it, they would be taken about as seriously as the wild-haired spokeswoman for the Raelian flying saucer sect when she announced her group had successfully cloned a human infant.

WHERE THE ELITE MEET

The Gnostic must forgive her enemies, and love them, precisely because they know not what they do. But did the ancient Gnostic adepts really see it in so compassionate a manner? What about their hermetically sealed categories of the "spiritual" ones, the "natural" ones, and the "carnal" ones? Isn't that to write people off? No, it is not. The seeming exclusivity is a rhetorical tool. It also occurs in the Parable of the Sower (Mark 4:3–20). The various soils are already what they are. By the soils' natures as rocky, bird-picked, thorn-infested, and fertile, the fate of the seeds is already set. If the gospel seed should land on thorny soil, it will and must be choked out. But then what's the point of telling the parable? Scrooge was right: "Why show me these things, if I am past all hope?"

It is just like Rudolf Bultmann's interpretation of the Gnostic "good shepherd" discourse in John chapter 10.[8] Those who *do* not hear the shepherd's voice calling them *cannot* hear it, since they *already* don't belong to the special flock (John 10:26). It appears to be a foregone fate, a deterministic dualism. But Bultmann sees that this is really a "dualism of decision." One must *decide whether* one hears the shepherd's call, whether one believes the word, and therefore belongs in the flock. In exactly this manner, one must *strive* to *become* good fruitful soil, to root out the thorns and stones, so that one may bear sixty or a hundred fold. And even so, one must decide whether one qualifies as a pneumatic ("spiritual one") or a psychic ("soulish one") or a carnal one. No one else can determine which you are. And you do not so much *discover* it as *decide* it.

And so the mission, the ministry, of the Gnostic is to guide the carnal and the natural ones to the plateau of pneumatic, Gnostic existence. It is the Gnostic's task to be a living lesson, teaching what the pious will never say: *that the spiritual quest and the intellectual quest are one.* The Gnostic must demonstrate that knowledge, too, builds up, because knowledge is love. To make clear that the one who thinks he knows but does not love does not yet know as he thinks to know (1 Cor. 8:2). The Gnostic says not, "This multitude that knoweth not the law is accursed" (John 7:49), but rather, "Father forgive them, they know not what they do" (Luke 23:34).

The Gnostic minister tries to have in himself or herself the mind that was in Christ Jesus who, though he was in the form of God, esteemed not equality with God a thing to be stubbornly clutched but condescended to the level of the mass. The charter of Gnostic ministry to the weaker brethren is the saying of Jesus, "Let the greatest among you be your servant." To know oneself the greatest is no conceit if it sends one into the service of all.

MY GOD IS FEAR

The weaker brethren are those superstitiously bound to the commandments of mere mortals or of the Demiurge. They fear that greater knowledge and freedom would mean nihilism and amorality. We read that, during the Civil War, on some Southern plantations slaves fought fiercely against their own liberators! Why? Because they were afraid to shoulder the burden of freedom.

The Gnostic is brother (or sister) to the weak, the superstitious, the legalistic, but he is the *stronger* brother. And he knows it is on the whole better to be strong than to be weak! She knows that there should come a day when one ceases nursing and becomes acclimated to solid food. Meat, not milk. The Gnostic minister must be like the patient nursemaid mentioned in 1 Thessalonians 2:6–8, attentive to when the baby teeth are ready to be replaced by adult incisors. One doesn't force-feed adult food and drink to the infant. Some years ago, the news carried a horror tale of a father who told his very young son to "Be a man!" and drink a bottle of Scotch. He did, and he died. But the Gnostic does not make the same mistake. One waits till the weaker brother himself becomes impatient with Mother Church's steady diet of pabulum. When a believer begins to see for himself the holes in the fabric of traditional religion, then he has knocked on the door. And the Gnostic's job is to open it, to indicate, yard by yard, the long path within. And this is one very positive result of the popularity of *The Da Vinci Code*: It has smoked out many people who, reading it, discovered that they were ready for something beyond what their churches had always spoon-fed them.

THE LONELY ROAD

The Gnostic mission, then, is not to catechize, not to indoctrinate. This voyage to *gnosis* is a quest the initiate must make for herself. No one can take her there. No one can give a free ride to the destination. At most one can prompt and prod forward.

Since the whole point of Gnosticism is that the truth is within, the ministerial role in spiritual guidance must be that of a Socratic midwife. Like a Zen master, one raises questions; one does not manipulate another into parroting one's own answers. What would be the point of that? Nor is there any point in trying to hide the fact that the road is a bumpy one through unfamiliar landscapes and fear-haunted woods. Remember, the one who decides to seek must expect to find something utterly unexpected, something that troubles and dismays because it threatens to undo every comforting illusion of the past. At such a time the Gnostic must simply be a faithful companion, not giving false comfort, saying, "Peace, peace!" when there is no peace—not yet, anyway. "Jesus said, 'Let him who seeks, not cease seeking until he finds, and when he finds, he will be troubled, and when he has been troubled, he will marvel; only then will he achieve mastery, and then let him rest'" (Gospel of Thomas, saying 2).

Do not the weaker brethren fear the meat of *gnosis* because they know it means leaving forever the nursery of comforting orthodoxy? They know the heretic is an outcast, and they fear to be alone. The Gnostic friend's support is affirmation, his patient friendship is a living reminder that there is a "goodly fellowship" of the heretics. If one ends up abandoning the "house of the Lord" for a "den of thieves," at least there's honor among thieves! For that is what Gnostics are—thieves. Their patron is Prometheus, the glorious Titan who dared steal fire from the very gods themselves. And he acted not for himself alone but for the masses of humanity who hitherto huddled in the darkness of ignorant superstition. There is a great need for experts like Professor Teabing to share what they know when the time is ripe, with individuals who are ripe to learn it. But it would sure help if the Teabings of the world had their facts straight first.

NOTES

1. See Hans Jonas, epilogue to *The Gnostic Religion: The Message of the Alien God and the Beginnings of Christianity*, rev. ed. (Boston: Beacon, 1963); and E. R. Dodds, *Pagan and Christian in an Age of Anxiety: Some Aspects of Religious Experience from Marcus Aurelius to Constantine* (New York: W. W. Norton, 1970).

2. H. Wheeler Robinson, *The Religious Ideas of the Old Testament*, 2nd ed. (London: Duckworth, 1956), pp. 75–76.

3. T. E. D. Klein, "Nadelman's God," in Klein, *Dark Gods* (New York: Bantam Books, 1986), p. 209.

4. Walter Schmithals, *Gnosticism in Corinth*, trans. John E. Steely (New York: Abingdon, 1971).

5. Walter Bauer, *Orthodoxy and Heresy in Earliest Christianity*, ed. Robert A. Kraft and Gerhard Krodel, trans. Philadelphia Seminar on Christian Origins (Philadelphia: Fortress, 1971).

6. Elaine Pagels, *The Gnostic Gospels* (New York: Random House, 1979); Karen L. King, *The Gospel of Mary of Magdala: Jesus and the First Woman Apostle* (Santa Rosa, CA: Polebridge, 2003); David M. Scholer, "Why Such Current Interest in the Ancient Gnostic 'Heresy'?" *Faith and Thought* 1, no. 2 (Summer 1983): 22–26; Robert A. Segal, ed., *The Allure of Gnosticism: The Gnostic Experience in Jungian Psychology and Contemporary Culture* (Chicago: Open Court, 1995).

7. H. P. Lovecraft, "Alienation," *Fungi from Yuggoth* (West Warwick, RI: Necronomicom Press, 1990), XXXII.

8. Rudolf Bultmann, *The Gospel of John: A Commentary*, trans. G. R. Beasley-Murray, R. W. Hoare, and J. K. Riches (Philadelphia: Westminster, 1971), pp. 374–75.

Chapter 5

CONSTANTINE'S CHRIST
The Development of Christology

*O*ne of the gross historical errors in *The Da Vinci Code* is the claim that, in the interests of imperial propaganda, Constantine and his vest pocket bishops abruptly replaced the hitherto-prevailing understanding of Jesus as a simple mortal with the mythic view of Jesus as a god who only seemed to be human. Professor Teabing befogs his friends with great gusts of the most flagrant misinformation on this point. The emperor Constantine, he says,

> was a lifelong pagan who was baptized on his deathbed, too weak to protest. In Constantine's day, Rome's official religion was sun worship—the cult of *Sol Invictus*, or the Invincible Sun—and Constantine was its head priest. Unfortunately for him, a growing religious turmoil was gripping Rome. Three centuries after the crucifixion of Jesus Christ, Christ's followers had multiplied exponentially. Christians and pagans began warring, and the conflict grew to such proportions that it threatened to rend Rome in two. Constantine

decided something had to be done. In 325 A.D., he decided
to unify Rome under a single religion. Christianity. . . . By
fusing pagan symbols, dates, and rituals into the growing
Christian tradition, he created a kind of hybrid religion that
was acceptable to both parties. . . . Nothing in Christianity is
original. . . . During this fusion of religions, Constantine
needed to strengthen the new Christian tradition, and held
a famous ecumenical gathering known as the Council of
Nicea. . . . At this gathering . . . many aspects of Christianity
were debated and voted upon [including] the divinity of
Jesus. . . . [U]ntil *that* moment in history, Jesus was viewed
by His followers as a mortal prophet . . . a great and powerful man, but a *man* nonetheless. A mortal . . . Jesus' establishment as "the Son of God" was officially proposed and
voted on by the Council of Nicea. . . . By officially endorsing
Jesus as the Son of God, Constantine turned Jesus into a
deity who existed beyond the scope of the human world.[1]

Most of this is utter nonsense. Let me count the ways. For one
thing, Constantine was indeed a Christian. In fact, there is reason
to doubt the traditional, semilegendary story of his dramatic conversion before the Battle of the Milvian Bridge, but that is not
because he was no Christian. On the contrary, it now appears Constantine was born and raised a Christian.[2] True, he was baptized on
his deathbed, but it was not against his will. He was merely hag-
ridden with fear of forfeiting salvation through any postbaptismal
slip-up. Many Christians were scared to death of this prospect, so
it was actually pretty common, at least by no means unusual, to
delay baptism till the deathbed. This anxiety would eventually lead
to the separate sacraments of repeated penance and extreme unc-
tion (deathbed anointing). But this solution did not yet exist.

How could this Christian emperor have served as Pontifex Maximus of Sol Invictus? He did so serve but simply because it was incumbent upon him as emperor of Rome, since the state religion, as Brown/Teabing says, was that of the Unconquerable Sun. Constantine managed to declare Christianity a *religio licitas*, a legal cult like Judaism or many of the mystery cults. He certainly did not even try to unify Roman society under a single religious canopy. And this is why he had to wear both religions' hats. It was his successor, Theodosius, who elevated Christianity to the position of the single state religion.

As for the assimilation of foreign, pagan elements into Christianity, this certainly did occur and on a scale pretty much comparable to that envisioned by Brown/Teabing. "Nothing in Christianity is original" is probably true. One can find all the maxims of Jesus in the literature of contemporary philosophy as well as among the rabbis. This fact should surprise no one except ultraorthodox Christians, who seem to imagine the world was under a blanket of moral darkness before Jesus. Beyond this, the notion of Jesus as a dying and rising savior god, the Gnostic idea of a heavenly being descending into this dark world to redeem his elect, the use of saving sacraments of bread and wine and baptism—all this was held in common with earlier mystery cults and was probably borrowed from them centuries before Constantine. The evidence is overwhelming, though conservative Christians remain stubborn in their refusal to admit it, at least publicly. How and why did such syncretism, such mixing of traditions and myths, take place? It is all part of the natural process of religious evolution in an environment, like that of the cosmopolitan world of antiquity, in which competing religions exist close together and trade adherents. An individual might belong to several of the current religions at the same time. That was common, and Constantine himself, as we have seen, was a prime example. In such a context, it would be impossible to stop each religion from rubbing off on the others. In the same way, we can trace, for example, Mithraic influence on the Attis cult. The cult of Sabazius seems to have been a fusion of Judaism and Dionysus worship.

Eventually (already in 1 Cor. 8–10) there is an attempt to prevent Christians from continuing easy participation in other religions' sacraments. This restriction of Christians to a single religious membership resulted in a more dedicated (if also more intolerant) membership. But ironically, it also meant that now you had a single direction of influence: If there were only pagans becoming Christians, which way is the interreligious influence going to go? Pagan converts to Christianity are going to bring with them their favorite elements of their old faith. It is all natural, inevitable, inescapable. To imagine that Constantine sat down with a focus group and a panel of advertising executives to cook the whole thing up is fully as arbitrary as to say, with traditional Christians, that Christianity as we know it emerged full-blown from the teaching of the historical Jesus.

This is not to deny that there were later attempts to conquer paganism by seizing and co-opting some of their features. For instance, you can find saints' healing shrines built over the healing shrines of Asclepius. You have to wonder if the bishops chose December 25 to celebrate Jesus's birth (no one had kept any record of it) just because Romans already celebrated Brumalia, the nativity of Mithras, on that day. It was an easy way of getting the flock to stop attending a fun pagan party: rather like the First Night program to provide nonalcoholic diversions on New Year's Eve. The widespread statues of Mary suckling or cradling the infant Jesus certainly owe something to the ubiquitous iconography of the Isis and Serapis faith. Things like this may well have been, as Brown intimates, cynical marketing decisions. But again, there is no reason at all to make it the fiendish scheming of a single mastermind.

Was there religious warfare in Constantine's day? Before his time, Decius and Diocletian had persecuted Christians with state power, and before that there had been sporadic lynchings of Christians by suspicious neighbors. But Constantine faced no interreligious crisis as Teabing suggests, nor did he try to fuse paganism and Christianity. The convocation of the Council of Nicea had nothing to do with any such scenario.

Nor did Constantine initiate or preside over the transformation of a merely human Jesus into a superhuman, divine Christ as Brown claims. As any seminary freshman knows (or used to know, until Green politics and encounter groups took over the theological curriculum), Nicene orthodoxy stipulated that the Word that was made flesh (John 1:14) shared the same divine nature as the Father, but not that he was no longer to be considered simultaneously human. Subsequent councils sought only to iron out the theological wrinkles. Many of us feel uneasy with these ancient formulae, but at least let us not misrepresent them.

EARLY CHRISTIANS, EARLY CHRISTS

Some early Christians believed that Jesus Christ was a supremely righteous man who had been adopted by God either at his baptism (Mark 1:11, "You are my Son") or at the resurrection. Acts 2:36 and Romans 1:3–4 certainly appear to preserve this understanding. The former has Peter proclaim: "Let all the house of Israel, then, know for certain that God has *made* him Lord and Christ, this Jesus whom you crucified," that is, subsequent to his crucifixion. Likewise, the latter passage: "the message concerning his Son, who was descended from David according to the flesh and designated Son of God in power according to the Spirit of holiness by his resurrection from the dead, Jesus Christ our Lord." Mark's gospel may be understood as implying this conception of Jesus. Notice that Mark has no miraculous birth narrative, but Jesus is simply shown appearing among the crowd of pilgrims to be baptized by John, and then he hears, apparently for the first time, the news from God that he is his Son. People who hold to this Christ concept are called *Adoptionists*.

This is the view closest to that which Dan Brown attributes to all early Christians before Constantine and the Council of Nicea. (Only he seems to imagine that people never called Jesus the Son of God in any sense at all until Constantine.) And it may indeed have been the earliest Christ concept, though there is no way to be sure. There is a kind of common sense to the idea that Adoptionism was first though. For instance, we find the Ebionite ("the poor") Jewish Christians upholding this view in the second century, even rejecting the doctrine of the virgin birth of Jesus, once they heard about it, as a foreign pagan element. It is possible, on the other hand, that the Ebionites were rather a later Judaizing sect that thought Jesus was held in too high esteem by other Christians who thought him a divine being and that the Ebionites wanted to cut him down to size. But this runs against the current of what usually happens in religions where an initially mortal founder (Muhammad, the Buddha, Moses, Mahavira) is sooner or later exalted to a divine status formerly restricted to the God whom the founder had served as a "mere" prophet.

There are a couple of New Testament texts that seem to try to deflate exaggerated estimates of Jesus. For instance, Mark 10:17–18, "And as he was setting out on his journey, a man ran up to him and asked him, 'Good master, what must I do to inherit eternal life?' And Jesus said to him, 'Why do you call me good? Surely no one is good, except only for God!'" Or John 12:44, "And Jesus cried out, saying, 'Whoever believes in me, believes not in me, but in him who sent me!'" Again, in John 14:9–10, "Have I been with you so long, Philip, and still you fail to recognize me? He who has seen me has seen the Father! . . . [Or] don't you believe that I am in the Father and the Father is in me?" Verse 10 sounds an awful lot like backpedaling from verse 9, as if some scribe had decided to take the Christology of the text down a peg by a bit of theological sophistry. But where to plug these passages into the evolving history of Christology? Do they attest a scaling back of an originally high Christology? Or rather an attempt by partisans of an earlier, more modest view, to rein in what are perceived as emerging exaggerations?

A good depiction of an Adoptionist portrait of Jesus would be *Jesus Christ Superstar* by Andrew Lloyd Webber and Tim Rice. There we behold a very human, sometimes petulant, Jesus who chafes at the weight of his sacrifice. He does not waver in his purpose, yet half his resolve is bitter resignation. He finds himself swept up in a destiny he can neither fully understand nor escape. And yet he himself is an unfathomable mystery to his enemies as well as his disciples, a "carpenter-king" larger than life as we know it.

Other early Christians believed Christ was a divine Spirit or angel who only seemed to appear in human flesh: "sending his own Son *in the likeness of* sinful flesh" (Rom. 8:3), "being born *in the likeness of* men" (Phil. 2:7). On the other hand, some passages oppose this view of Jesus: "By this [criterion] you will distinguish the Spirit of God [from its counterfeit]: every spirit [i.e., prophecy] which affirms that Jesus Christ has come in the flesh is of God, and every spirit which does not affirm Jesus [in this manner] is not from God. This is [instead] the spirit of Antichrist" (1 John 4:2–3). "Many deceivers have infiltrated the world, those who will not acknowledge the coming of Jesus Christ in the flesh" (2 John 7). They are called *Docetists* (from the Greek δοκεω, "to seem"). The mildest form of Docetism merely denied that the dying Jesus suffered any pain, as in the Gospel of Peter: "And they brought two evildoers and crucified the Lord between them. But he remained silent as if he felt no pain." Of course, this passage may mean only to depict the Stoic heroism of Jesus who would not give his foes the satisfaction of letting them see he was suffering, much like his silence in the face of interrogation (Mark 14:60–61, 15:5; Matt. 26:62–63, 27:12–14; Luke 23:9; John 19:9–10).

A stronger form of Docetism denied that Jesus died there at all, his place being taken by another man or even by a false vision of Jesus! The Koran says, "They denied the truth and uttered a monstrous falsehood against Mary. They declared: 'We have put to death the Messiah Jesus the son of Mary, the apostle of Allah.' They did not kill him, nor did they crucify him, but he was made to resemble another for him" (4:147). Islam seems to have inherited this version from Christian converts who might have read it in the Acts of John:

> When I saw him suffering, even then I did not stand by him in his suffering. Instead, I fled to the Mount of Olives, weeping at what had come about. And when he was crucified, Friday, at the sixth hour of the day, darkness enveloped the whole earth. And at once my Lord stood in the midst of the cave, shining with radiance that lit up the whole interior, and he said, "John! To the masses of people below, I am being crucified and pierced with lances and reeds, and I am being offered gall and vinegar to drink. But to you, I am speaking, and you must listen to what I say. It was I who placed in your mind the suggestion to come up into this mountain, so you might hear those things which a disciple ought to learn from his teacher, and a man from his God!"
>
> And having said this, he showed me a cross of light standing erect, with a crowd gathered round the cross, having no one appearance. But in the cross there was a lone form, a single likeness. And the Lord himself I saw above the cross, having no shape at all, but only a voice, nor was it the voice familiar to us, but one winsome and gentle and truly divine, saying to me, "John, it is necessary for someone to hear these things from me, for I will need one who will understand. I sometimes, for your sake, call this cross of light the Word, sometimes Mind, sometimes Jesus, sometimes Christ. . . . But this is not the cross of wood which you will see when you descend from here. Nor am I the one on the cross, I whom you do not see now but whose voice you hear. I was considered to be that which I am not, not being what I seemed to many others. But they will say of me something vile and unworthy."

Pretty much the same thing occurs in the Nag Hammadi Apocalypse of Peter: "When he had said those things, I saw him seemingly being seized by them. And I said, 'What do I see, O Lord, that it is you yourself whom they take, and that you are grasping me? Or, who is this one, glad and laughing on the tree? And is it another one whose feet and hands they are striking?' The Savior said to me, 'He whom you saw on the tree, glad and laughing, this is the living Jesus. But this one into whose hands and feet they drive the nails is his fleshy part, which is the substitute, being put to shame, the one who came into being in his likeness.'"[3]

We catch a hint of this version of Docetism in the Paul Schraeder/Martin Scorsese film *The Last Temptation of Christ* when, in the penultimate dream sequence, Jesus is freed from the cross and allowed to go his way. Even as the cursing, fuming, fist-shaking mob continues to behold him nailed helplessly above, the viewer sees Jesus walking away on tender, wounded feet from an empty cross. Another glimpse of Docetism may be found in Salvador Dali's famous crucifixion painting, where the spread-eagled body of Jesus floats in midair some inches from the cross.

The strongest version of Docetism, also attested in the Acts of John, is that Jesus had no real human form at all, with different people simultaneously seeing him differently!

For once he had called Peter and Andrew, who were brothers, he came next to me and my brother James, saying, "I need you! Come to me!" And my brother, on hearing it, said, "John—this child standing on shore and calling us! What can he want?" And I said, "What child?" And he replied, "That one, motioning to us!" And I answered, "We have kept watch at sea too long, my brother! You are not seeing straight! Can't you see it is a man standing there? Handsome, light-skinned, and smiling?" But he said to me, "Him I do not see, my brother. But let us go to shore, and we will learn what it is he wants of us."

And so when we had docked the boat, we saw him helping us secure the boat. And when we left there, inclined to follow him, I saw him this time as largely bald but with a thick and curling beard, while James saw him as a youth with only fuzz on his cheeks! So we were both uneasy and confused. What we saw: what could it mean? Subsequently, as we followed him, we gradually became only more confused as we pondered the thing. But next something even more amazing appeared to me, for I would try to catch him off guard, and never once did I see his eyes blinking; they were constantly open! And often he would appear to me as short and ugly, and then again as a man tall as the sky! Also, another marvel about him: when I reclined next to him at mealtime and leaned back against him, sometimes I felt his breast as smooth and soft, but other times hard as stone! Thus I was inwardly troubled and reflected, "How can I be experiencing this?" And as I thought about this, he turned and said to me, "John, you see yourself in me: if your own heart is tender, then I am tender to your touch; but if your heart is stony, then thus also will you find me."

The Acts of John is about as docetic as one can imagine any document being! It plainly denies that Jesus had a stable, corporeal form:

I will recount another glory, brothers. Sometimes when I would take hold of him, I encountered a solid, material

THE DA VINCI FRAUD

body, while other times when I touched him, the substance was immaterial, as if it did not even exist! And on any occasion he was invited by one of the Pharisees and attended the dinner, we went with him, and our hosts set a roll before each one of us, and he received one as well, and he would bless his own and divide it between us, and everyone was satisfied with so small a morsel, and our own rolls were left over untouched, which amazed our hosts.

And often, as I walked beside him, I wanted to see the impression of his foot, whether his foot left any print on the ground, for it appeared to me that he walked just above the ground, and I never saw a footprint.

One regularly hears that the Gospel of John represents the first line of defense against Docetism, but actually the text is strikingly equivocal, seeming to lean both ways. For instance, no sooner does it say (1:14) that "The Word became flesh" than it adds, "and pitched a tent among us," perhaps implying a nomadic, fleeting presence of dubious substantiality. In 4:6–7, Jesus is depicted as tired and thirsty, but by 4:31–32, he is refusing to eat; he has no need for physical food as long as he is nourished by doing the will of God! Here is the warrant for the ascetical saints of later centuries, ethereal souls who supposedly survived on nothing more than communion wafers. In chapter 6, verse 19, Jesus walks on water, which, as in Mark 6:48–49 and Matthew 14:26, naturally implies he is a bodiless phantom—or a god lacking physical density. On the cross he thirsts—or does he? It is all to fulfill the schedule laid out in scripture: "Jesus . . . said, to fulfill the scripture, 'I thirst'" (John 19:28). He invites Thomas to touch his wounds (20:27)—but he doesn't! It seems quite likely that the Johannine community was torn between Docetists and non-Docetists (who wrote the Epistles of John) and that each faction had its own version of the Gospel of John. Our cross-eyed text would be the result of later scribes combining readings from both!

It is possible for Docetism, or something like it, to have been the first version of Christology, but only if, as Paul Couchoud and others argued, Jesus began as a mythical deity and was only later imagined to have existed on earth sometime in the remote or recent past.[4] The Greeks vaguely imagined that Hercules, Asclepius, and others had lived fleshly lives on earth, though evidence indicates that originally both had been heavenly sun gods.[5] It may conceivably have been the same with the Jesus figure.

Still others believed that the Christ Spirit/angel entered into the man Jesus at the latter's baptism (Mark 1:10, literally, "descended into him") and departed at his crucifixion (Mark 15:34: "My God, my God, why have you abandoned me?"), and in the meantime, Jesus was the channeler for the Christ. We call this *Separationism.*[6] It would sure make sense of the exceedingly puzzling verse 1 Corinthians 12:31 ("Nobody can be speaking from the Spirit of God if he says, 'Jesus be damned!'") if it were aimed at Separationism. In view here would have been people who, like the Cainite Gnostics whom Origen describes, esteemed the Christ highly but reviled the earthly Jesus, his channeler, because they thought other Christians had made an idol of him. Similarly, 1 John 2:22 ("Who makes a habit of lying but he who denies that Jesus is the Christ? This is the Antichrist, he who denies the Father and the Son") would make a lot of sense if it meant to condemn those who believe Jesus was just the channeler for the Christ and not the Christ in his own right.

All these views were eventually condemned as heresies, which, however, by no means stopped people from believing them! A couple of centuries later, the evolving establishment church of Constantine took up the matter in a series of debates and councils, which we will survey. In all of them, the pendulum kept trying to settle in the middle between Jesus as a man and Jesus as divine.

CONTROVERSIES AND COUNCILS

The Nicene Creed was drafted to resolve the Christological controversy between the Arians (Arius, an Alexandrian presbyter or priest, Asterius, Eusebius of Nicomedia) and the faction favoring bishops Alexander and Athanasius, also of Alexandria. Neither of their Christological positions was identical with what would later emerge as "orthodoxy," nor was the debate simply over Jesus being either a mortal or an immortal, as Brown would have it. Both positions already took for granted that Jesus Christ was much more than a mortal man.

Athanasius held that Jesus Christ was the Word made flesh (John 1:14). The Word (Logos, the creative reason of God, a notion derived from Heraclitus, the Stoics, and Philo) was a separate person sharing the divine nature. The Word is also the Son. The Father begat or generated the Son, but this is a logical, not a chronological, priority. They have always been in a relationship of loving interdependence: The Son is "eternally begotten" by the Father, as Origen said. The Word is God's own wisdom through which he created all things. (Prov. 8:22–31, "From everlasting I was established, from the beginning, from

the earliest times of the earth. . . . When he established the
heavens, I was there. . . . Then I was beside him, a master
workman." John 1:3, "All things came into being through him,
and apart from him nothing came into being.") The Son took
on human flesh (not yet understood as a full human nature,
just a human body, which will later be considered heresy) in
order to save humanity.

Arius held that Jesus Christ was the incarnation of a heavenly being who had been the very first creature and through
whom as an agent or assistant God had made the rest of the
creation. (Ws. 7:24–27, "Wisdom . . . is a breath of the power
of God, and a pure emanation of the glory of the Almighty. . . .
For she is a reflection of eternal light, a spotless mirror of the
working of God, and an image of his goodness"; Sir. 1:4,
"Wisdom was created before all things"; Col. 1:15–16, "He is
the image of the invisible God, the firstborn of all creation. For
by him all things were created.") But, like the angels, he did
not share divine nature, the nature of the Father. Both before
and during his earthly sojourn, he learned wisdom and virtue
through discipline and suffering. At the resurrection, he was
given divine honor and dignity. He was adopted *by grace* as
"Son," "Word," "Lord," "Wisdom," even "God," because by his
perfection in virtue he had come to participate in these quali-
ties, which *by nature* belong to God alone. God's foreknowl-
edge told him from the beginning that Christ would successfully attain this perfection, and so scripture calls Christ "Son,"
"Word," "God," and so on by anticipation even before his
earthly life (e.g., John 1:1, "In the beginning was the Word."
Gal. 4:4, "But when the fullness of time came, God sent forth
his Son"). Technically, he wouldn't have been known as "the

Son" at the time described; the writers are merely taking into account the fact that the readers now know him as "the Son."

There were two essential Arian arguments. The first focused on three *scriptural* points. The outline of this schema of Christ being preexistent in heaven, yet later receiving even greater glory as a reward, is certainly to be found in Philippians 2:5–11 and in the Epistle to the Hebrews. The idea that the pre-existent Word was an agent of creation, and was himself created, can easily be inferred from John 1:1 ("and the Word was divine" or "the Word was a god") since the created status of Wisdom is explicit in the texts from the Wisdom of Solomon and Sirach that form the background of John 1. The notions of Christ's being perfected through endurance and suffering and of growing in wisdom are certainly found in Luke 2:52 ("And Jesus kept on increasing in wisdom") and in Hebrews 2:10 ("For it was entirely appropriate for him . . . to perfect the author of their salvation through sufferings").

Second, the Arians made three *theological* points. The idea of the Father begetting the Word smacked of Gnostic emana-tionism, a complicated scenario that envisioned God like the sun emitting a great number of derivative but still divine "rays." But, on the other hand, if the Word were *eternal*, he must be unbegotten, and this would seem to make Christ into God's *brother*, not his Son! Arians felt that to say the Son was in a relationship of "eternal generation" from the Father is a piece of incoherent sophistry, like a "square circle." And if God is Father *by nature*, and if the Son is Son *by nature*, then God must have been *forced* to beget the Son, and this is to reject God's sovereignty and freedom.

The central issue in the debate was undoubtedly the question of *soteriology*, the doctrine of salvation. The two sides began from a common presupposition about the nature of salvation. Both saw salvation as *theosis*, divinization or deification. Christ had made it possible for us to "become God." (Athanasius said, "God became man so that man might become God.") We could become immortal. By grace, that is, by adoption, we could become what God is by nature. In order to attain this, we must live a life of faith and good works. This remains the Eastern Orthodox view, which preaches unabashedly the doctrine of *synergism*: We must work with God for our salvation.

But as to the precise role of Christ in all this, the two views diverged. Athanasius held that Christ must be identified with God in order to make our deification possible. Human nature is mortal, therefore corruptible, because it is subject to change and decay (including moral decay, or sin). *Theosis*, deification of human nature, is made possible because, in Christ's incarnation, the unchanging eternal, divine nature unites with human nature and transforms it essentially. In Christ we experience this transformation. Christ must have been God incarnate, since otherwise the savior could not bring to humanity what humanity needs for deification: genuine deity. If he himself hadn't had it, how could he convey it to us? So Athanasius's key technical term for the relation of Christ to the Father was *Homoousias*, "of the same nature."

Arius, by contrast, believed that Christ must be identified with creatures in order to make our deification possible: He, precisely as a creature, attains the reward of deification in exactly the same way we do ("the pioneer and perfector of our faith"; "the firstborn of many brothers") and thus establishes the possibility of deification for the rest of creatures. No chemistry of essences and natures is needed; God simply effects the adoption as sons/daughters by his grace, that is, by fiat. Arius's operative slogan differed by one single letter: *"Homoiousias."* Christ was "of like nature" with the Father before the incarnation, then exalted by grace and in an honorific sense (like receiving an honorary degree) afterward.

One might assume that debates like this never leaked out of the ivory towers of theology, but it was not so. It appears that the Christological controversy was a matter of considerable public interest. Common people lined up on one side or the other, as if they were feuding fans of battling sports teams! We even hear that there were Arian drinking songs echoing in the dockside taverns of Alexandria! Imagine hardy seamen lifting a few to the success of Arianism! *"Oh . . . he's . . . not-one-with-the Fa-ther!"*

The Council of Nicea, in 325, summoned by Constantine, decided the issue by voting in Athanasius's favor. After the emperor's death, the decision was reversed, then reversed again, so that the initially victorious Athanasius was suddenly exiled, then recalled! Arian Christology, the belief that Jesus Christ was not fully God or man but a kind of archangel, survived among the barbarian Goths, evangelized by the Arian missionary Ulfilas. They lived in northern Europe from whence many later relocated to north Africa. Early passages of the Koran seem perhaps to reflect Arian Christology, and many Arian Christians finally converted to Islam. Today, the major Arian group is Jehovah's Witnesses. Arian Christology has also remained a favorite notion among certain English theologians.[7]

The aftermath of the Arian controversy was the debate over

precisely how *human* Jesus Christ was, granting his full divinity. Athanasius had pretty much taken the humanity of Jesus for granted without defining it. His disciple Apollinarius taught what he believed to be the natural implication of Athanasius's doctrine, namely, that Jesus Christ had only a human body of flesh and a human soul/mind, but *not a human spirit*. That, he reasoned, must have been "left open" to fit in the divine Logos. After all, it had to plug into the organism *some*place, right?

He was opposed by three theologians (boyhood chums, now ecclesiastical bigwigs), Gregory of Nyssa, Gregory of Nazianzus, and Basil of Caesarea, all from the Asia Minor province of Cappadocia, hence their collective nickname, the Three Cappadocians. These men argued that if Jesus saved us by becoming human, assuming humanity (i.e., taking humanity onto himself), and so raising us to the level of divinity, then in order to save our spirits he must have *had* a human spirit, not just the divine one. What, did he redeem only two-thirds of any human being? Their formula was "What is not assumed cannot be redeemed." So Jesus Christ must have been fully human as well as fully divine, not half and half like a mythical demigod.

The Council of Constantinople decided this issue in favor of the Three Cappadocians in 381. While this gathering promulgated no new creed, it did beef up the original draft of the Nicene Creed, adding extra material about the Holy Spirit ("the Lord, the giver of life, who proceeds from the Father. With the Father and the Son he is worshiped and glorified"), so that the version repeated in churches today is actually the Nicene-Constantinopolitan Creed.

To gain an idea of what an Apollinarian Jesus might have looked like, take a look at a scene from the Infancy Gospel of Thomas:

> And after some days, as Jesus walked with Joseph through the city, one of the children ran and struck Jesus on the arm. But Jesus said to him, "You have reached the end of the road!" And at once he fell to the earth and died. But when those present saw this wonder they cried out, "Where does this child come from?" And they said to Joseph, "It is not right for such a child to live among us!" As he departed, taking Jesus with him, they called out, "Leave this place! Or else, if you must stay with us, teach him to pray and not to curse; for our sons lose consciousness!"
>
> And Joseph called Jesus and began to admonish him: "Why do you call down curses? Those who live here are coming to hate us!" But Jesus said, "I know these words are yours, not mine, but for your sake I will be silent from now on. Only let them see the result of their own foolishness." And immediately those who spoke against Jesus were made blind, and as they wandered about they said, "Every word from his mouth is fulfilled!" And when Joseph saw what Jesus had done, he took hold of his ear in anger. But Jesus was annoyed and said to Joseph, "It is enough for you to see me, not to touch me. For you do not know who I am, and if you knew it, you would not vex me. Although I am with you now, I was made before you."

Here is a Jesus who had flesh and blood all right, since Joseph manages to box his ear, but he is a god dwelling in a human body, scarcely able to endure the inanities of the human race, among whom he is for the time being marooned! "What fools these mortals be!"

The story goes that Nestorius, bishop of Constantinople, was disturbed at hearing some of his parishioners praising Mary as the *Theotokos*, Mother of God. This made him reflect upon the Christological question, how are the divine and human natures of Jesus Christ related? He decided they could not be related in any way that would make it meaningful to call Mary's infant son "God." He is said to have exclaimed, "God is not a baby two or three weeks old!" Imagine the scene at home with the Holy Family: "Mary, can't you change God's diaper?" "Joseph, it's time for the Almighty's two o'clock feeding!" In the controversial 1985 French film *Hail Mary*, which sets the nativity story in the modern world, the Holy Family is setting off for a picnic in the country when all of a sudden, out of nowhere, young Jesus announces, to no apparent point, "I am he who is." Joseph's reaction: "Get in the car."

Nestorius was thought to have taught something to the effect that in Jesus Christ there were two subjects, divine and human, perhaps two persons, or something close to this. But according to his own rediscovered writings, admittedly not a model of clarity, Nestorius regarded Jesus of Nazareth as "the assumed Man" that is, assumed, or taken on, by the divine Word, the preincarnate Son of God. By the grace of God they formed one person with two natures. But Nestorius was misrepresented as teaching that Jesus and the Word were two persons sharing but a moral unity.

"Opposing" him (but actually holding to virtually the same view!) was Cyril of Alexandria, who argued that Jesus had been one person with two natures (divine and human) and that the personhood was divine, supplied from the divine side. This meant that, had there been no mission of incarnation for the

Word to undertake, there should have been no Jesus of Nazareth at all. The divine Word forms the nucleus of the Incarnation. This sounds sort of like Apollinarianism, but it isn't, since Cyril readily admits the human Jesus had a body, soul, and spirit. He was fully human, though he wouldn't have existed at all except for his divine destiny. On the other hand, it is not hard to see how Nestorius's position might be taken as opening the door to a kind of adoptionism or separationism. It bothered Cyril and his faction that Nestorians spoke of a "Word/man" Christology, not a "Word/flesh" Christology.

The Council of Ephesus decided in 431 in favor of Cyril. Of course this didn't really settle much; the Nestorian churches just picked up their marbles and left for home. Nestorian Christianity still thrives today, especially in Iran. Nestorius had been vilified, made a straw man against which to define orthodoxy. He did not actually espouse what is called "the Nestorian heresy," nor do today's Nestorians. In fact, one photograph of a gathering of Nestorians shows them holding up a big banner praising the *Theotokos*!

It is hard to picture the two-headed Jesus implied in the straw-man "Nestorianism" condemned by the council. To come up with an analogy, one must probably resort to the realm of comic book superheroes, a few of whom have a secret identity that is really an alter ego with whom they share consciousness, each in the background while the other is manifest. For instance, Dr. Don Blake strikes the ground with his cane and turns into and/or is replaced by the Mighty Thor, his cane replaced by a hammer. Billy Batson speaks the magic word "Shazam!" and is replaced by the adult Captain Marvel, with whom, however, he shares memories. Firestorm the Nuclear Man is a fusion between a high school student and his science professor, whose wizened, bearded head is shown hovering about the hero in ghostly form whenever that consciousness makes itself known with a word of advice. Presumably Cyril wanted to fend off something like this in the case of Jesus Christ.

Also, one wonders whether some of today's feminist theology, which disdains to call Jesus the Son of God and insists on dubbing him the Child of God, is not Nestorian in that it refuses to envision the incarnation "going all the way down." Just as Nestorius said, "God is not a baby two or three weeks old!" feminist theologians are saying, "God is not a male with a penis!"

Eutyches, pious Archimandrite of a monastery in Constantinople (not to be confused with Eutychus, the kid who fell asleep at Paul's long-winded preaching and fell out the window in Acts 20:7–12!), tried to explain how the two natures of Christ were related in one person. He admitted that the divine and human natures remained distinct from one another *going into* the union, until the point of the incarnation, namely, the impregnation of Mary. Afterward, Eutyches ventured, the two natures combined into a single nature (*monos physis*), unique to Jesus Christ. From there on in, Christ had a single nature. One person *from* two natures. The implied analogy is like salt and water: They fuse together into a new, single solution. Those who believe this are known as Monophysites.

Opposing Eutyches was Pope Leo, among others, Leo being the actual author of the formal response to Monophysitism, *Leo's Tome*. These Dyophysites (believers in two natures) insisted that the two natures *remained* distinct, inseparably united, never mingled or confused. The proper analogy here would be that of oil and water: Pour both into a blender and run it till Hell freezes over, and the oil is never going to mix with the water, even though not so much as a film of oxygen molecules separates them.

The Council of Chalcedon decided this one in favor of Leo and his colleagues in 451. Again, there was no actual resolution, since the numerous Monophysite churches went their merry way and exist till this very day. The Coptic Church, Ethiopian Orthodox Church, Armenian Orthodox Church, and so forth are Monophysite.

How to picture a Monophysite Jesus? That's a tough one, but maybe the best bet would be to picture Jesus as portrayed by Max von Sydow in *The Greatest Story Ever Told*. He speaks and acts always with the imperturbable serenity of a statue of the Buddha. He is floating through the pages of an epic, a self-consciously divine Messiah with nothing to say but sonorous pronouncements that already sound like momentous quotes as he is saying them (unlike, one may add, the Jesus in Pier Paolo Pasolini's *The Gospel according to Saint Matthew*, who seems to be just what he is: some guy videotaped in his backyard wearing a sheet and spitting out lines from the Bible!).

By contrast, a brilliant portrayal of the Chalcedonian two-nature Jesus who is really and significantly human as well as being truly divine is provided perhaps where most people would least expect it: in Schraeder and Scorcese's *The Last Temptation of Christ*. Ironically, this much-abused and misunderstood masterpiece takes the prize as the most orthodox Jesus film of them all! Where else will you find a depiction of a man who begins to sense deep inside that he is also God? Would such a realization go down easy? It would not. The ease with which religious conservatives seem to imagine the historical Jesus taking in stride the fact of his divinity shows that they are scarcely reckoning with a historical figure at all, rather just a character in a scripture, which, to them, is the really important thing. But *The Last Temptation of Christ* shows us an up-close view of a man tormented by something scarcely different from demon possession: divine incarnation! If the notion of God becoming a man was supposed to be as alien and scandalous to Jewish sensibilities as apologists are always assuring us it was (since they want to argue that Jewish disciples couldn't have just made it up), then mustn't it have been quite an identity crisis for a Jewish God-man to assimilate the two truths about himself? And so Schraeder and Scorsese, following author Nikos Kazantzakis, depict it. And that is why this film has real theological importance: It demonstrates, by means of artistic verisimilitude, that we *can* imagine a truly divine and truly human Jesus. Whether or not it is true, it cannot be easily dismissed as an artificial formula, a confusing bit of oxymoron.

Here, then, is one place where Dan Brown really lets his readers down. His completely false and misleading account of Constantine and the "invention" of the divine Christ is offered to the reader not as part of the fiction but as part of the factual research background. But it seems he could not manage to keep the two straight. And that is what I am trying to do in this chapter.

One last note: In any event, it is in no way clear that for Jesus to have had sex or begotten children, as many of these popular books say he did, would have been incompatible with either his sinlessness or his divine character. And this point is crucial to the Teabing hypothesis: The marriage of Jesus is supposed to be the bombshell to demolish historic Christianity. But would it? It would certainly surprise a lot of people, for whatever that's worth. But I am reminded of an anecdote told in class by my old mentor David M. Scholer. One day a woman in his church recounted a dream in which she saw Jesus roller skating and smoking a cigarette! Though the skating gave her no pause, the smoking did, but only for a moment. Then, she said, she realized Jesus was Jewish, and "I remembered: Jews smoke!" They also have sex.

Dan Brown seems unaware of the fact that there is no unquestioned unanimity of Christian opinion about Jesus's divinity and what it might mean. Controversy has never really died down, at least since the blossoming of Unitarianism and Socinianism at the time of the Protestant Reformation. And more recently than that, various waves of Liberal Protestant and Modernist Catholic thinkers have suggested thorough revisions of Christological doctrine. The most radical of these, perhaps, was the 1977 publication in Great Britain and America of the symposium *The Myth of God Incarnate*, in which a number of reputable theologians argued that it was time to jettison the whole idea of Jesus as the God-man. There was a bit of a flap about it for a while, but the biggest result was to provoke a few more books, opposing collections of essays carrying on the debate. Each side tried to reinforce the views of its clientele or maybe even to steal off a few sheep from the other flock. But the earth didn't shake. Nor would it if one could prove, as no one has ever done, that Jesus was married.

NOTES

1. Dan Brown, *The Da Vinci Code* (New York: Doubleday, 2003), pp. 232–33.

2. T. G. Elliott, *The Christianity of Constantine the Great* (Scranton, PA: University of Scranton Press, 1996), pp. 17–27, 29–38.

3. James Brashler and Roger A. Bullard, trans., "Apocalypse of Peter," in *Nag Hammadi Library in English*, ed. James M. Robinson, 3rd ed. (New York: Harper & Row, 1988), p. 377.

4. P. L. Couchoud, *The Creation of Christ: An Outline of the Beginnings of Christianity*, trans. C. Bradlaugh Bonner (London: Watts, 1939); G. A. Wells, *The Jesus of the Early Christians: A Study in Christian Origins* (London: Pemberton, 1971); Earl Doherty, *The Jesus Puzzle: Did Christianity Begin with a Mythical Christ?* (Ottawa: Canadian Humanist Publications, 1999).

5. Paul Veyne, *Did the Greeks Believe in Their Myths?* (Chicago: University of Chicago Press, 1988), p. 88: "the Greeks held their gods to be true, although these gods existed for them in a space-time that was secretly different from the one in which their believers lived."

6. Bart Ehrman, *The Orthodox Corruption of Scripture: The Effect of Early Christological Controversies on the Text of the New Testament* (New York: Oxford University Press, 1993), p. 14.

7. Maurice Wiles, *Archetypal Heresy: Arianism through the Centuries* (Oxford: Oxford University Press, 1996).

Chapter 6

LOOSE CANON

Who Picked the Books in the Bible?

Try to ignore the insufferable, patronizing tone; here is Professor Teabing's mini-catechism on the canon of scripture: "The Bible is the product of *man*, my dear. Not of God. The Bible did not fall magically from the clouds. Man created it as a historical record of tumultuous times, and it has evolved through countless translations, additions and revisions. History has never had a definitive version of the book."[1] Well, the translations point is a bit of a red herring. We can pretty well just go back, as Martin Luther and all subsequent translators have, to the original Hebrew, Aramaic (a little bit), and Greek. But Teabing, Dan Brown, is right about the rest of it. Dewey M. Beegle used to make the same point to those who claimed that, whatever problems we might be able to find in our editions of scripture, the "original autographs" were "inerrant and infallible." Beegle would counter, "*What* original autographs?" Because virtually every book of the Bible is a patchwork quilt.[2]

Some, like the Pentateuch, the Psalms, and Proverbs, began as compilations of earlier sources. Others began as collections of sayings, ledgers, prophetic oracles, speeches, and so forth, to which many more of the same sort, by nameless successors of the original prophets, were added over the generations. Some books (Matthew, Chronicles, 2 Peter) are supplemented versions of others (Mark, Samuel and Kings, Jude, respectively). And the major inference Teabing intends us to draw seems inescapable: There is no reason whatever to believe that either the origin or the growth of the Bible was supernatural in character. "The modern Bible was compiled and edited by men who possessed a political agenda—to promote the divinity of the man Jesus Christ and use His influence to solidify their own power base."[3] This, too, seems fair. The notion of an inspired scripture containing these books and no others is indeed a piece of mystification put forth by the self-appointed guardians of traditional faith, who have always sought to control what sacred texts we read and how we interpret them. That is the whole point of a canon (a "standard") of scripture.[4]

But we must part company with the pseudoerudite Dr. Teabag, ah, Teabing, when he keeps rambling on: "The Bible, as we know it today, was collated by the pagan Roman emperor Constantine the Great."[5] "Constantine commissioned and financed a new Bible, which omitted those gospels that spoke of Christ's *human* traits and embellished those gospels that made Him godlike. The earlier gospels were gathered up and burned."[6] Brown is a bit mixed up here. To be clear ourselves: Constantine was an intrusive amateur theologian who wanted things his way, and the notion of Christ as the Lord of the universe proved handy for him, as he positioned himself as Christ's almighty vicar on earth. But, as we have seen, the notion of a divine Christ was already quite old and no political creation. And Alexandrian bishop Athanasius, whose patron Constantine was, did indeed have major influence toward establishing the twenty-seven-book New Testament we use today. But, as far as we know, Constantine had no input in his list (see below). What Brown may be thinking of is the fact, reported by Eusebius, another favorite of Constantine (and the author of the "official" history of the church as written by the winners), that Constantine had fifty copies of scripture prepared (hand calligraphy!) on fine vellum for distribution through the major churches. Some scholars believe that the two fourth-century Bible manuscripts, Codex Sinaiticus and Codex Vaticanus, were among these. If so, it is interesting, as these do not match the canon list of Athanasius, indicating that the matter was still up for discussion. We knew that from Eusebius anyway, since he tells us where various groups lined up on this and that document and whether it belonged to scripture or not (again, see below). And the bishops of Constantine's faction (today's Catholic orthodoxy) did see to the destruction of many, many Gnostic and other writings, a terrible reproach for which we can never forgive them.

Another oddity in the Teabing tirade just quoted is the supposition that the Nag Hammadi and other pre-Constantinian gospels uniformly portrayed a merely human Jesus. If anything, the opposite is true. The Jesus of virtually all these writings is a fantastic and phantasmagorical being who functions mostly as a literary mouthpiece for outlandish doctrines no one alive today could espouse! (See chapter 4 on Gnosticism.) What, then, can Brown be talking about? One thing, and just one, in particular. He must be referring to that passage in the Gospel of Philip, which says Jesus used to smooch Mary Magdalene. Taking it out of context, Brown seems to think the Gnostic gospels portray Jesus simply as a cool guy. (See chapter 7, "Eighty Gospels?")

Many of these issues have remained unsuspected by most Christians, though they are no news to critical scholars. And thus we must thank Dan Brown for bringing them to the attention of such a wide audience. But, as ever, the problem is his admixture of gross misinformation. To collapse the history of the New Testament canon (which admittedly is anything but a textbook fallen from heaven) into the cynical scheme of an egomaniacal politician is on the same level with the ignorant claim of some that King James of England personally *wrote* the King James Bible! And as long as Professor Teabing has raised the issue, it is incumbent on us to try to sort out what really happened. In fact, the real story is much more fascinating and colorful than Brown's bogus version, and no less subversive of orthodox security.

MARCION INVASION

The history of a distinctively Christian scripture canon begins with Marcion of Pontus in Asia Minor. Traditionally dated as beginning his public ministry about 140 CE, Marcion may actually have gotten started earlier, just after the turn of the century. One ancient tradition/legend makes Marcion the secretary of the evangelist John, writing at the end of the first century. That story is probably not historically true, but no one would have told it if they did not assume Marcion had lived that early. It was a general tactic of early Catholic apologists to late-date the so-called heretics so as to distance them as far as possible from the apostolic period (in the same way as apologists today prefer the earliest possible date for the epistles and gospels, to include them within the apostolic period).

Marcion was the first real Paulinist we know of. It would later be a matter of some embarrassment to the church fathers that the earliest readers and devotees of the Pauline epistles were the Marcionites and the Valentinian Gnostics. We know of no Paulinists before these second-century Christians. The mid–first century existence of Pauline Christianity is simply an inference (admittedly a natural one) from taking the authorship and implied dates of the Pauline epistles at face value, as works representing a wing of first-century Christianity. But it is quite possible that the Pauline literature is the product of Marcionite and Gnostic movements in the late first and early second centuries. But even if most of the Pauline epistles are genuinely Pauline and from the first century, the most likely candidate for the first collector of the Pauline corpus remains Marcion. No one else in the time period would have had either the interest or the opportunity. No one was as interested in Paul as was Marcion. Why?

Marcion shared with his theological cousins the Gnostics the belief that the true God and Father of Jesus Christ was not the same deity as the creator and lawgiver God of Israel and of the Jewish scriptures. In this belief he was perhaps influenced by Zoroastrian Zurvanism, a dualistic doctrine, as Jan Koester suggests. At any rate he allowed that the creator God was righteous and just, but he was also harsh and retributive. His seeming grace was but a function of his arbitrariness: Nero might render a verdict of thumbs-up or thumbs-down as the whim moved him, and so with the God of Israel. Marcion deemed the Jewish scriptures historically true. He expected messianic prophecies to be fulfilled by a Davidic king who would restore Jewish sovereignty. But Marcion deemed all of this strictly irrelevant to the new religion of Christianity. In his view, which he claimed to have derived from reading Paul's epistles, Jesus Christ was the Son and revealer of an alien God who had not created the world, had not given the Torah to Moses, and would not judge mankind. The Father of Jesus Christ was a God of perfect love and righteousness who would punish no one. Through Jesus (and Paul) he offered the human race the opportunity to be adopted as his children. If they were Gentiles, this meant a break with paganism. If they were Jews, it entailed a break from Judaism and the Torah. Marcion preached a strict morality. For him all sex was sinful. Begetting children only produced more souls to live in bondage to the creator. Marcion believed Jesus had no physical birth but appeared out of heaven one day at the seeming age of thirty, already in a human body (like Adam—created as an adult but with a misleading belly button!), albeit a body of celestial substance. He taught and was later crucified. He had hoped his twelve disciples would spread his gospel of the alien God and his loving adoption of all who would come to him. But things went awry: The disciples, as thick-headed and prone to misunderstanding as they appear in Mark, underestimated the discontinuity of Jesus's new revelation with their hereditary Judaism and combined the two. This was the origin of the Judaizing heresy with which Paul deals in Galatians and elsewhere.

Marcion had noticed an oddity most Christians never notice as they read the New Testament: If Jesus had named the Twelve to succeed him and seemed satisfied with them, whence the need for Paul at all? And why should he come to eclipse the others in importance? The Twelve are for the most part merely a list of names. Not so Paul, whose letters have formed the basis for Protestant Christianity. Marcion saw a simple answer: The Risen Jesus saw how far off the track his disciples had quickly gone and decided to recruit another who would get the message straight. And this was Paul. To invoke a recurrent pattern in Christian history, think of Martin Luther, Alexander Campbell, John Nelson Darby, Joseph Smith, Charles Taze Russell, Victor Paul Wierwille, and others. All these believed that original, apostolic Christianity had been corrupted by an admixture of human tradition, and they believed they had a new vision of the outlines of true Christianity and set about to restore it. This is what Marcion thought already in the early second century. It shouldn't sound that strange to us. Like these men, Marcion succeeded very well in launching a new church, one that spread like wildfire all over and even beyond the Roman Empire. And the New Testament was his idea.

The emerging Catholic Church (that which would develop into the medieval church, which then subsequently split into Roman Catholicism and Eastern Orthodoxy) was by this time employing the familiar authority structure of scripture and tradition. The scripture was the Septuagint, the Greek translation of the Jewish scriptures (including the so-called apocryphal or deutero-canonical books of the Maccabees, Judith, Tobit, Sirach/Ecclesiasticus, Wisdom, Baruch, the Epistle of Jeremiah,

1 Esdras, etc.). This simply was "scripture." Tradition was, on the one hand, the growing body of sayings attributed to Jesus and stories about him and, on the other, the summaries of what was considered "apostolic" doctrine, represented in formulae such as the Apostles Creed. We find similar summaries in late second–century writers like Irenaeus and Tertullian. There were a number of early Christian writings of various kinds (gospels, epistles, apostolic acts, revelations, church manuals) that were written and circulated more or less widely, but these were at first more *expressions of* the faith than either the *source* or *criteria for* faith. That is not to say they were not important. Think of the writings of Calvin and Luther: They are very important to Calvinists and Lutherans who still study them, but no Calvinists or Lutherans would consider the wise writings of their founders to be scripture on the same level with the Bible. Admittedly, in practice the difference may evaporate, but that is just the technical distinction that is important here. The question that concerns us is precisely how the early Christian writings came to cross that line and join the category of scripture. The earliest Catholic Christians felt no need as yet for new scripture, since they found the Septuagint Bible adequate to their needs so long as they could use allegory and typology to read it as a Christian book, one about Jesus Christ and Christianity.

But this Marcion was not willing to do. He insisted on a literal, straightforward reading of the Jewish scriptures, refusing to treat them as a ventriloquist dummy and make them seem to speak with Christian accents. Theodore of Mopsuestia (350–428) had the same attitude, though he was no Marcionite. Read in a plain-sense fashion, Marcion recognized, the

Jewish scriptures had nothing to do with Christianity. (Even lacking his belief in two different biblical Gods, one can see his point when one thinks of the strained arguments needed in order to make various Old Testament passages sound like predictions of Jesus. And it is still quite common today to hear Christians contrast the severe God of Israel with the tender Father of Jesus.) So Marcion repudiated the Jewish scriptures. It wasn't that he disbelieved them; he didn't. They were just the proper scriptures of somebody else's religion that did not overlap with Christianity as he understood it. Nor was Marcion anti-Semitic or even anti-Judaic! For him, Judaism was a true religion on its own terms; it's just that it wasn't the religion of Jesus Christ or the Apostle Paul.

Anyway, without the Septuagint Bible as his scripture, Marcion felt the need to compile a new scripture that would teach Christian faith and morals authoritatively. So he collected the early Christian writings he felt served the purpose. These were paramountly the Pauline epistles, except for the Pastorals—1 and 2 Timothy and Titus—because these did not yet exist. They were written in reaction to Marcion and other "heretics" in the second century. As for the rest, Marcion had shorter, earlier versions of the texts than ours. Likewise, he had one gospel, corresponding to a shorter version of our Gospel of Luke, though he knew it simply as "the gospel." Catholic writers decades later would claim that Marcion had edited and censored the texts, cutting out any material that served to link Christianity with its Jewish background. Marcion no doubt did do some small amount of editing, textual criticism, as it seemed to him, but it rather seems that Catholic apologists padded out the texts with their own added material, claiming that their own versions were original and should be adopted instead of the Marcionite text. Marcion called his scripture the *Apostolicon* ("the Book of the Apostle").

THE FIRST COUNTER-REFORMATION

If Marcion had been merely some eccentric, people like Justin Martyr, Irenaeus, and Tertullian would not have bothered with him. But he rapidly became a force to be reckoned with, since Marcionite, Pauline Christianity spread far and wide. The relationship between Marcion and the Catholic leaders of his own day is strikingly paralleled in the uneasy relations between Paul and the Jerusalem apostles in Galatians and 2 Corinthians. The Catholic Church sought to co-opt Marcionism/Paulinism late in the second century by, as anticipated just above, adding material to the Pauline texts and Luke, harmonizing Pauline Christianity with Judaism in the manner still familiar today, insisting that Christianity was the rightful heir to God's covenant promises with Israel and the Jewish people. Had Marcionism triumphed, I dare say we would have seen more peaceful Jewish-Christian relations, since neither side would have been perceived as coveting the heritage of the other.

How did the Catholic Church respond to the Marcionite Sputnik of a specifically Christian scripture? Where Marcion relegated the Jewish scriptures to the Jewish religion and replaced them with a distinctly Christian scripture, the Catholic bishops decided to retain the Jewish Bible (reinterpreted in a Christian manner) and to add a new set of writings onto it. They certainly had no objection to having a set of books that would speak overtly of Christian faith and practice. Remember, they already had them. It was just a question of making it official, making them part of the Bible. So they took over the Pauline letters, adding the Pastorals and interpolating the others to bring them into closer accord with Catholic teaching. Marcion's gospel became our Gospel of Luke (adding chapters 1–3, the Nazareth synagogue sermon, the Prodigal Son, the Tower of Siloam and Pilate's massacre of the Galileans, the "Wisdom saith" speech, the Triumphal Entry, the Wicked Tenants, the resurrection debate with the Sadducees, the prediction of Spirit baptism, and the ascension). To balance and dilute Luke, Catholics added Matthew, Mark, and John (already written, of course, though John had to be extensively reshuffled and interpolated, as Bultmann showed, before it could pass as sufficiently orthodox).

Wanting to restore the clout of the Twelve, Catholics made a late and lame attempt to represent them in the canon alongside Paul. The Acts of the Apostles sought to co-opt Paul and make Peter his twin (so as to bring both sides together, one devotees of Paul's memory, the other of Peter's), as well as to imply that the Twelve in general played some important role. If they ever had, their labors were among Jewish Christians in Palestine, and their work was largely forgotten after 70 CE and the destruction of Jerusalem. A group of three anonymous epistles from "the Elder," a master of traveling missionaries late in the first century, was ascribed gratuitously to John son of Zebedee. Two spurious Petrine writings (1 and 2 Peter, by different pseudonymous authors) were chosen out of the much larger bin of Petrine apocrypha surviving today (the two Apocalypses of Peter, the Gospel of Peter, the Journeys of Peter, the Acts of Peter, the Preaching of Peter, the Letter of Peter to Philip, etc.), as was a letter by someone named James (the Brother of the Lord? Son of Zebedee? Son of Alphaeus? Or any other James?) and another by one Jude. This gave us the core of the Catholic canon, though its exact outlines would take some centuries to be settled.

THE A LIST

For Irenaeus (115–202), bishop of Lyons and major opponent of Gnosticism, the Christian Testament included the four gospels, the Pauline epistles, and Acts. He used, but seems not yet to have regarded as scripture, 1 Peter, 1 John, either 2 or 3 John (he does not say which, but he mentions another Johannine epistle), Jude, and Revelation. He makes no mention of Hebrews, 2 Peter, or James. Twenty years later, Tertullian (160–mid–third century), a follower of Irenaeus, had the same list, but for him, all of these books were part of scripture. Tertullian also used Hebrews and the Epistle of Barnabas, though we cannot tell if he regarded them as canonical. And he thought 1 Enoch ought to be included in the Old Testament. (The first Christian we know of who referred to the Jewish scriptures as the Old Testament was Melito of Sardis in the last third of the second century. And Clement of Alexandria [160–215] was the first to call the Christian scriptures the New Testament.)

While Irenaeus considered the books just listed to be authoritative and canonical, he does not seem to have predicated that authority upon any divine inspiration. As he saw it, their authority stemmed from their privileged historical position, their character as foundational documents of the apostolic age. Again, Tertullian has carried things a significant step further, locating the authority of the New Testament books specifically in their apostolic authorship. They did not simply come from the dawn age of the church; they had to carry the authorization of having been composed by Jesus's apostles or their delegates. Here he is thinking of Mark and Luke, who for this very purpose were imagined to have been disciples or assistants of Peter and Paul, respectively. (Irenaeus has his predecessor, Papias, bishop of Hierapolis about 130, already linking Mark to Peter in this way, but he is probably fudging it. "Papias" seems to have functioned as an all-purpose source of convenient "traditions," licenses to make this or that "apostolic" as needed.)

Clement of Alexandria had no closed canon. He made frequent reference not only to our four conventional gospels but also to the Gospel according to the Hebrews and the Gospel according to the Egyptians, to apocryphal as well as to canonical Acts, to the Epistles of Clement and Barnabas, the Preaching of Peter, the Shepherd of Hermas, and others. And (if Morton Smith is to be believed) he used a secret edition of Mark. So far, the New Testament books were considered authoritative because apostolic. It was Clement of Alexandria's successor Origen (185–251) who first considered them inspired writings as opposed to writings of inspired or authoritative writers, an important distinction even in twentieth-century scripture debates. Origen reasoned that, since a book either was or was not inspired, then it behooved the church to decide which ones, and no others, belonged in the Bible. But he himself did not make the judgment call. He only saw the need.

Eusebius, the great church historian and propagandist for Constantinian Christianity, makes it clear that precise canonical boundaries were still a matter of dispute in his day (mid–fourth century). He tells us how, in the discussions of contemporary theologians, the available writings fell into four categories. First, there were what he regarded as *genuine apostolic* books: the four conventional gospels, the Pauline epistles, with some disputing Hebrews, 1 John, 1 Peter, and Acts. Some include Revelation in the category (Eusebius was no fan of it, though!). Second, there were generally *disputed* books: 2 and 3 John, Jude, James, 2 Peter, some say Hebrews. (The Pauline authorship of it was still up for grabs—Origen had admitted "God alone knows" who wrote Hebrews.) Third were the "*spurious*," that is, possibly pseudonymous in authorship, but still acceptable and usable: the Gospel according to the Hebrews, the Acts of Paul, Shepherd of Hermas, Apocalypse of Peter, the Didache (Teaching of the Twelve Apostles to the Nations), Barnabas, and some say the Revelation of John. (Eusebius thought one "John the Elder," not John the son of Zebedee, wrote it.) Fourth were outright *heretical forgeries*: Acts of John, of Andrew, Peter, Thomas, and so on and the Gospels of Peter, Thomas, and Matthias. It is evident that the canon question was still wide open.

The Muratorian Canon, a fragmentary writing from Rome, has generally been placed in the second century, but some now argue it dates to the fourth, and it lists all our New Testament books except for Hebrews, James, 1 and 2 Peter, while adding the Apocalypse of Peter and the Wisdom of Solomon (!). It mentions and rejects the Shepherd of Hermas.

BONFIRE OF THE HERESIES

The first known list of our twenty-seven New Testament writings appears in the Paschal (Easter) Letter of Athanasius to his diocese in 367 CE. He lists them and warns his flock to use these and no others. One immediate result of this encyclical was to prompt the brethren of the Monastery of Saint Pachomius in Egypt (the very first known Christian monastery) to hide away their copies of books banned from the list. These they buried in a cave in leather satchels, where they rested in oblivion till 1945 when accidentally discovered by a peasant farmer. The monks knew the inquisitors would be coming around again to see if the encyclical had been obeyed, and they did not want to hand over their precious copies of the Gospels of Thomas, Philip, Peter, the Egyptians, Mary Magdalene; their Revelations of Zostrianos, James, Melchizedek, Seth, Shem, Dositheus, and others; their Epistles of Peter and James; their Apocrypha of John and James; and so forth to be burned. Their library attests an astonishing range of Christian scripture still in use at the time. We have only these and a very few other copies of the excluded books because the Constantinian authorities carried out a systematic purge of the writings deemed heretical as per Athanasius's encyclical. (Others, like the Shepherd of Hermas, survived outside the canon since they were not considered dangerous, just not official.)

The list of Athanasius, he who championed *Homoousias* Christology at Nicea, was officially adopted ("received") by the local Synod of Hippo in 393 and again by the Synod of Carthage in 397. But this hardly meant that from there on in everyone used our New Testament list. Surviving manuscript codices of the New Testament (and there are a great many) from the next few centuries continue to include other (less heretical) books and/or to lack some of the ones on the list. Scribes apparently did not feel particularly bound to conform to the Athanasian norm. Why should they? No ecumenical council ruled on the matter until the Counter-Reformation Council of Trent! In general, though, it would be fair to say that by about 400 CE, the Western Mediterranean churches used the Athanasian canon, remaining grudgingly reluctant about Hebrews. It took another two centuries until the Eastern churches were ready to accept Revelation as canonical. Even today, in the Monophysite churches of Armenia and Ethiopia, the New Testament canon contains books like 3 Corinthians, Clement, Barnabas, and so on.

At the time of the Protestant Reformation, Martin Luther had the opportunity to reshape the canon simply by virtue of the fact that he was preparing the official German edition of the Bible for Protestants. It was up to him what would go into it. So he rejected the Old Testament Apocrypha, partly because not all survived in their original languages. Since he argued scripture was authoritative only in the original Hebrew and Greek, not in the Greek Septuagint or the hitherto-official Latin Vulgate, he couldn't consider a book canonical that survived only in translation. Some, though, he disdained because of practical or theological matters. Still, he did not condemn them, and even the Puritans continued to read them for edification. The King James Bible included these books till 1823, when printers dropped them.

But Luther also reshuffled the New Testament canon, restricting Hebrews, James, Jude, and Revelation to an appendix. James he called an "epistle of straw," while he said Revelation deserved to be taken out and thrown in the Elbe River! None of these books adequately conveyed the doctrine of salvation by grace through faith alone, Luther's theological plumb line. Needless to say, Lutherans did not see fit to follow their master at this point. It was only in the nineteenth century that the question was reopened by Friedrich Daniel Ernst Schleiermacher and later by Adolf von Harnack. Schleiermacher urged that theologians continue to sift the canonical from the apocryphal even within the bounds of the New Testament, while Harnack said it was now finally time to follow Marcion and cut loose the Old Testament. Perhaps the most astonishing Protestant remark on the canon question came from Willi Marxsen, a twentieth-century German theologian, who noted that Protestants have implicitly sawn off the branch they sat on when they rejected the tradition of the church as the norm for faith and practice in favor of "scripture alone." How? Simply by ignoring the fact that the contents of the canon were purely a matter of church tradition, not of scripture! The Bible doesn't tell us what ought to be in the Bible; tradition does, and it is this latter that Protestants claim to reject. Uh-oh.

MAKING THE CUT: CRITERIA

As a matter of tradition, the selection of the books for the canon was a gradual and to some degree haphazard process. It was the result of a piecemeal accumulation of local tradition and usage, and then a comparison of such local versions and usages by larger councils. Certain surviving remarks give us a good idea of what considerations guided the mostly anonymous Catholic bishops and theologians in the second, third, and fourth centuries. There were four criteria often or generally brought to bear. Some will sound familiar by now. I will discuss them in order of descending importance, noting how one has a tendency to collapse into another.

First, *catholicity*: Was a book known and used liturgically all over the empire? If it was not, it was dubious, since a real apostolic writing should have had time to circulate more widely. The fewer quarters of the church in which it was known, the greater the likelihood of its being a recent forgery. ("Why didn't we hear about this 'Gospel according to Wally' till now? I smell a rat!") Little 3 John had trouble on this score, but it made it in because it was evidently by the same author as the popular and renowned 1 John, so they figured it was its tiny size that caused it to be largely lost in the shuffle. In practice, the criterion of catholicity meant that the more widely known the book, whatever its contents, the better its chances were, because long familiarity and wide readership meant that there had been more opportunity for any "heretical" rough edges to have been worn away by theologians' clever reinterpretations. But if it was unfamiliar, something that sounded heretical would jump right out. This is what happened to the Gospel of Peter. Bishop Serapion was asked to come to look over a copy of this gospel in rural Syria, where it was popular. He had never heard of it, so he took a look and saw no problem. But then someone advised a second look, and he picked out signs of Docetism, the belief that Jesus had only seemed to suffer on the cross while remaining divinely impassive. So the book was condemned. Had he grown up hearing it read every Sunday, in a familiar context, he would never have noticed any problem any more than the Syrian congregations who were familiar with it did. And the less widely known a book was, the easier politically it was to dump it, since it would have fewer partisans to be offended by its omission.

Second, *orthodoxy*: Did the writing conform to the rule of faith, the emerging creed? But again catholicity could overrule this, since any unorthodox element could be reinterpreted provided the book were widely enough beloved (which is why no one yelps at the numerous Gnostic, docetic, and adoptionistic verses in Paul's letters!). But evidence of Docetism could sink a book, as with the Gospel of Peter or the Acts of John. But it might be something as simple as citation of other books no longer considered canonical. Barnabas cited 1 Enoch as scripture and didn't make it, while Jude cited 1 Enoch and did squeeze in (though someone tried to replace it with 2 Peter, which incorporates most of Jude but cuts his references to the Assumption of Moses and 1 Enoch!). Or a book might be rejected not because it actually taught some heresy but because it risked letting the camel's nose in under the tent flap. In this way, late apocalypses like the Shepherd of Hermas were dangerous because they were of later vintage, and if one could accept them, then there was no longer any clear reason not to accept the prophetic rantings of the Montanist prophetess Maximilla! Other books were finally rejected, not so much because of their content but because of guilt by association, that is, long or notorious use by heretical sects. The Gospel of Thomas was probably excluded mainly because Valentinians and Manicheans used it. Theirs were by no means the only ways to read the book, and had it been included in the canon, it would not sound heretical to anyone now. The familiar Gospel of John almost shared Thomas's fate because it was so popular among Gnostics, one of whom, Heracleon, wrote the first known commentary on it. The anti-Montanist Gaius thought the Gospel of John must have been written by Gnostics, perhaps by Cerinthus himself! A whole group, dubbed by their enemies "the Alogoi" (a pun: opponents of the Logos gospel/ witless ones), opposed John's canonization. And it *was* probably Gnostic in origin! As Bultmann shows throughout his commentary, it has been somewhat toned down by an "ecclesiastical redactor."

Third was *apostolicity*—was it written by an apostle or the associate of an apostle? We have already seen how important this criterion was. But this was a wax nose easily twisted. If a book was widely known and deemed orthodox, then an apostolic byline could be created for it. In this way, to secure entrance into the canon, the anonymous Epistle to the Hebrews was ascribed, rather late, to Paul. Or if it was too late for that, some tenuous link might be forged between the ascribed authorship and some apostle, as when Irenaeus made Mark Peter's secretary and Luke Paul's. If a book sounded just too blatantly unorthodox, despite a clear apostolic authorship claim (like numerous books attributed to Thomas, Peter, Paul, Matthias, James, John, etc.), it could be dismissed as a forgery. Or a case of mistaken identity, as when Eusebius, who had once embraced the millenarian teaching of Revelation, first ascribed it to John son of Zebedee, but once he rejected the doctrine, he decided the Revelation must have been the work of another John—the Elder, not one of the apostles at all—and thus not to be taken so seriously!

Similarly, one is forced to wonder whether Matthew's gospel received that "apostolic" ascription because it was by far the most popular of the gospels, while "Mark" and "Luke" were damned with the faint praise of noble but subapostolic names by those ecclesiastical editors who first titled them. They fell short of the "apostolic" Matthean standard and so merited lesser authoritative names/titles. By the time the drastically different John was added to the equation, Gaius, remember, suggested Cerinthus for its author as a way of condemning the Gnostic heresy he perceived it to contain. To go all the way to grant it a fully apostolic pedigree was an orthodox counterblast. Had no one gone all the way to the extreme of ascribing the book to Cerinthus, neither would anyone have gone to the opposite extreme of suggesting the Apostle John as its author. It is exactly parallel to the criticisms aimed at the erotic Song of Solomon in the first century among the rabbis. Shouldn't such a piece of pornography be summarily ejected from the canon, that is, from public reading? No, came the reply; in fact, the book is especially holy, rendering the hands of anyone who touches it ritually unclean, that is, temporarily taboo from mundane contact. From one end of the pendulum swing to the other.

Fourth, *numerology*. Irenaeus was desperate to include Matthew, Mark, Luke, and John and equally zealous to crowd out the Valentinian Gospel of Truth. So he reasoned that there can be only four canonical gospels, because there are four winds, four compass directions, four Argus-eyed chaemeras in the heavenly throne room in Revelation. And the perfect number seven (the number of the planets known to the ancients, each worshiped on one day of the week) was reflected in collections of epistles. Paul's were first organized by the hebdomad of recipient churches: Rome, Corinth, Galatia, Philippi, Thessalonika, Colossae, and Ephesus. But this arrangement threatened to leave little Philemon out in the cold, to say nothing of the Pastorals. But once these (ostensibly addressed to individuals) were added, one counted epistles, not recipients, and this brought the total up to thirteen (with two each, of course, to Corinth and Thessalonika). Hence the "need" to make Hebrews a fourteenth Pauline epistle, resulting in two sevens. (If not for the number business, one could as easily have ascribed it to Apollos or Clement or Barnabas, as some did, since these were Pauline proxies, like Luke.) There was a version of the Ignatian epistles containing seven of them, and the Revelation is prefaced by seven epistles. And this is no doubt why there are seven letters in the "Catholic/General Epistles" grab bag (James; 1 and 2 Peter; 1, 2, and 3 John; Jude).

SCRIPTURE AS TRADITION

In retrospect what we see is a process, first, of *expansion* of the canon in reaction to Marcion, and then a *contraction* of the canon to exclude the books of Montanists, Gnostics, and others. Every religion has had debates over the contents of its canon. Different sects, or subdivisions of religions, have different canons, even if it is only a matter of which individual books they put the major emphasis on. But it is well to ask just what is the point of delimiting a canon. The point is to restrict the number of possible sources of divination or doctrine, to limit the number of available voices one may consult and must obey. If you don't want the flock considering certain doctrines, you'd best omit any scriptural texts that might be understood as teaching them.

By the same token, hand in hand with the defining of the canon, comes the governing of interpretation by an authoritative elite. Until the Second Vatican Council in the mid-1960s, the Roman Catholic Church discouraged Bible reading by the laypeople, lest it unleash sectarian fanaticism, every Bible reader becoming his own pope. To the extent that Protestants have avoided this danger it is because individual Protestants have been content to stay within the limits set by the interpretive tradition of their pastor or denomination. Notice how the late 2 Peter both knows a Pauline canon/collection *as scripture* (3:15–16) and admonishes the reader never to presume to engage in personal interpretation of scripture (1:20), since it is a perilous task that has already led many into soul-blasting heresy (3:16)? Tertullian set forth his Prescription against Heretics, where he advised fellow Catholics never to get embroiled in scripture arguments with heretics, since the heretics might well win! What one had to do instead was to deny the heretics' right to appeal to scripture in the first place. Scripture is authoritative only when interpreted through the filter of apostolic tradition!

Today's biblicists are, then, caught in a double, and doubly fatal, irony. First, the contents of the Bible whose infallibility they idolize have been set by fallible mortals like themselves, not by some miracle of revelation. They are dependent for their Bible's table of contents on the unquestioned traditions of men, which in principle they claim to disregard. Second, they continue to quote the Bible as if it were their sole authority when in fact they control the reading of the texts by their own traditions of orthodoxy, condemning as heretical any who venture a different interpretation. In fact their notorious terror at the prospect of the higher criticism of the Bible amounts to an unwillingness to allow the Bible to speak with new voices. Teabing is basically right about this one: The supposedly divine Word has human fingerprints all over it.

NOTES

1. Dan Brown, *The Da Vinci Code* (New York: Doubleday, 2003), p. 231.

2. Dewey M. Beegle, *The Inspiration of Scripture* (Philadelphia: Westminster: 1963), pp. 17–40.

3. Brown, *Da Vinci Code*, p. 234.

4. Frank Kermode, "Institutional Control of Interpretation," in Kermode, *The Art of Telling: Essays on Fiction* (Cambridge, MA: Harvard University Press, 1983), pp. 168–84.

5. Brown, *Da Vinci Code*, p. 231.

6. Ibid., p. 234.

Chapter 7

EIGHTY GOSPELS?

Leftover Gospels outside the Bible

CRUNCHING THE NUMBERS

We have seen that Dan Brown's expert on the Bible and early Christianity rarely knows exactly what he's talking about. He'll say something with a point to it, but he then invites the skeptic to dismiss it out of hand because of the egregious errors in which he wraps it. "Because Constantine upgraded Jesus's status almost four centuries [*sic*: surely he means three!] *after* Jesus's death, thousands of documents already existed chronicling His life as a *mortal* man."[1] Among these he numbers the Dead Sea Scrolls, which, in fact, never mention Jesus by name if at all, and the Nag Hammadi documents, which certainly do not depict a human or humanistic Jesus.[2]

Later, it looks like considerably more of these writings—in fact, most, maybe all—survived the book burnings because they are buried with Mary Magdalene's mummy, like packing paper, one supposes. Teabing starts christening these not-so-lost books "the Sangreal documents."[3] They "include tens of thousands of pages of information. Eyewitness accounts of the Sangreal treasure describe it as being carried in four enormous trunks. In those trunks are reputed to be the *Purist Documents* [yet another title!]—thousands of pages of unaltered, pre-Constantinian documents, written by the early followers of Jesus, revering Him as a wholly human teacher and prophet."[4] In that case, it seems safe to hazard the guess that they don't capitalize "He" and "Him" as Brown does! In any event, this all comes from *The Hiram Key*, as we have seen, a completely fanciful source.

The number shrinks considerably elsewhere in the book: "More than *eighty* gospels were considered for the New Testament, and yet only a few were chosen for inclusion—Matthew, Mark, Luke, and John among them."[5] No, Professor Teabing, there's no "among them." Unfortunately, those are the only four that made the cut.

These tantalizing remarks naturally make one wonder what sort of thing might be contained in the Purist Documents or Sangreal documents (or whatever we are to call them). Luckily, Teabing provides a couple of peeks: "Another explosive document believed to be in the treasure is a manuscript called *The Magdalene Diaries*—Mary Magdalene's personal account of her relationship with Christ, His crucifixion, and her time in France."[6] This is just hilarious, though one suspects unwittingly. Brown is descending to the level of the supermarket tabloid "scoops" such as archaeologists discovering love letters from Jesus to Mary. Or maybe it is a tip of the hat to an earlier dime novel, *The Magdalene Scrolls* by Barbara Wood (1978). In any case, here Mary Magdalene has become a first-century Jackie-O!

One can find all extant samples of noncanonical gospel literature assembled, with good introductions, in Robert J. Miller's *The Complete Gospels*.[7] But while it's this book you're reading, let me provide my own take on some of the most interesting gospels.

THE "LOST" GOSPEL Q

"Also rumored to be part of the treasure is the legendary '*Q*' *Document*—a manuscript that even the Vatican admits they believe exists. Allegedly, it is a book of Jesus' teachings, possibly written in his own hand.... Why wouldn't Jesus have kept a chronicle of his ministry? Most people did in those days."[8] It is hard to know where to begin! Brown probably got the idea that Mary Magdalene is wrapped up in Q from *The Hiram Key*. Those authors, Christopher Knight and Robert Lomas, misunderstand what Q is supposed to be. They have somewhere got the notion that it was a source document drawn upon by all four canonical gospels. Brown doesn't understand what it is either. He seems to think it is supposed to be a notebook of some kind, containing Jesus's basic preaching material, which he would check off after each gig to make sure he didn't use the same material on the same audience twice! And Brown says such books were common. Not so. But in any event, whether Jesus kept such a thing or not, that is not what Q is supposed to be. What is it, then?

The one-letter title stands for the German word *Quelle*, or "source" (German scholars first came up with the theory), and Q is the sayings source used by Matthew and Luke in addition

to their using Mark. To slow down: When one compares
Matthew, Mark, and Luke in detail, it quickly becomes evident
that they are not independent works. Somebody has been
copying from somebody else. Much material is shared between
them, quite often verbatim. And where they differ, it looks like
the kind of difference you have when one writer edits another.
These are called redactional changes. Most of Mark reappears
in both Luke and Matthew, but Luke and Matthew also share
a considerable amount of material that does not appear in
Mark. Most scholars accept that the pattern of dependence was
as follows. First, there were two major Jesus documents: Mark,
largely a narrative, and Q, almost entirely a set of sayings.
There are occasional parallels between the two, enough to suggest Mark might have picked up a few things from Q and
rewritten them. Later, Matthew and Luke independently
decided to combine the two well-known Jesus books and to
add material of their own. So Matthew combined Mark and Q,
adding much new material. Luke combined Mark and Q, but
in a different order, also adding new material of his own creation. (John seems to have made some use of Mark and Luke,
maybe of Matthew as well, but not of Q, which may have been
lost by his day.) Thus the contents of Q are no mystery. There
may well be other collections of teachings of Jesus buried out
there somewhere, but if we want to talk about Q, we are
talking about a hypothetical literary source whose contents we
know because we can distill them from Matthew and Luke. If
we couldn't, we wouldn't even be talking about Q. So, contrary
to Brown and Teabing, we already have Q. We've always had it.
It's just parts of Matthew and Luke.

This is not to say the subject of Q is not of considerable

interest. Helmut Koester, James M. Robinson, Burton L. Mack, and others have drawn attention to a profound implication of there being a gospel composed only of sayings. Keep in mind, it is apparently a self-sufficient gospel in which some ancient Christian body expressed what it thought was most important—and it makes no mention of miracles, Jesus's crucifixion, or a resurrection! What kind of Christians, when faced with the prospect of committing to paper what they wanted people to know about Jesus, would assemble just his sayings? Presumably a variety hinted at in the Gospel of Thomas, saying 13, when Matthew says to Jesus, "You are a wise philosopher." We have no right to assume this early group even knew about the death of Jesus, much less believed in it as the vehicle for human salvation! Recent discussion of Q and its implications has indeed had a major impact on the way scholars are revising their understanding of Christian origins.

It is true that there do remain some scores of gospels that were unknown or distasteful to the nameless compilers of the canon. Mary Magdalene's kiss-and-tell memoirs happen not to be among them, but these books are interesting nonetheless, and I propose to survey them here. I will have more or less to say about each depending on its relative importance or interest.

THE GOSPEL OF THOMAS

This document is the only surviving example of the sayings gospel genre, though we have reason to believe there were others, including the Q source. There are but stray narrative bits in Thomas, which are there to set up the sayings. And yet it is not quite right to say that Thomas's sayings just hang time-lessly in the air with no narrative framework (like those col-lected in the Book of Proverbs). Depending on how one understands the phrase "the living Jesus" at the start of the book, the ensuing sayings may be intended as a (primitive ver-sion of a) revelatory Resurrection discourse like the Pistis Sophia, The Dialogue of the Savior, or The Epistle of the Apos-tles. These books presuppose some sort of Passion and Easter Narratives and propose to enlighten the reader on special eso-teric teachings given by Jesus to the elite among his disciples before his final ascension, the sort of thing hinted at in Acts chapter 1 but not made explicit there. We may read Thomas as providing a collection of such resurrection teachings.

But does this not conflict with the fact that many of the say-ings in this collection are other versions of sayings attributed to Jesus during his Galilean teaching ministry in the tradi-tional gospels? Yes and no. Actually, it just goes to vindicate Rudolf Bultmann's observation that early Christians made no distinction such as today's historians like to make between remembered sayings of a historical Jesus and inspired prophetic oracles issued in the early Christian congregations by prophets uttering a word of wisdom or word of knowledge in the name of the Risen Lord.

Why is this gospel connected to the name of Judas Thomas, Judas the Twin? Many in early Syrian Christianity supposed that Thomas, being, after all, *someone's* less important twin brother (otherwise the *other* brother would have been dubbed "ditto," Didymus or Thomas, i.e., the Twin), was actually the twin of *Jesus*. (Mark 6 does list a brother named Judas.) But just as often this brother relation was understood to be spiritual and figurative, Thomas being the paramount example of (or a fictional-ized symbol of) the Christian who achieves Jesus's own level of spiritual advancement. This was something considered impossible by emerging institutional Catholicism, whose dogma of inescapable Original Sin functioned as a stifling, self-fulfilling prophecy for those catechized to believe it, thus ensuring the hierarchy would never work itself out of a job.

Since the Gospel according to Thomas was discovered among a cache of overtly Gnostic documents at Nag Hammadi, scholars have assumed it, too, is a Gnostic product. In recent years, Stevan L. Davies and others have pointed out how mild the esoteric character of Thomas is compared with full-fledged Gnostic texts like the Pistis Sophia.[9] While some sayings do seem to teach Gnostic doctrines like the preexistence of the soul and implicit reincarnationism, others inculcate strict Torah observance. Some sayings hotly repudiate belief in a future coming of the Kingdom of God, while others plainly teach it. Some sayings teach antisexual Encratism; others presuppose the Jewish Platonism of Philo.

Is Thomas dependent on any or all of the traditionally canonical gospels? There is a lot of overlap. But the verbal similarities are considerably looser than those between, say, Matthew and Mark or Luke and Mark. The situation is similar to that of John and the Synoptics, where the dependence is much looser, the rewriting considerably freer—if there is dependence at all. Scholars including Helmut Koester, Stevan L. Davies, and Stephen J. Patterson argue vigorously and plausibly that Thomas presents us with an independent and often earlier, more authentic, version of those Jesus sayings it holds in common with Matthew, Mark, or Luke. The key to the debate is whether close reading of Thomas's sayings reveals any of the distinctive marks of Matthew's or Luke's redactional style. That is, we think we can often pinpoint just how and where Matthew and Luke have retouched their Markan and Q source materials, and if we were to find in Thomas something that appears to retain the editorial marks of Matthew or Luke, this would count as evidence that the compiler of Thomas had derived the sayings in question from those Gospels, not just from free-floating oral tradition. If Thomas seems to be quoting Matthew's version of a saying, then Thomas is later than Matthew and used Matthew. And this is what I think did happen. I believe there are sufficient signs to indicate that Thomas follows Matthew and Luke. And yet Thomas certainly seems to be a collection of variegated materials, many derived from oral tradition rather than written sources. But we don't have an either-or dilemma here. Oral tradition of the sayings of Jesus continued to thrive for a long time after the gospels were put down in written form, and we learn from Papias that at least some Christians continued to prefer what they considered the living voice of apostolic tradition to what they could find in books. What I think happened in the case of Thomas is that its compiler did three things.

First, he relied upon memory quotations of material he had once read or heard read from Matthew and Luke, having no copy at hand as Matthew did of Mark when he was writing his own gospel. In other words, through memory quotation, necessarily imprecise, and more so as time goes on, the written gospel materials reentered the stream of oral tradition, not once, but many times. And Thomas represents a second written crystallization of some of these sayings. Second, the compiler wrote down various sayings he had heard in word-of-mouth tradition, whether attributed to Jesus or not, many of them plainly ascribed to Dame Wisdom, speaking as she does in Proverbs 9, and then ascribed them to Jesus. Third, he coined a number of sayings of his own and redacted or reshaped others.

Those who consider Thomas independent of Matthew and John tend also to make it early. Koester and Davies both place Thomas around 50 CE, earlier than any other surviving gospel. If I am correct, and Thomas does in fact owe a debt to Matthew and Luke, such an early date is impossible.

But there are other reasons for the suggestion of an early date of writing. First, the Christology of Thomas is pretty much *nontitular*. That is, it refrains from calling Jesus the Son of God, the Son of Man, the Christ, and so forth. For Davies and Patterson this implies that Thomas comes from the dawn age of Christianity when Christian devotion to the slain and resurrected Jesus had not yet articulated itself in the form of divine titles with which to crown Jesus. But I think the compiler and his coreligionists were reacting to such titles, repudiating them out of a Zenlike fear that such titles will serve to make believers substitute a dogma about Jesus for the Living One himself. See saying 43, "His disciples said to him, 'Who are you, that you say these things to us?' Jesus said to them, 'Do you not know who I am from what I say to you?'"

Similarly, some point to the (supposed) lack of futuristic eschatology (expectation of the soon-coming end of all things) as a sign of early date. But it may be that Thomas, where it does repudiate futurism (and that is not consistent), is not innocent of it but rather reactive against it. In this case, Thomas is relatively late because its readers and writers have seen the world so far outlast the apocalyptic deadlines set for it that such timetables can no longer be taken seriously. The Kingdom of God can no longer be realistically expected to come from without, so from now on it must be sought within. So we might date Thomas roughly contemporary with John—the mid-second century.

THE GOSPEL OF PETER

Toward the close of the second century (ca. 190–200), the congregation at Rhossus, about thirty miles from Antioch in Syria, was found to be using a gospel ascribed to Peter. Someone thought this untoward and complained to Bishop Serapion, who at first thought it no serious aberration. But a second complaint caused him to take a closer look. Suspecting Marcionite influence, he sought out local Docetists of some type (Gnostics?) with whom he was apparently on cordial terms, and he borrowed some of their writings, perhaps including commentaries on the Gospel of Peter itself. Doing his homework, he finally decided the text in question was heretical. He then wrote the congregation as follows:

> For our part, brothers, we welcome both Peter and the rest of the apostles as we would Christ himself, but, as seasoned men, we reject the writings that spuriously carry their names, knowing that we never accepted such writings. As for me, when I visited you, I assumed you all held fast to the true faith, so I saw no particular need to examine the gospel some circulate under the name of Peter. I said, "If this is all that is

troubling you, let it be read." Since that time, however, I have been told more: that its partisans' minds were sunk in some snake-hole of heresy. Now I shall make sure to pay you another visit, so, brothers, expect me soon. But we, brothers, mindful of what sort of heresy Marcion belonged to, . . . were enabled by students of this very gospel, that is, successors of those who first circulated it, those we call Docetists, for most of the ideas are their doctrines, [I say,] using [works we borrowed] by them, [we] were enabled to go through [the gospel] and discover that, while most of it was in fact quite compatible with the genuine teaching of the Savior, some things had been added.[10]

A fragment of the Gospel of Peter was discovered in 1884 in a tomb in Akhmim, Egypt, bound in a small book along with part of 1 Enoch in Greek as well as a fragment of the Apocalypse of Peter.

M. R. James dated the Gospel of Peter at about 150, and most even today follow him. This judgment depends upon too early a date for the traditional four gospels. Peter's date depends on theirs because it is obvious that Peter uses all four of the others, drawing upon each for various details. But John Dominic Crossan has given strong reasons for thinking that Peter uses a fifth gospel source, one older than Matthew, Mark, Luke, and John, which they seemed to have used also.[11] It would have been a Passion gospel pure and simple (unlike Peter, of which only the Passion section happens to remain), and Crossan calls it the Cross Gospel. He admits, however, that later editors have added to Peter other material taken from Matthew, Mark, Luke, and John.

THE GOSPEL OF MARY

This second-century Nag Hammadi gospel is a pretty standard Gnostic "revelation" to the reader as to the proper strategy needed in order to elude the watchful Archons who would bar the fleeing soul's heavenward ascent. The important thing about it is the ascription of it to Mary Magdalene. Not only is it credited to her, but she appears in an opening scene in which she must defend her apostolic authority for the teachings, from Jesus, she proposes to impart. We may be sure that this narrative sequence, which is lively and full of interest, reflects the position, and the uphill battle, of prophetesses in the Gnostic communities as elsewhere. At least she does finally prevail here, as women did generally in "heretical" groups like the Marcionites and Gnostics, taking refuge from the abuses of emerging orthodox authorities who sought to snuff out their ministry.

As to the actual content, about half of which is lost due to manuscript damage, there are two ways to understand the point of the guided tour of the heavenly spheres. First, we might just be reading someone's learned speculations, put forth for curiosity's sake. This is what we are reading in Jewish apocalypses like 1 Enoch, where Enoch is shown (with us looking over his shoulder) the regions of heaven where the snowflakes and the raindrops and the hail stones are stored, and so on. Second, and more likely, we are to memorize the details of the gauntlet that we will have to pass through after death so as to be ready with the right response at the right moment. This is the function of works like the Egyptian and Tibetan Books of the Dead (the Papyrus of Ani and the Bardo Thödöl, respectively). But the point of such books is pretty much that implied in the old joke where the lad asks mommy why grandpa is so feverishly studying the Bible, and she replies, "He's cramming for his finals!" The Tibetan Book of the Dead implicitly warns the reader he or she had best cultivate certain spiritual attitudes while there is still time. This is because the soul will have to withstand the vision of two groups of deities on the intermediate plane: the peaceful deities and the wrathful deities. The first will dazzle; the second will terrify. But the book calls upon the soul to recognize in both the mere figments of his own innermost self, then he will be able to get past them and on into liberation. These deities are obviously counterparts to the Gnostic Archons who seek to turn back the ascending soul. What is the difference between the peaceful and the wrathful deities? The first are viewed in the light of the soul's good karma; the second are distorted through the warped lens of bad karma. So it is really the individual's own works, good or bad, and his disposition that he must deal with as he seeks liberation. Karen L. King's *The Gospel of Mary of Magdala* is very helpful in enabling the reader to grasp the same dynamic in this gospel: The evangelist is really talking about an *inner* ascent of moral and spiritual progress. If the Gnostic must ascend through seven heavenly spheres, the Yogi must awaken the Kundalini (the spiritual force coiled within) and make it ascend up the spine through a set of seven chakras, "circles," or centers of psychic power. Ultimately the outer ascent of the one and the inner ascent of the other are two enabling metaphors for the same essential process.

THE GOSPEL ACCORDING TO THE HEBREWS

The Gospel according to the Hebrews occupies a special place on the margins of the traditional canon. Its associations in early Christianity were heretical, to be sure, explaining why it did not gain admittance to the canon. But not very heretical, for the book was the favorite of various Jewish-Christian sects who held the Torah and Jesus equally sacred and found no difficulty in combining the two. The emerging Catholic Church uneasily tolerated this position. It was certainly more to its liking than Marcionite Christianity, with its thorough repudiation of Judaism. And the scholars of the church held the Gospel according to the Hebrews at arm's length, but hold it they did. We find various major figures commenting on it, bringing it to bear on the interpretation of canonical passages where light might be shed. Even those who would not brook its presence in the official canon (and that was not everybody, even in Catholicism), still did not deem it a false gospel. Copies of it circulated on into the early Middle Ages, though it is, so far as we know, no longer extant.

From the several mentions of it and quotations from it in the early Church fathers, we know a good bit about the book. It was a shorter version of Matthew, and many (like Jerome) even considered it to be the Hebrew or Aramaic original of our Greek Gospel of Matthew. This it cannot have been, since the latter patently makes verbatim use of the Greek Mark. Still, there is some relation. Nicephorus tells us exactly how much shorter Hebrews was than canonical Matthew, about twenty-four hundred words. Several other ancient writers provide a handful of juicy passages they thought worthy of preservation and of comparison with canonical Matthew. Numerous others made comments on short notes, variant readings, very slight differences from canonical Greek Matthew. These quotations and notices have often been compiled for the modern reader.

THE GOSPEL ACCORDING TO THE NAZARENES

Also some kind of revision of Matthew, this gospel was written during the second century and used by Jewish-Christian Nazarenes around Beroea. One distinctive feature of this gospel is its note that the man whose hand is healed in Matthew 12:9–14 explains his plight to Jesus: "I was a mason, working with my hands to gain my bread. Please, Jesus, restore me to health, so I need not eat my bread in shame." We also read how, coincident with Jesus's death, not that the Temple's veil was torn but that its great lintel collapsed and shattered. In the Nazarene version of the Parable of the Talents (Matt. 25:14–30), we read that one servant (assimilated to Luke's Prodigal Son?) squandered the master's money on debauchery, while the second invested it, and the third buried it.

The most interesting surviving feature of the Gospel according to the Nazarenes is a scene set in the home of Mary in Nazareth: "Behold, the Lord's mother and brothers said to him, 'John the Baptist is baptizing for the remission of sins. Let's go and be baptized by him!' But he said, 'What have I done that I need his baptism—unless by saying this I speak in ignorance?'" There is a version of this in Thomas, saying 104, "They said, 'Come, let us pray today and let us fast.' Jesus said, 'Why? What sin have I committed? Or how have I been overcome? But after the bridegroom has left the bridal chamber, then let people fast and pray.'"

Also striking is a saying like that of the seventy-sevenfold forgiveness (Matt. 18:21–22), with the addition, "For even in the prophets, after being anointed with the Holy Spirit, somewhat of sin was found."

THE GOSPEL ACCORDING TO THE EBIONITES

This was another Jewish-Christian gospel, probably based on Matthew but taking care to add elements (in a stylistically cumbersome and redundant manner) from Luke and Mark as well. At least it appears so in the opening scene, which, as in Mark, is the baptism. The Ebionites rejected the Virgin Birth doctrine and with it the Matthean and Lukan nativities.

Ebionites were also vegetarians and therefore rejected animal sacrifice. And yet they espoused, against Paul, a staunch observance of the Torah! How could that be? They took seriously Jeremiah 7:22, "I never spoke to your ancestors or issued any commandment concerning burnt offerings and sacrifices in the days when I brought them out of Egypt!" Then where did the endless Levitical laws of sacrifice come from? "How can you boast, 'We are wise, for the Law of Yahweh is with us'? No, look: the lying pen of the copyists has turned it into a lie!" (Jer. 8:8). Ebionites understood this to mean that, though the Torah was divinely inspired of God, the text had been seriously tampered with, riddled with misleading interpolations. They held a variation on the Gnostic theme of Jesus as the divine Revealer. For the Ebionites this meant first and foremost that Jesus's task was to reveal which were the true biblical passages and which the corruptions. And sacrifice loomed large among the latter. Hence the Ebionite Jesus said: "I have come to abolish sacrifices, and if you do not leave off sacrificing, the wrath of God will not cease from you." John the Baptist, then, could not have eaten locusts, since even they are animal flesh of a sort, so the Ebionite gospel depicts him eating only wild honey. Jesus can scarcely have deigned to eat of the Passover lamb, so in this gospel he recoils from the very idea: "Do I desire at this Passover to eat flesh with you?"

Written in Greek, as incongruous as it may seem, the Gospel according to the Ebionites cannot be much later than the canonical gospels since Irenaeus (ca. 180) has heard of it.

THE GOSPEL ACCORDING TO THE EGYPTIANS (1)

Clement of Alexandria preserves just a few brief quotations from this Egyptian gospel, enough for us to tell it was composed by and used for Encratite Christians, people who equated sexual reproduction with original sin, perhaps because it trapped otherwise pure souls in bodies of sinful flesh, or possibly because the primal Adam-Eve division occasioned the further splintering of the human race into classes and groups who enslave, exploit, and oppress one another. These Christians believed one must repent and be baptized into identity with Christ the New Adam, the one who restored the primordial oneness of Eden before the Fall. Such people strove to live a life of gender equality by dissolving traditional social structures and family roles, and living heedless of government in their own anarchist conclaves, as they waited for the second advent of Christ. Women functioned as prophets in their movement (as we see also in the Acts of Paul, another Encratite document); accordingly, in the Gospel of the Egyptians, Salome appears as a close disciple and revealer of the esoteric revelation of Jesus. Salome was an extremely common name in the Holy Land, but it seems reasonable to identify this Salome with the woman disciple of Jesus mentioned in Mark 16:1. Since she also appears in Secret Mark, which also features themes of esotericism and initiation, Stephan Hermann Huller has suggested that what Clement calls the Gospel of the Egyptians is actually the same document as the Secret Gospel of Mark, another Egyptian work.[12]

THE GOSPEL ACCORDING TO THE EGYPTIANS (2)

Also titled the Holy Book of the Egyptians concerning the Great Invisible Spirit, this book has nothing in common with any known gospel form or with the material quoted by Clement as from a Gospel according to the Egyptians. Most likely the copyist had heard of the book Clement mentions but never saw it and jumped to the conclusion that he had been referring to this book with a similar title. This one, discovered at Nag Hammadi, outlines the salvation history of Sethian Gnosticism. Its divine savior is not Jesus Christ but Seth, messianic son of Adam. A scribe has arbitrarily inserted forms of the name Jesus twice, but the book is the product of Jewish Sethian Gnosticism, which may be related to Dositheanism, founded by Dositheus, a disciple of John the

Baptist. It is a good example of the kind of Gnostic theological discourse that Catholic Christianity eventually simplified for use in the doctrine of the Holy Trinity.

THE ORACLES OF OUR LORD

Somewhere around 150, Papias, bishop of Hieropolis in Asia Minor (close to the New Testament cities of Colosse and Laodicea), compiled a kind of scrapbook of reports he had gathered about Jesus and his teachings. Eusebius disdained the book, saying that it included "certain strange parables." One prediction of the abundance of nature in the coming millennium seems to have been lifted almost verbatim from the Second Apocalypse of Baruch and then misattributed to Jesus. The book disappeared long ago.

THE EPISTLE OF THE APOSTLES

Here is a second- or third-century collection of creedal formulas and paragraphs from theological treatises dressed up superficially as postresurrection teachings of Jesus. It appears to be an attempt to co-opt the Gnostic genre of revelation dialogues to reinforce Catholic doctrine, a case of trying to beat the enemy at his own game. Interestingly, this book considers Peter and Cephas to have been separate apostles, not two names for the same one. Also, it shows how easy and natural it seemed, even for centuries after Jesus, for the pious to place their own words in his mouth, truckloads of them!

THE PROTEVANGELIUM OF JAMES

The title of this book, which was also known as the Gospel or Book of James, reflects a theory that it was the source of the nativity stories of both Matthew and Luke, that both of those evangelists drew elements from this supposedly earlier, fuller version (a "protogospel"). That is hardly likely, however, since in that case Matthew's and Luke's nativity stories would look a great deal more alike. Instead, we have to conclude that this book, written, it seems, toward the end of the second century, draws on and harmonizes the divergent nativities of Matthew and Luke.

The spotlight is as much on Mary as it is on Jesus. We see here the beginnings of Roman Catholic and Eastern Orthodox anxiety about the sexuality of Mary the mother of Jesus. No one had thought of the Immaculate Conception of Mary yet, but the Protevangelium is much concerned to vindicate her perpetual virginity, and to that end it dramatizes the theory that Mary and Joseph had only a legal marriage so as to avoid having Jesus born illegitimate. It posits the clever solution that Joseph was an old widower with four sons and some daughters (Mark 6:3), while Mary was quite young. The two had a completely Platonic "spiritual" marriage as was common among second-century ascetical Christians.

We also owe to the Protevangelium the idea that the "stable" in which Jesus was born was a cave. Jerome believed he was staying in it, near Bethlehem, many years later.

THE INFANCY GOSPEL OF THOMAS

If nature abhors a vacuum, so does popular piety. Early Christians just could not abide not knowing what the Son of God must have been doing before he began his public ministry. If all one had was Mark's gospel, the answer would be: nothing special. Jesus's boyhood and young adulthood would have been presumably even less eventful than most since he was busy being righteous. (Granted, Mark has him appear at a baptism of repentance, but as everyone knows, it is only the righteous whose conscience impels them to such rituals.) For Mark, the "action" started only once Jesus was endued with power from on high, at the baptism. Matthew and Luke have begun to compromise this picture, since they have added a miraculous birth story and so made Jesus a demigod right from square one. Thus it comes as no surprise when Matthew has Jesus already know he is God's Son before he is baptized and when Luke portrays him at twelve years old as a child prodigy—no real child at all, but a godling in childlike form. Once this precedent was established, Christian curiosity was given the green light, and the pious imagination went wild concocting stories of what the divine boy Jesus might have done, would have done, and finally *did* do. Such stories are filled with contempt for the dull-witted adults around Jesus. The point is to glorify Jesus at their expense; they must, like Mark's disciples, be fools, or Jesus's preternatural wisdom cannot shine the brighter.

One may say that the spiritual level of the stories of the Infancy Gospel tradition is not very high. The young Jesus is ruthless, not to say capricious, in his application of divine power. He does not suffer fools. The gospel saying that best fits him is Mark 9:19, "O faithless generation! How long am I to be with you? How long must I endure you?" The stories are none of them elevated beyond the level of 2 Kings 2:23–24, where the prophet Elisha rids himself of the nuisance of mocking children by summoning she-bears to rip them to bloody tatters. More than anyone else, the young god Jesus must remind us of blue-skinned Krishna, a godling who plays jokes on his devotees, only Jesus has less of a sense of humor!

Though most of the individual episodes and anecdotes in Infancy Thomas do not require any particular setting (come to think of it, just like most stories and sayings in the familiar adult gospels!), on the whole the book has been constructed as a great patch to fill a perceived hole in Matthew: What happened while the Holy Family was sojourning in Egypt, then when they returned? We seem to be brought up more or less even with Luke 2:41 by the end of the book. The Infancy Gospel of Thomas is the earliest of its genre and goes back, at least in some basic form, to the late second to early third century.

THE ARABIC INFANCY GOSPEL

Actually titled The Book of Joseph Caiaphas, this gospel stems from somewhere in the fifth to sixth century, hence too late even for Teabing's stash of Sangreal documents. It combines much material from both the Infancy Gospel of Thomas and the Protevangelium of James, adding a section recounting *Arabian Nights*-style miracles worked by Mary during the Holy Family's sojourn in Egypt. One interesting distinction of the book is its explicit mention of Zoroaster: He is said to have predicted the birth of Jesus, and it is this oracle that led the Magi to come looking for him in Bethlehem! The book exists only in Arabic, but it was probably composed in Syriac.

THE INFANCY GOSPEL OF MATTHEW

A product of the eighth or ninth century, this one is derivative of both the Infancy Gospel of Thomas and the Protevangelium of James, apparently adding some material from the Arabic Infancy Gospel as well.

THE SECRET GOSPEL OF MARK

Morton Smith claimed that, while cataloging manuscripts at the monastery of Mar Saba in 1958, he ran across a fragmentary copy of a letter written by the great second-century theologian Clement of Alexandria. It purported to answer the questions of a certain Theodore relative to a hush-hush document, a secret edition of the Gospel of Mark, whose circulation was restricted to the advanced members of the church. It seemed there were various, even *more* secret, versions in circulation, and the Carpocratian Gnostics were citing a copy that implied Jesus was in the habit of initiating new converts into the Kingdom of God via homosexual rituals ("naked man with naked man"). Such scandalous elements Clement dismissed as fabrications, though he did consider authentic a passage that he quotes, providing a simpler Markan counterpart of the Johannine resurrection of Lazarus.

Many scholars accept Smith's claims at face value, but there has always been deep suspicion that Smith faked the whole thing. Specifically, it appears he may have cooked up the idea inspired by a then-recent mystery novel called *The Mystery of Mar Saba*, in which a hoaxer claimed to have discovered (at the Mar Saba monastery no less!) an ancient document in which Nicodemus confessed to absconding with the body of Jesus and helping Joseph of Arimathea to bury it elsewhere.

THE GOSPEL OF TRUTH

We knew of this gospel through the attempts of Irenaeus of Lyon to discredit it, but it was not until a copy finally turned up among the Nag Hammadi codices in 1945 that we had a chance to read it for ourselves. It is the work of Valentinus, the greatest of the second-century Gnostic theologians, he who claimed to be a disciple of Theodas, Paul's disciple. It is not a narrative about Jesus; the title comes from the fact that the phrase "The gospel of truth" leads off the book, and ancient books were often called by their initial words. The book is actually a meditation on the nature and implications of the Christian message as Valentinus understood it. It would then be analogous to the Epistle to the Hebrews. It is fascinating in that it omits reference to the elaborate theological features of Valentinian belief as we know them from later theological debates. Perhaps it was an early work of Valentinus, before he himself had elaborated its implications. Or maybe it was Valentinus's attempt at his own *Mere Christianity*.

THE GOSPEL OF PHILIP

This work is neither a connected treatise like the Gospel of Truth nor a narrative like the familiar gospels. Again, it is not a set of sayings like Thomas. It seems rather to be a collection of notes, perhaps sermon notes, compiled by a Valentinian Gnostic. The book reminds one of the aphoristic philosophy of Wittgenstein. Philip sets forth a surprisingly sophisticated theory of language and signification. Richard Arthur discerns certain Dosithean elements in the book. Most scholars date Philip in the second century, quite reasonably, given the clear Valentinianism of it. But Barbara Thiering has made the case for a first-century date, pre-70, based partly on the apparent hostility toward Gentiles the book displays, which would seem to fit best amid the Jewish-Gentile Christian struggles that are ubiquitous in Acts and the Pauline epistles.

THE GOSPEL OF BARNABAS

Muslims today consider this long text to be the original gospel as delivered to Jesus (which seems a bit unlikely since it takes a retrospective look at Jesus). It is a peculiar work, combining a synthesized gospel harmony with a great deal of other narrative and teaching material. In its present form, it dates from the late sixteenth century and is likely the work of an apostate monk, one Brother Marino, who had worked for the Holy Office of the Inquisition. Strangely, the book depicts Jesus as a prophet, but no messiah. That dignity it reserves for Muhammad when he should arrive. But then Barnabas cannot be the work of a Muslim, since Muslims believe Jesus, not Muhammad, was the messiah! Nor is it likely that a man who worked with the Holy Office would not have been aware of this. The Gospel of Barnabas also shows pronounced Jewish-Christian, Ebionite features, such as advocacy of Jewish dietary laws and opposition to Paul.

The best solution to the long-standing puzzle is that offered by Rod Blackhirst, namely, that this long medieval work was based on an earlier Ebionite text (or traditions) filtered through the syncretistic Carmelite hermit brotherhood, a very ancient group predating the arrival of Latin monasticism in the region.[13] Tracing their pedigree (whether or not fictively hardly matters) to Elijah and the Rechabites (Old Testament Jewish ascetics mentioned in Jeremiah 35), the Carmelites had a mixture of Jewish, Christian, and Muslim beliefs, and if there is anyone liable to reshape Jesus as an Elijah-like forerunner for someone else, it would be them.

THE WISDOM OF JESUS CHRIST

The most interesting thing about this second- to third-century Gnostic revelation text (discovered at Nag Hammadi) is the valuable insight into the artificiality of the whole post-Resurrection dialogue genre. No reader can seriously entertain the notion that any of these dialogues actually preserves quoted material, whether from a waking encounter with the Risen Jesus or from a dream vision. Every one of them is flagrantly a case of the author simply putting his or her own ideas into the mouth of Jesus in order to pull rank by using his name. Of course, we witness the same phenomenon in the New Testament gospels (which is why, for instance, several different opinions as to the validity of fasting are ascribed to him). As it happens, we are able to corroborate such literary judgments very definitely in the case of the Wisdom of Jesus Christ because we also find among the Nag Hammadi texts the original source of this one, namely, Eugnostos the Blessed, a theological treatise that matches this one almost word for word. A redactor has simply snipped up Eugnostos the Blessed into answers by Jesus to artificial questions by the disciples, which the editor himself has supplied.

THE DIALOGUE OF THE SAVIOR

Many scholars today believe that this Nag Hammadi Gnostic revelation dialogue incorporates several distinct sources, though that is hardly obvious from a surface reading. One of the supposed sources is held to be a Thomas-like or Q-like set of sayings of Jesus, which have been placed, almost totally absorbed, one might say, in the present context. It seems just as likely, however, that the book is the work of a Gnostic writer who remembers certain sayings from hearing the gospels (Matthew, Luke, John, and especially Thomas, possibly the Gospel according to the Egyptians) read in Gnostic meetings and peppers his own creation with them to give it an air of authenticity. The result is quite intriguing in any case, containing both a semi-philosophical creation myth and a revelation of the challenges facing the ascending soul of the Gnostic.

PISTIS SOPHIA

This, the granddaddy of Gnostic revelation dialogues, incorporates two similar third-century sources depicting interviews of Jesus after the resurrection by his disciples. Both are taken up with wearying details of what the ascending Gnostic may expect on his postmortem heavenward journey. The title refers to a female divinity, one of the emanations from the Supreme God. She is "Faith-Wisdom," often called simply "Sophia" in other Gnostic texts. Jesus here tells the story of her fall and redemption. Though the book is of the greatest value for our understanding of Gnosticism (it was about the only document we possessed that was actually written by Gnostics before the Nag Hammadi discovery), it is very tough going, making the Book of Leviticus look like a page-turner. One need not be a defender of the orthodox faith to ask oneself whether the exclusion of this bit of "chloroform in print" was a shame.

THE BOOKS OF JEU

These two second- or third-century texts are much like the Pistis Sophia in that in them Jesus explains the Gnostic doctrines of fall and creation, as well as the specific information needful to attain final salvation in the teeth of the opposition of the Archons (evil angels). Again, the resemblance to the Tibetan Book of the Dead is pronounced in that here we have all manner of specifics, names, formulae, baptisms, and so forth, with which the spiritual champion must equip himself. It is preparation for the ordeal the soul will face upon dying.

Like Pistis Sophia, these texts were known before Nag Hammadi, and like Pistis Sophia, they are mighty slow going. Unusual for such books, the Books of Jeu contain diagrams! Copying these books cannot have been easy. Finally, the name "Jeu" has nothing to do with either Jesus or the Israelite King Jehu, still less with Jews. It refers to the ultimate Godhead and is presumably another form of the divine name "Iao," though this is usually assigned to the Demiurge.

TOLEDOTH JESCHU

The Toledoth Jeschu, or Generations of Jesus, is a Jewish antigospel, extant in several variant versions, portraying Jesus as a false prophet and magician. The usual account of the Toledoth Jeschu is that it is a nasty parody of the Christian gospels, a safe way for Jews to vent their resentment for their hideous treatment at the hands of Christians. The texts are often considered to be late, medieval compositions, and thus historically worthless. But the wide distribution of various language versions and manuscript fragments, together with the numerous parallels with second-century Jewish-Christian polemic preserved in Tertullian, Celsus, and elsewhere, imply, as Samuel Krauss and Hugh J. Schonfield demonstrate, a date for the original version of about the fourth century, the 300s CE, with numerous of the traditions underlying it going back even further.[14] Schonfield takes another step and suggests that the Toledoth Jeschu was based on a prior Hebrew gospel circulated among Jewish Christians. The reason for this is that the text treats Jesus with much more respect than one would expect if the Toledoth were merely a burlesque on a false prophet. It has certainly been worked over by a redactor hostile to Christianity; Jesus is regularly called "that bastard," in a taunt against the virgin birth doctrine, but one would expect much, much worse, the sort of thing we do in fact encounter in later Talmudic references to Jesus the false prophet. Again, the huge number of Christian "testimonia" (proof texts from the Old Testament) marshaled to prove Jesus was the Messiah would be exceedingly strange in a work that started out as a lampoon of Christian messianism, all the more since none of these proof texts is ever refuted!

One of the chief points of interest in this work is its chronology: It places Jesus's activity at about 100 BCE. This is no mere blunder (though it is not hard to find gross anachronisms elsewhere in the text). Epiphanius and the Talmud also attest to Jewish and Jewish-Christian belief that Jesus had lived a century or so before we usually place him.

SUFI SAYINGS OF JESUS

Some ancient writers found it difficult to distinguish between early Christian preachers and their Cynic counterparts. Cynicism was a post-Socratic philosophy begun in the late fourth century by Antisthenes of Athens, a direct disciple of Socrates, who taught in the Cynosarges building in Athens, and by Diogenes of Sinope, a wandering sage who adopted the roaming dog (κυνος) for his ideal. The name "Cynics" may have come from either root. Cynics taught that one ought to live in accord with nature by reason, rejecting with scorn and humor all social conventions and material possessions. Diogenes went about naked or "clothed" in a barrel or a tub. Cynics generally adopted the distinctive garb of a tunic or loincloth, a cloak, a shoulder pouch, and a staff, nothing else, especially not money. They were mendicant beggars and claimed to have been sent by God (Zeus) to witness to mankind that we may live as unencumbered and carefree as the lilies of the field and the birds of the air, that we have as little need for possessions, jobs, marriages, or government, as animals do. They loved their enemies and refused to retaliate when beaten. They flouted common decency with relish.

It is hard to miss seeing the similarity between Cynic teaching and many of the sayings attributed to Jesus in which he orders disciples to renounce job, possessions, family, and worldly cares, instead leaving all things in the hands of a caring Providence, imitating the creatures of the wild. Indeed, there is no other religious or philosophical movement in antiquity that provides such close parallels with the most characteristic and radical sayings of Jesus. It seems most likely that the Mission Charge of the Synoptics (Mark 6:8–11; Matt. 10:5–23; Luke 9:3–6, 10:2–12) frets over whether Christian missionaries may take with them a staff, a cloak, a shoulder bag, and so on, mainly in order to differentiate them from similar-appearing Cynic apostles.

Was the historical Jesus a Cynic? It is by no means impossible, as Gerald Downing, Burton L. Mack, John Dominic Crossan, David Seeley, and others have argued. Cynics had long been active in areas adjacent to Palestine, and it was a cosmopolitan age when Hellenistic culture penetrated Jewish Palestine. But as the case of Proteus Peregrinus (see Lucian of

Samosata's satire *The Passing of Peregrinus*) shows, Cynics were attracted to Christianity and even wrote what came to be Christian literature. Thus the sayings attributed to Jesus that sound like Cynicism may have been originally unattributed Cynic maxims brought into the Christian movement by Cynic converts and subsequently attributed to Jesus.

At any rate, it is striking that the Sufi mystics of medieval Islam venerated Jesus in much the same terms as the Cynic hypothesis casts him: an ascetical hermit who wandered homelessly though accompanied by disciples. These sayings may have been coined by Sufis and attributed to Jesus, who after all has high standing in all forms of Islam. But it is also likely that some or even many of these sayings came to the Sufis from their Syriac monkish forbears, and then the possibility presents itself that this sayings tradition may come from still earlier in the Christian movement. In large measure, they present a pre-Christian, pre-Christological vision of Jesus as a Cynic-like ascetic, just as Mack, Downing, and the others understand him. Thus it may be, not that the Christology has been trimmed from them, but rather that it has not yet been added! Though the largest share of these sayings appear in al-Ghazali's *Revival of the Religious Sciences*, a twelfth-century Sufi work, there are indications that the Sufi author may have derived them all from a sayings source with earlier Christian roots.

THE GOSPEL OF NICODEMUS

Early defenders of the Christian faith, especially Tertullian and Justin Martyr, challenged readers skeptical of their claims about Jesus to go and corroborate them by checking the "Acts of Pilate," the official report of the case, which these authors simply assumed must be somewhere on file in Rome. During the reign of Maximin, a document purporting to be the relevant file did surface, but it was a piece of anti-Christian propaganda. It appeared between 311 and 312. Christians expunged it when they got the opportunity. This lost text may have been a hostile smear against Christian claims, or conceivably it may have been the real thing. We cannot know. At any rate, in the fifth or sixth century, a new work called the Acts of Pilate appeared. It was also known as the Gospel of Nicodemus, which tips one off immediately as to its sympathies. In it Pilate interrogates a series of witnesses for Jesus, including people he has healed. Eventually he hears the reports of Roman soldiers and others who have seen the Risen Jesus himself. There is even a report of the Harrowing of Hell, a major medieval theme, first expounded here: After his crucifixion and before his Sunday morning return, Jesus went, in spirit, to Hell and trashed the place, sending its wardens, Beelzebub and Satan, scurrying before his fury. He rescued the elect (Adam, David, Isaiah, et al.), who were only now permitted to go to heaven, since only now had redemption been won on the cross. Then Jesus departed, "leading captivity captive," and leaving their Satanic majesties holding the bag.

THE APOCALYPSE OF PETER

The Nag Hammadi library contained an Apocalypse of Peter quite different from the one we already had, which was a typ-

ical tourist guide to the afterlife. In the Nag Hammadi Apocalypse of Peter, Peter is with Jesus in the Jerusalem Temple when
the savior vouchsafes his chief disciple a series of visions. In
them Peter beholds various enemies, both members of the
Jewish establishment in Jesus's own day and future Christian
rivals, including both the Catholic/orthodox institutional
church and competing Gnostic sects. He also sees an advance
view of the crucifixion, which he is told is a docetic sham even
though the blind (both conventional Christians and their enemies) believe the real Christ was crucified. The book seems to
come from the third century, based on the hinted state of
ecclesiastical conflict it tries to depict.

THE PREACHING OF JOHN

This intriguing document comes to us as part of a larger work
(itself somewhat fragmentary) called the Acts of John. This
portion provides the apostle's ostensible recollections of Jesus.
It seems likely that the Jesus material originally formed a separate work, the Preaching of John. As such it is implicitly a
kind of rival or counterpart to the Gospel of John. The
Preaching of John attempts to set forth a consistently docetic
version of the story of Jesus.

The Preaching of John was no abstract treatise written by a
speculative theologian off in an ivory tower somewhere.
Rather, it was a scripture that guided the life of a pious sect. We
can be sure of this because of the inclusion in the text of the
liturgy for the Round Dance of the Savior, a celebration analogous to the Eucharist and the ritual washing of the feet. It

would no doubt be most impressive to see the rite performed today. What sort of a community stands behind this text? Were they full-fledged Gnostics? The hallmark of Gnosticism was an elite grasp of saving truths not to be shared with the rank and file. Not only does the Preaching of John have something of a Gnostic (not just a docetic) tinge, but also John says he was laughing to scorn the poor chumps who imagined they were crucifying the real Christ. That rings of the contemptuous Gnostic elitism bemoaned in 1 John 2:9–11 ("Anyone who claims he is in the light and hates his brother is in the darkness still," etc.). Also, the lyrics to the Round Dance of the Savior pictures the angels and Powers of the Ogdoad, the Eighth Heaven, participating invisibly in the rite, implying a Gnostic world picture.

As to authorship: ancient writers grouped together five works—the Acts of John, Acts of Paul, Acts of Peter, Acts of Thomas, and Acts of Andrew—as all being the works of a Gnostic teacher Leucius (another form of the common name Luke). While they do all share certain important features, they were certainly not the products of a single author. The strategy behind this disingenuous claim was to make it appear that these writings represented the wild imaginings of a single mischievous author rather than being repositories of widespread early Christian belief. We thus have no idea who really wrote any of them. But it is well worth noting that at least here in the Preaching of John we have a sample, albeit fictive, of what "memoirs of the apostles" (as Justin Martyr called the gospels) would have looked like. Though we read in Eusebius that Mark represents the recollections of Peter and Luke of Paul, these texts do not at all read like apostolic table talk. By contrast, the

203

Preaching of John does sound, formally at least, like an eye-witness's reminiscences. The Preaching of John is not actually apostolic table talk, but the Gospel of Mark is not even trying to sound like it.

THE APOCRYPHON OF JAMES

Presenting itself (fictively) as a secret writing, not to be shared around by the recipient, this writing takes the superficial form of a letter from one of the two or three apostles named James.

The premise is that, while the apostles were busy all together in one place, writing down what Jesus had privately revealed to each one of them, the writer James, along with Peter, experienced a private return of Jesus from heaven. He tells them he is about to ascend again and challenges them to join him, even to get there in advance of him, if they wish! There is much exhortation, some of it surprisingly orthodox for what otherwise appears a solidly Gnostic text: "Truly I say to you, no one shall be saved unless they believe in my cross. But those who have believed in my cross, theirs is the Kingdom of God."

The most important thing about the Apocryphon (or Secret Book) of James may be the valuable clue it gives as to how books like this came to be written. It was not, of course, the original apostles who wrote them but rather mystical sectarians and monks who gathered to meditate, hoping to induce visions of the heavens and of Jesus, hoping he might reveal the soul's secrets to them. Then, each would write down what came to him, and they were circulated under the name of Jesus and/or apostles.

THE GOSPEL OF THE SAVIOR

This gospel must be reconstructed from a pile of fragments. It stands astride the divide between Gnosticism and emerging Orthodoxy (much like the Apocryphon of James) in that, while it seems to presuppose the Gnostic world picture, it places great emphasis on Jesus's impending crucifixion. The book depends heavily on both Matthew and John, though it also seems to be in touch with continuing oral tradition. It may come from the late second, early third century.

OXYRHYNCHUS PAPYRUS 840

The following fragment of a gospel had been inserted into a locket to serve as an amulet worn around the neck. It was discovered in the tombs of Oxyrhynchus, Egypt, in 1905. It contains the end of one episode and the entirety of another. From this we can tell this must have been a gospel very close in style and form to the New Testament gospels. Free of heavy-handed Gnostic fustian, this gospel is really a shame to have lost. Here is the primary episode:

> And he took them with him into the very place of purification and strolled about the Temple court. And a chief priest named Levi, a Pharisee, joined them and said to the Savior, "Who gave you permission to march into this place of purification and to view these sacred utensils without having ritually bathed yourself, or even having your disciples so much as wash their feet? As it is, you have entered the Temple court, this place of purity, in a state of defilement, although

[the rule is that] no one may enter and view the sacred utensils without first bathing and changing his clothes."

At once, the Savior stood still with his disciples and answered: "How is it then with you? I see you, too, are present in the Temple court. Does that mean you are clean?"

He answered him, "Indeed I am, for I have bathed myself in the pool of David, having descended by one stair and ascended by the other, and I have donned white and clean clothes, and only then did I presume to come here and view these sacred utensils."

Then the Savior said to him, "Woe to you, blind man without sight! You have bathed yourself in waste water in which dogs and pigs lie all night and day. You have scrubbed your skin raw, just as prostitutes and dancing girls perfume, bathe, chafe, and rouge theirs in order to awaken the lust of men. Within, they are full of scorpions and every variety of wickedness. On the other hand, my disciples and I, whom you charge with failing to immerse ourselves, have in fact been baptized in the living water that comes down from heaven. But woe to those. . . ."

This one would be worth about a million Pistis Sophias!

NOTES

1. Dan Brown, *The Da Vinci Code* (New York: Doubleday, 2003), p. 234.

2. By Barbara Thiering's esoteric decoding of the Dead Sea Scrolls, they do refer to a purely human Jesus, but her whole point is that this is anything but apparent on a casual surface reading, and Brown gives no hint of having anything like her approach in mind.

3. Brown, *Da Vinci Code*, p. 256.

4. Ibid.

5. Ibid., p. 231.

6. Ibid., p. 256.

7. Robert J. Miller, ed., *The Complete Gospels: Annotated Scholars Version* (Sonoma, CA: Polebridge Press, 1992).

8. Brown, *Da Vinci Code*, p. 256.

9. Stevan L. Davies, *The Gospel of Thomas and Christian Wisdom* (New York: Seabury, 1983).

10. Eusebius, *Ecclesiastical History* 6:12:2–6.

11. John Dominic Crossan, *The Cross That Spoke: The Origins of the Passion Narrative* (San Francisco: Harper & Row, 1988).

12. Stephan Hermann Huller, "Against Polykarp," unpublished MS.

13. Rod Blackhirst, "Barnabas and the Gospels: Was There an Early *Gospel of Barnabas*?" *Journal of Higher Criticism* 7, no. 1 (Spring 2000): 1–22.

14. Samuel Krauss, *Das Leben Jesu nach jüdischen Quellen* (Berlin: S. Calvary, 1902); Hugh J. Schonfield, *According to the Hebrews* (London: Duckworth, 1937).

Chapter 8
MARY MAGDALENE
Female Apostle?

Mary Magdalene looms very large in *The Da Vinci Code* as in many of the pseudoscholarly works Dan Brown's novel draws upon. And one suspects this accounts for quite a bit of the popular interest in the book, since Mary has also become a symbol for Christian feminism, and the novel encourages such a stance. One of the virtues of the novel is that, despite its misinformation on several points, it has given much wider exposure than ever before to the wealth of early Christian texts in which the Magdalene plays a surprisingly prominent role. And yet the average reader of Brown and his predecessors is likely in no position to sort the factual wheat from the spurious tares in Brown's field without some assistance.

FRAGMENTS OF THE MAGDALENE

Mary Magdalene is a tantalizingly enigmatic figure in all four canonical gospels. Mary Magdalene, we discover, was one of a number of wealthy female disciples of Jesus, who traveled with his entourage and paid for their food and accommodations (Mark 15:40–41; Luke 8:1–3). Though this kind of arrangement would be common enough in Hellenistic Mystery Religions, where the devotion of wealthy women to their gurus was notorious (see Juvenal's *Sixth Satire* and Plutarch's *Advice to the Bride and Groom*), the situation is really unparalleled as far as we know in Judaism. Mary Magdalene seems even to have been the leader of this group of women since she has the top spot when any of their names are listed, and hers is the only name appearing in all these lists (Mark 15:40–41, 47, 16:1; Matt. 27:55–56, 61, 28:1; Luke 8:2–3, 24:10). What does it mean that the group of women even *had* a leader? (Perhaps her later status as the leader of a Christian sect or movement has been read back into the time of Jesus.) Mary also is said to have been a recovered demoniac, healed by Jesus. There is something decidedly odd about this, too, as she is not merely said to have been demon possessed, a genuine affliction even if modern psychology has different ways of accounting for it. No, we read that *seven* demons had gone out of her, and this detail marks the whole thing as legendary. Short of *Ghostbusters* technology, how would you know how many there were? It's not like cavities at the dentist.

And as if that rap sheet were not enough to overcome, Christian legend casts the Magdalene as a reformed prostitute as well. Despite this, Christian speculation all the way up into nineteenth-century Mormonism and *Jesus Christ Superstar* has made her Jesus's (at least would-be) lover. (Interestingly, if Jesus had married an ex-harlot, this would make him another like Hosea—whose wife, Gomer, however, was still turning tricks for a little extra cookie-jar money—and Joshua, who rabbinic lore said married Rahab, the Belle Watlin of the Old Testament.)

In the rest of the New Testament and in orthodox Christianity of the next few centuries, Mary Magdalene has been tacitly relegated to president of Jesus's "ladies' auxiliary," though some gospel accounts make her the first witness of the risen Christ. Yet all these are only intriguing scraps. One receives the impression that these details are the lingering after-echoes of some great explosion.

We gain a very different impression when we turn to Gnostic Christian documents excluded from the canon. There Mary Magdalene appears as a, or even *the*, prime revealer of the secrets of Jesus. She is his closest disciple and the greatest of the apostles! How did two such clashing portraits of this woman arise and coexist? Does either represent the historical Magdalene?

THE GNOSTIC TEXTS

First, let us review the relevant Gnostic texts and see what we can make of them. Perhaps the most famous text is the concluding saying (114) of the Gospel of Thomas (first or second century CE).[1] "Simon Peter said to them, 'Tell Mary to leave us, for women are not worthy of (eternal) life.' Jesus said, 'But I shall teach her how to become male, so that she too may become a living spirit like you fellows. In fact, every woman willing to make herself male will enter the Kingdom of Heaven.'"

Some see in this text a terrible antiwomen slam, dealing

Mary Magdalene a backhanded compliment. Be that as it may (and I will return to the point presently), it is certainly remarkable that Mary as an individual is elevated to occupy at least the same level as the male disciples. Even if the text is not much help to Christian feminism, it certainly exalts Mary Magdalene, and that is the point here.

In the Gospel of Mary (second century CE), Mary Magdalene is the chief revealer to the other disciples, relating a resurrection vision in which Jesus explained the course of the liberated spirit on its way back to God. She encourages the male disciples to take up the missionary task Jesus has assigned them: "Then Mary stood up, greeted them all, and said to her brethren, 'Do not weep and do not grieve or lose your resolve! His grace will empower you and protect you. Instead let us praise his greatness, for he has prepared us and made us into men'" (9:13–21).

Then she imparts her revelation. When she is done, Peter and Andrew scoff at Mary's gibberish. Peter says:

> "Did he really speak privately with a woman and not openly to us? Are we supposed to turn about and listen to her? Did he prefer her to us?" Then Mary wept and said to Peter, "My brother Peter, what do you think? Are you saying I thought this up myself in my imagination, or that I am lying about the Savior?" Levi intervened and said to Peter, "Peter, you have always been hot-tempered. Now I see you contending against the woman as if she were one of our adversaries. But if the Savior made her worthy, who are you indeed to reject her? Surely the Savior knows her very well. That is why he loved her more than us. Rather let us be ashamed and put on perfect humanity." (17:16–18:16)

(Note the parallels to the Thomas saying: Jesus has made her "worthy" and made them all "men.")

The Dialogue of the Savior (second or third century CE) also knows Mary Magdalene as a preeminent revealer; she draws forth revelations by her astute questioning of the risen Christ. "She spoke this way because she was a woman who knew all things" (139:11–12). "Mary said, 'Tell me, Lord, what purpose has led me this far: to benefit or to suffer loss?' The Lord said, '[You are here] because you reveal the greatness of the Revealer'" (140:15–18). Similarly, the earlier of the two documents composing the Pistis Sophia (200–250 CE) depicts a kind of "press conference" with the Risen Christ among the disciples. Again, Mary is prominent. "Peter said: 'My Lord, that's enough questions from the women! We can't get a word in edgewise!' Jesus said to Mary and the women: 'Give your male brethren a chance to ask a question'" (vi:146). The later, lengthier section, the main documentary basis for the Pistis Sophia (250–300 CE), places even greater emphasis on the primacy of Mary: She asks fully thirty-nine of the forty-six questions addressed to the living Jesus.

> What happened when Mary had heard the Savior say these words ["Whoever has ears to hear, let him hear"] was that she gazed intently into the air for a whole hour. She said: "My Lord, give me the word, and I will speak freely." And Jesus, full of compassion, answered, saying to Mary, "Mary, blessed are you, because I will fully instruct you in all the highest mysteries of heaven! Speak freely, you whose heart is raised to the Kingdom of Heaven to a greater degree than all your brothers." (i:17)

Peter loses his temper: "And Peter interposed and said to Jesus, 'My Lord, we will put up with no more from this woman, for she monopolizes the opportunity to speak. None of us gets the chance, because she lectures incessantly!' (i:36) [But then:] Mary came forward and said: 'My Lord, it is because my mind overflows with insights and always moves me to speak up and supply the solution! . . . I am afraid of Peter, because he threatened me and hates our whole sex!'" (ii:72)

The Gospel of Philip (250–300 CE?) speaks of Mary as analogous to the heavenly Wisdom, mother of the angels.

> And the companion of the [Savior is] Mary Magdalene. [But Christ loved] her more than [all] the disciples [and used to] kiss her [often] on her [mouth]. The rest of [the disciples were offended] by it [and expressed disapproval]. They said to him, "Why do you love her more than all of us?" The Savior answered and said to them, "Why do I not love you like her? When a blind man and one who sees are both together in darkness, there is no difference between them. When the light comes, then he who has sight will see the light, and he who is blind will remain in darkness." (63:34–64:9)

The Philip passage steps lightly. "Kissing" was often used as a euphemism for sexual intercourse, and this same gospel elsewhere says that "it is by a kiss that the perfect conceive and give birth" (59:2–3).[2] Later, we are assured that the implied sexual intercourse is purely spiritual and metaphorical in nature (76:6–9; 82:1–10).

Finally, one more depiction of Mary Magdalene as the special recipient of post-Easter revelations occurs in the Greater Questions of Mary, yet another Gnostic dialogue. The text, like that of a shorter but similar dialogue, the Lesser Questions of Mary, is not extant, but orthodox heresiologist Epiphanius preserved a particularly juicy tidbit: "They aver that he gave her a revelation: after taking her aside to the mountain and praying, he brought forth from his side a woman and began to unite with her, and then, believe it or not, holding his semen in his hand, he showed that 'This is what we must do to be saved.' Then, when Mary fell to the ground in shock, he raised her up again and said to her: 'Why did you doubt, O you of little faith?'" (*Panarion* 26.8.2–3).[3]

Notice the recapitulation of the Edenic splitting of Eve from the side of Adam, as well as the intercourse between them. Here is a charter either for Gnostic libertinism or for the sacrament of the Bridal Chamber, where the soul unites with Christ. This latter was some sort of mysterious initiation rite administered by Syrian, Jewish, and Gnostic Christians. No one knows exactly what it was.[4]

MAKING MARY MALE?

Elisabeth Schüssler Fiorenza shows how virtually the same "becoming male" terminology familiar from Gnostic texts occurs in the writings of the first-century Alexandrian Jewish philosopher Philo.[5] There it is more fully explained and in such a way that it makes sense of the Gnostic use of the terminology we find in Thomas 114. For instance for Philo, spiritual development by ascetical effort is "becoming male" because Philo denominates the rational soul as "male," the irrational soul (i.e., emotions, appetites) "female." A person who integrates these elements and thus finds God's grace to grow spiritually has "become one." See the Gospel of Thomas: "They shall become a single one" (saying 4). As for "becoming male," what it might mean for an early Christian woman apostle is clear from the Acts of Paul, where Thecla shaves her hair and "tailored her mantle into a cloak in the male style." Paul then charges her, "Go, and teach the word of God" (11:25, 40, 41). She is to preach the gospel of celibacy: "Blessed are the continent, for only to them shall God speak" (11:5). Here is a woman who becomes an apostolic preacher by renouncing sexuality and becoming as a man in appearance![6]

FOREBEAR OR FIGUREHEAD?

Most scholars who discuss these texts have focused on whether they are part of a pro-women argument aimed by Gnostics at the orthodox bishops. Mary Magdalene, some suggest, was appropriated as the mouthpiece for pro-women Gnostic views because she was known by all as a prominent female gospel character, not one of the Twelve, characters who had already been claimed by the orthodox. She is female and a "leftover" character. This is Elaine Pagels's view: The "secret texts use the figure of Mary Magdalene to suggest that women's activity challenged the leaders of the orthodox community, who regarded Peter as their spokesman."[7] Pheme Perkins rejects this theory as arbitrary, though she also seems to assume that the texts tell us nothing of the historical Mary. Perkins agrees

Mary has become a purely literary mouthpiece, but she thinks the women's issue was not particularly in view: "We are skeptical of those who use this picture of Mary to claim that Gnostics upheld community leadership by women in opposition to the male dominated hierarchy of the orthodox Church. . . . Mary is the hero here not because of an extraordinary role played by women in Gnostic communities, but because she is a figure closely associated with Jesus to whom esoteric wisdom may be attached."[8]

Elisabeth Schüssler Fiorenza sides with Pagels: "The debate between various Christian groups on primacy in apostolic authority is reflected in various apocryphal texts which relate the competition between Peter and Mary Magdalene. . . . Those who claim the authority of Andrew and Peter . . . argue against the teaching authority of women," while their opponents "appealed to the women disciples as scriptural precedents and apostolic figures."[9] Karen L. King sums up the dilemma well. What she says about the Gospel of Mary applies equally well to all these texts: "Does the final scene in the *Gospel of Mary* reflect actual conflict between the historical figures of Peter and Mary? . . . Or were Peter and Mary . . . only narrative representatives for opposing Christian groups or differing theological positions?"[10]

The common assumption is that Gnostic writers merely "used" Mary as a symbolic figure, a "precedent," much as modern Christian feminists do when they argue that Mary Magdalene was *in a manner of speaking* an "apostle" since "apostle" means "sent one," and she was "sent" to proclaim the news of the resurrection to the Twelve.[11] Those who argue that way seem to mean that *solely on the strength of her activity on Easter morning* she can now serve as a kind of literary precedent for women in ministry. But, however one answers the question of a pro-women polemic underlying the Mary Magdalene texts, might one not also argue that Mary Magdalene did, in fact, carry on an apostolic ministry in circles receptive to her, circles that eventually contributed to the great Gnostic movement of the early Christian centuries? King thinks so: "The strength of this literary tradition, attested as it is in multiple independent witnesses, makes it possible to suggest that historically Mary may have been a prophetic visionary and leader within some sector of the early Christian movement after the death of Jesus. This much may be said of Mary of Magdala with a high degree of historical probability."[12]

MAGDALENE MOUTHPIECE

But I think the evidence points in a different direction. I agree with Pheme Perkins: Mary Magdalene is merely a literary mouthpiece in these texts. We might compare Mary Magdalene, Gnostic apostle, to Joseph of Arimathea, pressed into service (albeit centuries later, though that is beside the point) as the apostle of an indigenous Celtic Christianity ostensibly planted by this New Testament figure centuries before Roman Catholic missionaries set foot on the British Isles bearing their popish evangel. According to certain of the grail legends (see chapter 2, "The Holy Grail"), Joseph had received the cup of the Last Supper from the Risen Jesus. Joseph then took the grail to Gaul, where he established the second table of the grail (the first, of course, having been that of the Last Supper). Later still, he took it to Glastonbury, England. Eventually King Arthur would build the famous Round Table as the third table for the grail. Is there any historical basis to this story? Not a chance, but that did not stop the tale from providing after-the-fact justification for Celtic, non-Catholic Christianity, as it still functions for some sectarians today. Why was Joseph of Arimathea chosen for the honor? Simply because, like Mary Magdalene, he was a gospel character close to Jesus, but not one of the Twelve, who had been irrevocably claimed on behalf of the Catholic Church. It seems to me that Mary Magdalene is another like Joseph of Arimathea. Her apostleship is a later propaganda argument on behalf of one side in a theological dispute between Catholic and other types of Christianity. Furthermore, the very parameters of the debate, which assume that the Twelve are synonymous with apostolic authority, marks the role of Mary in the Gnostic texts as secondary, historically inauthentic. For in the lifetime of the historical Magdalene, such a monolithic authority structure, such a "Catholic" conception of the Twelve, could not yet have existed.

THE NEW TESTAMENT EASTER STORIES

Can we follow the trajectory we have plotted through the Gnostic texts further back into the canonical gospels? This is important because, depending on what we find there, we might discover a first-century basis for Mary Magdalene as a historical apostolic figure.

The trail would seem to lead directly to John 20:1, 11–18, a story in which Mary Magdalene is the first to see the Risen

Christ at the empty tomb or anyplace else.[13] Christ tells her little by way of revelation, whether Catholic or Gnostic, but the striking thing is that he tells her to let the male disciples know he is ascending to his Father. In other words, by the time they receive the report, he will have departed! He tells Mary, in short, to tell them good-bye! This certainly implies Mary is the only one to have seen the Risen Lord. The other apostles are excluded as recipients of Easter appearances just as surely as Acts excludes Paul from true apostleship on the same basis. Can this story originally have been an independent one, placed in the context of John 20 in order to obviate the surprising implications of Mary having been, according to the underlying tradition, the *sole* witness to the risen Jesus?

Raymond E. Brown suggests that it was John 20:1–18, the appearance to Mary *in its canonical form*, as the first in John's series of resurrection episodes, that inspired the use of Mary as a revealer in the later Gnostic texts.[14] This is once again to make the link with Mary Magdalene a purely *literary* one. To make the case that Mary Magdalene's apostolic importance to Gnostic groups in the next couple of centuries stemmed from an actual apostolic claim on her part, one would need to make the John 20:1, 11–18, episode historical in nature. One would need to say something like this must have happened to form the basis for any actual claim Mary may have made to apostolic status. And this claim would have continued to be reflected in the later Gnostic texts not because of literary borrowing but because of historical memory. Is this likely?

The very preservation of the original unit John 20:1, 11–18, might be said to presuppose a context in which a group of early Christians cherished and passed down the story of Mary's *unique* Easter revelation, thus a circle of Christians for whom Mary was the chief apostle. How else could the original, independent episode have survived long enough for the fourth evangelist to co-opt it? This would be a powerful argument in favor of the hypothesis that Mary Magdalene was an apostle. But is it a viable understanding of the passage? I used to think so and said so in an article some fifteen years ago. Now I am not so sure. I fear that a brief survey of the Easter traditions of the gospels is in order if we are to be in a proper position to evaluate these claims.

WARP AND WOOF

It is vital that we understand the range of techniques that were in play among the four evangelists in composing their empty tomb and resurrection narratives. *First,* later gospel writers freely rewrote their predecessors, Matthew rewriting Mark, and so forth. *Second,* they padded the stories by rewriting, without attribution, Old Testament scripture texts. *Third,* they borrowed common miracle stories from the cults of rival saviors like Asclepius, Apollonius, and Pythagoras, all of them Sons of God. *Fourth,* they parodied polemics aimed at the Christian resurrection doctrine by outsiders.

Mark's is the earliest gospel, and he has followed the Passion of Jesus Christ with a story of his empty tomb's discovery by Mary Magdalene and other women followers (Mark 16:1–8). A mysterious "young man" tells them Jesus is risen. As Charles H. Talbert has shown, such a tale fits neatly in the same class with other current stories in which the loved ones of a vanished and/or slain hero cannot find his body, only to be informed by a heavenly voice or an angel that he has been taken up.[15] Scholars, unconsciously continuing to take the story as history even when they say they know better, puzzle over the failure of the frightened women to convey the angel's message. They were ordered to tell Peter and the others to go to Galilee to await Jesus. But they didn't. Then how is it *we* are hearing the story?

Well, of course, the same way we hear what Jesus prayed to the Father in the Garden when there were no witnesses present to overhear and repeat it! Mark has simply created both scenes out of whole cloth. He is the omniscient narrator. All right, then, but why have the story end on such an odd note? Well, of course, for the same reason he has Jesus tell his inner circle of disciples, who have just witnessed the visitation of Moses and Elijah atop the Mount of Transfiguration, to keep mum about it—till the resurrection occurs. For the same reason Jesus tells them not to reveal his messiahship. For the same reason the Risen Jesus appears only to small groups in locked rooms. This is a technique of clever imposture whereby a narrator "explains" why some innovation of his is true *anyway*, even though no one remembers ever hearing it before! So Mark has added something altogether new to his readers: the story of the discovery of the empty grave of Jesus, who has been assumed into heaven like Hercules or Asclepius or Romulus or Enoch or Moses or Elijah—you get the picture.

LUKE'S LOOSE ENDS

Luke used most of this material, but he planned on including some resurrection appearances, so he arbitrarily had the women relay the message (this time received from *two* men) to the disciples. They will eventually see the Risen One in Luke 24:34–43, though the women do not. For his raw material, Luke has borrowed familiar legends of the epiphany of a divine savior. The story of the disciples meeting Christ on the road to Emmaus (Luke 24:13–35) closely matches a story we read from a source already three or four centuries older than Luke in which the Savior Asclepius, incognito, joins a couple returning home disappointed after a pilgrimage to his holy shrine. There they had hoped to gain relief from a much-delayed pregnancy, but the god had been of no help. To remedy their despair and faithlessness, he heals her on the spot (from what is revealed as a false pregnancy), makes his identity known, and vanishes from their sight.

To this Luke adds a rather incoherent episode in which Jesus suddenly pops into the midst of his disciples and demonstrates what he has just belied: his corporeal solidity! It is distinctly parallel to an episode preserved in Philostratus's *Life of Apollonius of Tyana*, wherein his disciples have given the sage up for dead, having abandoned him before his trial before a Roman tyrant. But here he is, all of a sudden in their midst! Is he a ghost? No, he assures them, extending his meaty hands for them to touch, just as Jesus does in Luke 24:36–43. His ascension into heaven from the Mount of Olives is clearly borrowed from Josephus's account of Moses's assumption into heaven. So Luke has supplemented Mark in the same way

Mark supplemented the version of the story he had inherited: Just as Mark borrowed the form of the standard exaltation story, so Luke added some typical epiphany and ascension stories. Luke has changed the role of Mary Magdelene only enough to facilitate the (fictive) continuation of the story: She hears the angelic tidings and does obey the command to convey them.

MATTHEW'S MOSAIC

Matthew faced the same challenge Luke did. He had Mark in front of him and didn't like the way it ended. He, too, wanted to present resurrection appearances, but where was he going to get them? He did not think of borrowing legendary prototypes from rival gods. He expanded Mark's narrative as he had so many times at earlier points in the story, by fudging it from scripture. He created a half-baked version of an appearance (Matt. 28:16–20) upon a Galilean mountain he says, by way of afterthought, that Jesus had directed them to, though we had heard nothing about it. The speech (vv. 18–20) about receiving universal authority over all nations and so on comes, as Randel Helms shows,[16] right out of two contemporary Greek translations of Daniel 7:14, the vision of one like a son of man receiving sovereignty over all peoples, tongues, and nations. This is scarcely an appearance story at all: all summary, no scene.

But what of Mary's role? Matthew has embellished the scene elaborately in order to parody an anti-Christian slur to the effect that Jesus's body was gone from the tomb ("if you say so!") only because his wily disciples had made away with it. Matthew swallows and digests this polemic, turning it into a piece of comedy, based, again, on Daniel: Just as the Babylonian guards who cast Shadrach, Meschach, and Abed-Nego into the incinerator keeled over from the terrible heat (3:22), so did analogous Roman sentries collapse (Matt. 28:3–4) before the radiance of a mighty angel. Where did *he* come from? He is Mark's humble "young man" reinterpreted as the "fourth man" present in the furnace with the three Hebrew youths, one "like a son of God" (Daniel 3:25).

But Matthew seemingly was not quite sure he had gotten Mark's "young man" right—suppose it was *not* an angel, but rather the Risen Jesus himself? So Matthew, who adds a second Gadarene demoniac to Mark's solo madman (Matt. 8:28 vs. Mark 5:1), a second blind man to the lone Bar-Timaeus (Matt. 20:30 vs. Mark 10:46), a second donkey to Mark's single beast (Matt. 21:1–7 vs. Mark 11:1–7), now adds a second version of Mark's young man, the Risen Christ (28:9–10). That he is merely a literary doublet, though, is obvious from the fact Matthew invents no new lines for the character, having him merely reiterate the command of the angel! This detail is of the utmost importance for our inquiry; it means that *the appearance of the Risen Christ to address Mary Magdalene is a literary product created as a kind of harmonization by Matthew.*

JOHN'S EASTER EVOLUTION

John uses at least three of the techniques I have described to expand the narratives he had inherited from Matthew and

Luke. The analysis of John's Easter section, chapters 20–21, is especially complex because, as all critical scholars agree, chapter 21 is a supplement to chapter 20, recapping the original ending of the book (20:30–31, "Jesus also performed many additional signs before the eyes of his disciples, which, however, are not included in this book; but these have been included to convince you that Jesus is the Christ, the Son of God, so that, believing it, you may come alive in his name") in 21:25, a paraphrase: "And there are many additional feats Jesus performed, which, if one were to record them all, would flood the very world with books!" But that is not all: it appears as well that somewhere along the line someone has beefed up chapter 20 as well, adding the Doubting Thomas episode (20:24–29); all the disciples are assumed present in 20:19–23, but suddenly we read that Thomas was not there! That is a condition of the second story, not the first.

In the same way, John 20:1, 11–18, Mary Magdalene's exchange with the two angels and with the Risen Jesus, appears to have been shoe-horned into a story in which, as in Luke, the women see the empty tomb and tell the men, without seeing Jesus himself.[17] Verse 2 has Mary Magdalene run to tell the male disciples that the tomb is empty, whereupon two of them return without her. But she is somehow "back" at the tomb in verse 11! This same verse would open the question of why the two male disciples missed seeing the two angels, since all there was to be seen in the tomb in verses 6–7 were the discarded grave clothes. Did the angels hide at first? Or arrive late? Also, if the story were originally cut from the same cloth as its present context, why is Mary told not to touch Jesus in verse 17, while Thomas is told in verse 27 just the opposite? And in the section 20:2–10, Mary is said to have visited the tomb with the other women (v. 2) as in the other gospels, while in John 20:1, 11–18, she is alone. The most important incongruity is that verse 17, despite its other difficulties, at least means that the ascension is imminent, but, instead of ascending, Jesus goes on to make several other appearances in the next chapter and a half!

In the appearance to Mary, are we dealing with an independent episode preserved and inserted here in John's Easter complex? It will be easier to make a judgment once we briefly survey the kind of material surrounding it. That may help us to see the sort of thing the evangelist and/or redactor did with his material in general. The report of the women prompting the visit of Peter and his colleague to the empty tomb (John 20:2–10) has Johannine fingerprints (John's favorite vocabulary and conceptuality) all over it, and it appears to be a Johannine rewrite of Luke 24:9–12 ("the women . . . told this to the apostles, but the report struck them as an empty tale, and they did not believe them. But Peter got up and ran for the tomb. He stooped to peer inside and saw the linen wrappings lying abandoned. And he returned home, baffled as to what might have happened"). John has added the second disciple on the basis of Luke 24:24, "*Some* of our group went to the tomb." (Some important manuscripts of Luke lack 24:12, Peter's inconclusive visit, but it does not matter whether this verse was a subsequent addition; even if it was, John may have read the longer version.)

BARNACLES ON THE JOHANNINE HULL

John 20:19–23 can be naturally understood as John's rewrite of Luke 24:36–43, the main difference being that Jesus's *solid* hands and *feet* (Luke) become his *wounded* hands and *side* (John), to adjust the originally Lukan scene to the details of John's crucifixion account, where, alone of all the gospels, Jesus gets wounded in the *side*.

The Doubting Thomas scene is borrowed from, or at least cut from the same cloth as, contemporary stories such as we read, again, in Philostratus, where, weeks or months after the final ascension of Apollonius to heaven, a group of his devotees are together in one place praying and studying. One of them announces that he just cannot bring himself to believe in immortality, all the more since he has long been beseeching Apollonius for proof, but so far in vain. The others tolerate his unbelief, until one day they hear him exclaiming, to no one visible, "I believe you!" Their flabbergasted gazes tell him they do not share his vision, so he explains that the venerable Apollonius has appeared, just now, to him alone, to convince him to believe in eternal life, much like John 20:30–31, which makes the same point concluding the Doubting Thomas story.

John 21:1–19, the miraculous catch of fish, also appears in Luke 5:1–9. In both versions, Peter and company have failed to catch any fish until Jesus bids them cast the net as he directs, whereupon they find their fraying nets strained to the breaking point. Then, he tells Peter to follow him, in Luke as an angler for souls, in John as a shepherd of souls. Luke has plugged the story into Mark 1:16 and 17, to explain why Peter, Andrew, James, and John would have been willing to abandon home and livelihood. John's version, too, has the disciples at work fishing and does not say they have *returned* to fishing. Maybe the redactor has made it into a resurrection story. In any case, the story originally featured Pythagoras, and in that version the sage did not cause the great catch but rather used his mathematical acumen to "guess" the number of fish just hauled ashore by fishermen. Pythagoras was a vegetarian and made a deal with the salty fellows: If he could tell the correct number of fish, they would set them free. He did, and so did they. This explains why, despite the uncanny presence of the resurrected Son of God, the disciples in John 21 take the time to count the fish! It is a vestige of the Pythagoras tale, where it mattered. This is why the number is provided, 153, to no apparent purpose, at least until one realizes that 153 was one of the sacred "triangular numbers" venerated by the Pythagoreans! Did John derive the story from Luke, or from Pythagoreanism? We don't know. But John does seem to be either rewriting Luke or borrowing a contemporary miracle story, if not somehow both.

The awkward dialogue between Jesus and Simon Peter in John 21:20–23 ("If I should want him to remain behind till I come, how is that any business of yours?") is another attempt to domesticate and to defuse a hostile anti-Christian jibe. We find one form of the polemic in 2 Peter 3:4, "What happened to the promise of his coming? Ever since the (church) fathers died off, the world has continued on as it always has since the day it was made!" You see, the early belief that Jesus should return before his generation passed (Mark 13:30) had already shrunk its line of defense, as more early disciples died, down to promising that only *some* should live to see it (Mark 9:1). Finally, it had been reworked as the claim that at least *one* member of that generation should endure to the end ("The saying circulated among the fellowship that the brother in question should not die," John 21:23a). But he did, and the great weight of vindication that had rested upon his shoulders came crashing down. The only way John's redactor could think of to get off the hook was to call the whole thing a gross misunderstanding: "But Jesus did not actually tell him he would not die," only that even if such an enormity were to be true, it would be no concern of Peter's. What we have here is a move akin to Mark's statements that this or that report had to be hushed up till an opportune time. It is all disingenuous revisionism.

ONCE MORE INTO THE BREACH

This brings us at last to the Magdalene encounter in John 20:1, 11–19. We can deconstruct the passage by marking how John employs three of the standard techniques to construct the passage. First, it surely seems as if he has copied Matthew's splitting of Mark's "young man" into an angel *and* the Christ. Only John has also cast Luke's two men in the scene, making them explicitly angels a la Matthew. Notice that, again, Jesus vouchsafes nothing to the women, or woman, but a verbatim repetition of the words of the angels. And he implicitly negates the item of Mary clasping Jesus's feet from Matthew 28:9, telling her not to hold onto him (20:17a). So John has rewritten a predecessor, namely, Matthew.

He has also supplemented it with scripture, adapting for Jesus the parting words of the angel Raphael in Tobit 12:18–21, "I came, not as a favor on my part, but as sent by the command of our God. So praise him forever and ever! All this time, I only appeared to you and never ate nor drank, but you were beholding a vision. And now, render thanks to God, for I am ascending to him who sent me."[18] Raphael refers, inclusively, to "our God," a mutual allegiance, just as Jesus speaks of "my Father and your Father, my God and your God" (20:17b). Like Jesus in John 20:17, he says he will momentarily "ascend" to "him who sent me," a ubiquitous Johannine phrase. The otherwise puzzling command not to touch him, as Helms suggests, recalls the Docetism (see chapter 5, "Constantine's Christ," for more on Docetism) of Raphel's phantom human semblance and probably derives from it. The Risen Jesus is "untouchable."

And John turns to his own advantage yet another antiresurrection jibe, one familiar from Tertullian and the sources of the Jewish antigospel Toledoth Jeschu (see chapter 7, "Eighty Gospels?"), namely, that, while the disciples might not have maliciously stolen Jesus's corpse, the caretaker of the garden in which he was buried (John 19:41) must have transferred it from its temporary interment (for the sake of the encroaching Sabbath) to some other location. John has taken a story in which it really *was* the gardener of whom Mary inquired, and substituted Matthew's resurrected Jesus for him.

Finally, is John 20:1, 11–18, an older, independent unit of tradition that John has inserted here in an alien context? Remember, if it is, then we would have the historical root of the apostolic claim of Mary Magdalene. There certainly are, as we have seen, ample signs that two stories have been fused together as we read John 20:1–20, but which is earlier? I take John 20:1, 11–18, to be the original Johannine text, with John

20:2–20 (the Lukan-derived visit of Peter and his companion) as the subsequent addition, clumsily patched in. Then someone added the Doubting Thomas tale onto the end of that one. And everything in chapter 21 is additional, too. This means that the episode in which Mary seems to be the sole witness of the departing Jesus, even though a literary invention of John based on pieces of Matthew and Luke, was originally intended to be the sole resurrection scene in John's gospel. Later scribes supplemented it, layer upon layer. In this case, we need not take the clash between Jesus's telling her to tell the Twelve good-bye on the one hand and the subsequent appearances to the Twelve on the other as a sign of John's making new use of an older story. No, there was no pre-Johannine unit of tradition depicting Mary as the sole witness to the resurrection. John himself cobbled together the scene from bits of earlier gospels.

What does this review of the gospel Easter stories portend for the question of Mary Magdalene as an apostle? I hope to have demonstrated, against my own earlier theory, that the crucial passage John 20:1, 11–18, has apparently been composed by the Fourth Evangelist or one of his redactors on the basis of Matthew's redaction of Mark, plus a rewrite of Tobit 12:18–21, plus a turnabout of the rumor that Jesus's body had merely been moved to an unknown location. The story is scarcely even about the Magdalene, much less about any supposed Magdalene Circle of Christians. Mary comes second-hand from Matthew and appears in John just to recognize Jesus and to verify his identity for the benefit of the reader.

BLACK MAGIC WOMAN

While any notion of Mary Magdalene as an apostle must be tenuously pieced together from gospel fragments that appear on the surface to say nothing of the sort, there are two familiar characterizations of the Magdalene that are overtly stated in the gospels. First, Mary is said (Luke 8:2; Mark 16:9) to have been possessed at one time by seven demons. We sometimes read that demon possession was a put-down commonly aimed at those perceived as heretics. The evidence cited for this generalization comes from John's gospel. There, Jesus's opponents cry out, "You have a demon!" (7:20) and "Are we not right in saying that you are a Samaritan and have a demon?" (8:48) and "He has a demon, and he is mad; why listen to him?" (10:20). And thus some urge that Mary gained the false stigma of having been possessed because she was a teacher of doctrines rejected by authorities of her day. And if that were so, runs the argument, Christians of a later date who had forgotten the Magdalene controversy might have misunderstood the "demon" charge and taken it literally.

But I do not think that will work. These texts from John seem to make more sense as accusations that Jesus *possesses* demons rather than being possessed *by* them. Indeed, isn't that precisely the point in Mark 3:22–23, "He has Beelzebul, and it is only by the ruler of the demons that he expels demons"? The theory of exorcism was that the mightiest magicians could "bind the strong man," then "despoil him of his possessions" by ordering him to send his subordinate devils packing. This rationale is still visible beneath a layer of redaction in Mark 3:27. On second reading, the passages from John seem to mean the same thing. They are accusations that Jesus is no saint but a mere magician. This is only reinforced by the jibe that he is "a Samaritan" as well as "having a demon." There, he is being compared to the infamous Simon Magus, the magician. Thus we seem to be left with no parallel text that would allow us to understand Mary the demoniac as garbled version of "Mary the heretic, Mary the Gnostic."

It is striking that the demoniac Mary business enters the gospel tradition only in a very late stage, that represented by Luke's rewriting of Mark (chapter 8, verse 2) and the interpolated Markan Appendix (Mark 16:9). And as I have pointed out already, both passages have Jesus casting seven demons out of her, a sure mark of legend, folklore, or pious imagination. Where did the legend of Mary's sevenfold possession come from, and why so late? We will see in just a moment.

ONLY HER HAIRDRESSER KNOWS FOR SURE

As is well known, Mary Magdalene has always been painted as a prostitute. Many or most scholars today reject this tradition because they can find no basis for it in the canonical gospels. That seems to imply it is a rather late legend, the product of clever interpreters combining various gospel characters about whom little is said. Early commentators gratuitously identified Mary Magdalene with both Mary of Bethany (John 12:1–3) and the "sinner" of Luke 7:36–38, both of whom are shown anointing Jesus with expensive perfume. And certainly that is no evidence at all.

But I think there *is* early gospel evidence for Mary's earlier career as a prostitute. It is hidden in plain sight, preserved in the very epithet "Magdalene" itself. We know that Jewish anti-Christian satire ridiculed the doctrine of the virgin birth of Jesus by claiming that Jesus was the illegitimate son of Mary of Nazareth by a Roman soldier named Pandera. It seems obvious that "Jesus son of Pandera" is a cruel pun derived from "Jesus son of the *parthenos* (virgin)." Similarly, they confused Mary of Nazareth with Mary Magdalene and punned that "Magdalene" meant not "of Magdala," supposedly a village in Galilee, but rather *m'gaddla*, "the hair curler," a euphemism for a brothel madam, since elaborate hairstyling was regarded as the mark of a prostitute.[19] If "Mary the hairdresser" was Jesus's mother, then he was the son of a Roman soldier and a Jewish prostitute. In this pun, we probably have the starting point of the tradition of Mary as a prostitute. But my guess is the rabbinical satirists intended no pun at all. The only liberty they took, probably more of a mistake, was to identify the two Marys. As J. B. Lightfoot suggested long ago, Aramaic-speaking Christians already referred to Mary as "the Madame," "the Hairdresser." And this epithet survived in the long-lived tradition of Mary the reformed prostitute.

Unlike Mary the demoniac, Mary the Madame (Magdalene) is attested early in the gospel tradition, as early as the character herself, in the Markan Passion narrative (Mark 15:47; 16:1). So when and why was the demoniac image added onto the earlier prostitute image? I think that later Christians grew uncomfortable with the importance assigned a whore in the sacred narrative, even a reformed one, and they sought to wash her of that stigma by reinterpreting *"m'gaddla"* as a reference to her hometown, assuming there was a town named Magdala. In just the same way, some scholars argue that "Jesus the Nazorean" originally denoted Jesus's membership in the ascetical Nazorean sect, represented today by the Nasoreans or Mandaeans of Iraq. Once Christians became uncomfortable with a divine being (as they eventually considered him) being a disciple of mere humans they conveniently reinterpreted "Nazorean" as "Nazarene," the one from Nazareth (a town, however, unattested in any roughly contemporary record). Again, "Iscariot" originally was an epithet for Judas, meaning either "the False One" or "the Dagger," but the gospel writers seem no longer to realize this, taking it as another hometown name, as if it meant "Judas of Kirioth" (implict at John 13:26). So it was a common kind of reinterpretation.

DO YOU KNOW THE WAY TO MAGDALA?

Was there even a town called "Magdala" for Mary to have hailed from? That is highly doubtful. The King James Version of Matthew 15:39 mentions "Magdala," but better manuscripts and modern translations read "Magadan." Where did Matthew find this information? Not in Mark, for Mark's version of the story (8:10) reads "Dalmanutha." No town with either name appears either in the Old Testament or any other pre-Christian records. Codex Bezae, a fascinating manuscript with many valuable variant readings, has "Melagada" instead of Dalmanutha at Mark 8:10. There is even a marginal scribal note advising how copyists might make "Melagada" into "Magada," something a bit closer to "Magdala": "Insert *dal* after the *g*, erase the *da*."[20]

All this may sound quite strange to anyone familiar with recent writings on Mary Magdalene. Some scholars wax bold to inform us about the details of Mary's hometown even down to its economics.[21] Where did they get this "information"? First, from anachronistically late writings like the Jewish Talmuds, written centuries after Jesus.[22] Second, by arbitrarily identifying various Galilean towns or archaeological sites with "Magdala" even though no ancient record does. You can't just say that every time Josephus mentioned the fishing village of Taricheae he really meant Magdala. This is the kind of "Pin-the-tail-on-the-Bible" archaeology William Foxwell Albright and his disciples were famous for practicing: "If the Bible says it existed, then it must be there *some*place! There's a set of ruins over there? *Bingo!* By golly, we've discovered Kadesh-Bilga-meth!" This sort of thing is frowned upon today, except, of course, when the results happen to come in handy.

The greatest irony in the use of such late sources to secure a place name meaning for "Magdalene" pops up in the Talmud, where we read how "Magdala was destroyed because of prostitution" (*y. Ta'anit* 4, 69c).[23] Don't you see what has happened here? The transformation of the epithet "Magdalene" meaning "harlot" into meaning "from Magdala" has carried with it the telltale echo of the original. Now "Magdala" has become a second Sodom, Mary implicitly being rescued like Lot, only because she (must have) repented before it was too late!

Now we can see why later Christians substituted demon possession as the negative condition from which Jesus must have redeemed Mary. You see, being a prostitute was a freely willed career choice. Demon possession was not. The demoniac was a victim, not a sinner. Thus, Mary as a prostitute appears early in the gospel tradition, while Mary the demoniac appears much later.

DISTAFF APOSTLE?

What can we say about the historical likelihood of Mary Magdalene being a prominent Christian leader, perhaps even esteemed by her admirers as an apostle? Much is made of this possibility in *The Da Vinci Code*, where, as in today's gospel scholarship, it has become something of a dogma. What is the evidence on which a positive judgment might be based? King, as we have seen, takes the widespread second-century occurrence of Mary as a resurrection visionary and interlocutor with the Risen Jesus to imply that there was a historical Apostle Mary. But my analysis of the Easter traditions rules out such an inference as far as I am concerned. It seems likely to me that the whole role of Mary as a resurrection visionary stems from John 20:1, 11–18, which, in turn, is a Johannine rewrite of Matthew 28:9–10. From this mustard seed has the whole tree sprung.

MESSIANIC QUEEN?

Finally, is it possible for Mary and Jesus to have been married or at least to have been romantically involved? This notion, too, is central to *The Da Vinci Code*. Of course it is possible. As we have seen, the Gospel of Philip says, "Now Mary was the favorite of the Savior, and he often used to kiss her on the lips." It is obvious that the erotic imagery is being used metaphorically in such passages, and yet who can discount the possibility that here, as in other cases, some notion, originally taken in a physical, material sense, has been "docetized," its offense to squeamish readers removed by "not taking it literally"?

Again, there is something quite suggestive in the gospel depiction of Jesus traveling with unattached women (Mark 15:40–41; Luke 8:1–3). We are reminded of some of the Apocryphal Acts of the Apostles, where Andrew, Philip, Paul, and others preach the celibate version of Christianity and attract high-born women to follow them. As might be expected, this has the effect of alienating their husbands, since the women are now too sanctified to sleep with them. And the husbands can be excused for suspecting their wives have been seduced by some Svengali using their devotion cynically as an entrée to enjoy sex with them all. For instance, in the Acts of Philip, the irate husband of convert Nicanora gives her an ultimatum: "It will be a fine thing for thee to be cut off by the sword, or to see thee [thrust] from beside me [for] committing fornication with these foreign magicians; for I see that thou hast fallen into the madness of these deceivers."[24] The female following of Jesus in the gospels looks like nothing so much as this, leaving us to consider whether, a la the suspicions of the husbands in the Apocryphal Acts, Jesus had been using the group of women as his harem. And in view of parallel cases from the whole history of Utopian cults and communities, we cannot dismiss the possibility.

Still, possibility is not probability, as it seems to have become for upholders of the Teabing hypothesis. The notorious tendency of conservative apologists and New Age paperback writers alike is to leap from mere possibility to the right to believe. "If there might be space aliens, we can assume there are." "If the idea of Atlantis is not impossible, we can take it for granted." "If the traditional view of gospel authorship cannot be definitively debunked, we can go right on assuming its truth." No, you can't. And though Jesus might have had sex with one or many women or men, the mere possibility is of no help. He might have been a space alien, too. Some think he was. But historians don't.

NOTES

1. It is customary to date this gospel to about 150 CE, still a very early date, but recently there have been attempts to show that Thomas may very well be a first-century CE document. See especially Stevan L. Davies, *The Gospel of Thomas and Christian Wisdom* (New York: Seabury, 1983).

2. D. A. Carson, *Exegetical Fallacies* (Grand Rapids, MI: Baker Book House, 1984), p. 53, explains the conclusions of Robert Joly, *Le vocabulaire chretien de l'amour est-il original? Φιλειν et Αγαπαν dans le grec antique* (Brussels: Presses Universitaires, 1968), who shows how the similarity between *kuneo* (to kiss) and *kuno* (to impregnate), especially in their identical aorist form *ekusa*, led to all sorts of sexual puns.

3. This passage is still so shocking to pious ears that M. R. James refused to translate it! "Epiphanius in *Her* xxvi. 8 quotes the Lesser Questions of Mary: but I must be excused from repeating the passage." In *The Apocryphal New Testament* (Oxford: Clarendon Press, 1972), p. 20. (Actually, it is the *Greater Questions*, not the *Lesser*, to which Epiphanius refers. James was nodding.)

4. Gilles Quispel, "The Birth of the Child: Some Gnostic and

Jewish Aspects," in *Eranos Lectures 3* (Dallas: Spring Publications, 1987), pp. 25–26. If one were to accept Morton Smith's *Secret Gospel of Mark* as a genuine ancient document (I do not), it must be admitted it would be tempting to trace the sacrament of the Bridal Chamber back to the rites of homosexual initiation Smith claims (*The Secret Gospel: The Discovery and Interpretation of the Secret Gospel according to Mark* [New York: Harper & Row, 1973], p. 114) Jesus practiced, since it would certainly make sense of the fact that men accepted the female role in a hidden ceremony with Christ as the male! But this must be left as mere speculation unless and until more evidence comes to light.

5. Elisabeth Schüssler Fiorenza, *In Memory of Her: A Feminist Theological Reconstruction of Christian Origins* (New York: Crossroad, 1984), p. 276. Fiorenza is dependent on the work of R. Beor, *Philo's Use of the Categories Male and Female* (Leiden, The Netherlands: Brill, 1970).

6. For sheer interest's sake, attention ought to be drawn to a striking parallel (?) in the Mahayana Buddhist scripture *Saddharma-Pundarika* (*Lotus of the True Law*). Sariputra says to the daughter of the Naga-king Sagora, who is seeking to become a Bodhisattva, "'It may happen, sister, that a woman displays an unflagging energy, performs good works for many thousands of Aeons, and fulfills the six perfect virtues [*Paramitas*], but as yet there is no example of her having received Buddhaship.'" Contrary to expectation, however, she does receive this distinction: "At that same instant, before the sight of the whole world and of the senior priest Sariputra, the female sex of the daughter of Sagara, the Naga-king, disappeared; the male sex appeared and she manifested herself as a Bodhisattva" (Xl:51). H. Kern, trans., *Saddharma-Pundarika, or Lotus of the True Law* (New York: Dover Publications, 1963), pp. 252–53.

7. Elaine Pagels, *The Gnostic Gospels* (New York: Random House, 1979), p. 64.

8. Pheme Perkins, *The Gnostic Dialogue* (New York: Paulist, 1980), p. 136.

9. Fiorenza, *In Memory of Her*, pp. 304, 306.

10. Karen L. King, *The Gospel of Mary of Magdala: Jesus and the First Woman Apostle* (Santa Rosa, CA: Polebridge, 2003), p. 86.

11. E.g., Letha Scanzoni and Nancy Hardesty, *All We're Meant to Be* (Waco, TX: Word, 1975), p. 59; Paul K. Jewett, *Man as Male and Female* (Grand Rapids, MI: Eerdmans, 1976), p. 169; Virginia Ramey Mollenkott, *Women, Men & the Bible* (Nashville, TN: Abingdon, 1977), p. 19.

12. King, *Gospel of Mary of Magdala*, p. 142.

13. Rudolf Bultmann, *Theology of the New Testament*, trans. Kendrik Grobel, vol. 1 (New York: Charles Scribner's Sons, 1951), pp. 295–96, shows how 20:2–18 was at first a distinct story unto itself.

14. Raymond E. Brown, *The Community of the Beloved Disciple* (New York: Paulist, 1979), p. 154.

15. Charles H. Talbert, *What Is a Gospel? The Genre of the Canonical Gospels* (Philadelphia: Fortress, 1977).

16. Randel Helms, *Gospel Fictions* (Amherst, NY: Prometheus Books, 1988), pp. 140–42.

17. Rudolf Bultmann, *The Gospel of John: A Commentary*, trans. G. R. Beasley-Murray, R. W. Hoare, and J. K. Riches (Philadelphia: Westminster, 1971), p. 682.

18. Helms, *Gospel Fictions*, pp. 146–47.

19. The pun occurs in the Babylonian Talmud, *Hagigah*, 4b. See Bernhard Pick, *Jesus in the Talmud* (Chicago: Open Court, 1913), pp. 15–16; F. F. Bruce, *Jesus and Christian Origins outside the New Testament* (Grand Rapids, MI: Eerdmans, 1974), p. 58. Jane Schaberg (*The Resurrection of Mary Magdalene: Legends, Apocrypha, and the Christian Testament* [New York: Continuum, 2002], p. 55) is fully aware of the suggestion (originally made by J. B. Lightfoot), which I am merely

reiterating here, that "Mary Magdalene" originally denoted "Mary the Harlot," but she just notes it to drop it. For her and her semi-mystical meditation on Mary as a Virginia Woolf analogue "Mary the Harlot" is a dead end.

20. Frank R. Zindler, "Where Jesus Never Walked," *American Atheist* (Winter 1996–97): 41–42, dependent upon D. Paul Glaue, "Der älteste Text der geschichtlichen Bücher des Neuen Testaments," *Zeitschrift für neutestamentliche Wissenschaft und die Kunde der älteren Kirche* 45 (1954): 103.

21. Schaberg, *Resurrection of Mary Magdalene*, pp. 47–64; Richard Atwood, *Mary Magdalene in the New Testament Gospels and Early Tradition*, European University Studies Series XXIII, vol. 457 (New York: Peter Lang, 1993), pp. 21–25; Marianne Sawicki, "Magdalenes and Tiberiennes: City Women in the Entourage of Jesus," in *Transformative Encounters: Jesus and Women Re-viewed*, ed. Ingrid Rosa Kitzberger (Leiden, The Netherlands: Brill, 2000).

22. Of course, I, too, am repairing to the Talmud, but in my case it is only a matter of lexical information. If, on the other hand, one is willing to siphon "historical" information about Jesus, Mary, or "Magdala" from these texts, one might as well go the whole way with Brown, Teabing, Biagent and the rest, taking one's data from *The Golden Legend*. One is already on the same train, and one might as well hang on for the next station.

23. Schaberg, *Resurrection of Mary Magdalene*, p. 55.

24. Alexander Roberts and James Donaldson, eds., *Ante-Nicene Christian Library*, vol. 16: *Apocryphal Gospels, Acts, and Revelations*. Edinburgh, UK: T&T Clark, 1870), pp. 304–305.

Chapter 9

A CHRISTIAN GODDESS?

Mary Magdalene and the Sacred Feminine

GOD AND MAMMY

To a great degree, *The Da Vinci Code* tends to exploit the radical chic fringe of religion and religious studies. Is the book's advocacy of Christian goddess worship another case of this? Is the very notion of "rediscovering" a Christian goddess just an opportunistic gimmick employed to bring liberal Christianity into fellowship with neo-paganism? There are many individuals, men and women, attracted to both Protestant Liberalism and neo-paganism at the same time, and they welcome such a rationale for healing their theological schizophrenia. If they do not finally have to choose between, shall we say, God and Mammy, all the better. But that is neither here nor there as far as the task of New Testament research is concerned. It shouldn't matter whose interests or whims may be served by one's possible conclusions. The question is, regardless where a theory comes from or whose bread it butters, is there any evidence for it? And in the present case, it seems that there is.

JESUS ADONIS

We must begin with an old and despised theory of Christian origins, already mentioned in this book more than once, namely, that the resurrection of Jesus Christ from the dead is of a piece with the celebrated resurrections of other Near Eastern savior divinities, including Osiris, Dionysus, Attis, Adonis, Tammuz/Dumuzi, and Baal. The vigor with which conservative Christian apologists have attacked this theory is an index of its strength and of the wide-ranging character of its implications. Consider first the mythic parallels.

OSIRIS

Jealous of his brother Osiris's sister-bride Isis, Set (god of the desert) contrived to assassinate Osiris (god of the grain harvest). This he accomplished by means of a clever subterfuge. At a feast, Set arranged for someone to haul in a mysterious and elaborate sarcophagus. No one admitted to having had it delivered. So Set suggested all present lie down in it to try it on for size. The first to fit it should receive it as a prize. Of course, it had been designed to fit Osiris's dimensions, and Set's minions were ready to act as soon as Osiris reclined in it. They rushed forward with hammers and pegs to nail the casket shut, then spirited it away before anyone understood what was happening. They cast the box into the Nile, which took it far away until it was found and used as a pillar in a building. Isis set out to find her husband's body and did find it. But Set stole it away and this time cut it into pieces, distributing them all over the land. Isis (and her sister Nephthys, Set's wife) went in search of the pieces and, in some versions, found all of it but the penis, which Isis magically reconstructed from clay. She anointed her husband's corpse with unguent, and he returned from the dead.

She had intercourse with him to produce a son, Horus, the falcon of the sun, who would serve as Osiris's reincarnation on earth while Osiris himself assumed office in the netherworld Amente, the heaven of Egyptian mythology, as lord of the living and the dead. Later, Horus would kill Set in battle. These beliefs are pre-Christian, attested many centuries earlier among the Pyramid Texts, where it says that the interred shall share Osiris's resurrection even as they have shared his death. The myth was also still alive and circulating in early Christian times, as we can see both from the enormous popularity of Isis and Osiris initiation across the empire and from the summary of the story in Plutarch's *Isis and Osiris*. It is notable that the worshipers of Osiris sealed their identity with him by means of a sacramental feast of bread and beer, which naturally symbolized his body and blood, seeing that he was the god of grain. Nor is Osiris any stranger to the biblical tradition, since the patriarch Joseph married into the family of the Osirian priesthood (Gen. 41:45, "On" = Osiris). In fact, the story of Joseph itself sounds like a reworked version of the Osiris myth.

DIONYSUS

According to the salvation myth of the Orphic religion (which began in the sixth century BCE), Dionysus Zagreus was the son of Zeus, born as a hunting deity. He was murdered and devoured by the Giants (monstrous offspring of Uranos, and consigned by him to nether darkness inside the earth till Zeus freed them). Athena alerted Zeus to the attack, but by the time the father of gods and men could intervene, all that was left was the beating heart, which Zeus promptly swallowed. He reduced the Giants to ash with his vengeful thunderbolts, and then he created the human race from this dust. On the one hand, this resulted in human beings possessing an inner spark of the divine (from Dionysus) and an outer body of crude flesh (from the Giants). Orphism proposed to help them awaken the divine spark within. Subsequently, on the other hand, Dionysus of Thebes, the more familiar version of the god, was reborn from Zeus's thigh. "Dionysus" means "Young Zeus" and implies a still earlier version of the myth in which he represented the resurrection of Zeus himself, who was believed on Crete to have been gored to death by a wild boar, like Adonis.

Orpheus, the inspired poet who told of these events, was also party to a resurrection myth. He entered Hades to retrieve his dead wife, Eurydice, and with the permission of the gods, he took her by the hand and led her to the surface. But he failed because he did not obey the gods' command not to turn and look at her till they reached the surface. He lost her again and forever after lamented the loss in song. The poet swore never to marry again, and the female worshipers of Dionysus, the Maenads, took revenge by tearing him limb from limb, much as the Giants had dismembered Dionysus Zagreus. Forever after, the frenzied worshipers of Dionysus sacramentally reenacted his death by ripping live animals to pieces and devouring their bloody remains.

ATTIS

Attis was a Phrygian youth beloved of Cybele, the Cave Mother. (These seem to have been a local variation on Adam and Eve.) He betrayed her by marrying the local princess of Pessinus (the cult center). Cybele learned of his treachery and appeared, unwelcome, at the wedding, sending all the guests fleeing in terror, including the groom. Attis, awash in bitter self-reproach, sat beneath a tree and in remorse castrated himself, his blood darkening the flowers he sat on and accounting for the purple color of violets from that day forth (just as the death of Jesus reportedly etched the cross in Dogwood blossoms). But, in some versions of the myth, Cybele forgave her lover, whom she found having bled to death. And she raised him from the dead. The resurrected Attis is depicted dancing.

Attis cultists ritually relived his fate by castrating themselves in frenzied public ceremonies, then tossing their testicles into the lap of a silver statue of Cybele, symbolically fertilizing her womb, the womb of nature. In the yearly celebration of his mysteries, his priests would carve a small effigy of Attis and then affix it to a stripped pine trunk. This they would ritually inter in a cave or vault, then keep vigil till, after three days, the Hilaria, the day of rejoicing, dawned. Then they would retrieve the image and announce to the waiting crowd, "Rejoice, you initiates! For your god is saved! And we, too, shall be saved from ills!"

ADONIS

Adonis was a Syrian deity, whose name is obviously another form of Adonai, "Lord," a biblical name for God. His tale is basically another version of Attis's, only it is the Greek goddess Aphrodite whom he loves and who loves him. He is unfaithful to her, and she takes revenge, unleashing a fierce boar, which gores Adonis. But she can't stay mad and raises Adonis from the dead.

DUMUZI/TAMMUZ

Another very ancient, prebiblical myth of the resurrected god comes from Mesopotamia, where it was told to explain the death of vegetation in the fall and its return in the spring. In this one, it is a young god named Dumuzi who dies and descends to the netherworld. He represents the spirit of vegetation, and so his departure causes all greenery to wither. But his lover Ishtar burns with a love stronger than death. She undertakes to make the journey to Sheol alive, and she must face many dangers on the way. In the course of her adventure, she herself is killed but rises from the dead. Finally, she reaches him, and she has more luck than Orpheus. She successfully brings Dumuzi up from the dead, restoring the life of plants, while she takes his place. Every winter he goes back, and she comes up.

Ancient peoples believed they ought to take no chances, so they did not merely commemorate the change of seasons; they cooperated to make sure it kept happening on schedule. So Mesopotamian women would ritually mourn for the slain Dumuzi, anticipating his return. Dumuzi's worship thrived also in nearby Israel and Judah, where he was called Tammuz, lending his name to one month of the Hebrew calendar. It appears that the Song of Solomon originated as the liturgy of the cult, though the names have been trimmed in light of the evolution toward Jewish monotheism. The only way it could keep its place on the shelf of sacred literature was to omit the names, now considered idolatrous. But it remains pretty easy to recognize Ishtar Shalmith in the "Shulammite" (Song 6:13) and Tammuz in her lover who is also her brother (4:9).

BAAL

Baal ("Lord") was a title received by the Canaanite and Amorite storm god, also called Aleyan and Hadad. He was the son of El ("God") and one day set out to defeat the death monster Mot. In this he failed and was devoured. But when his consort Anath discovered the bloody field (reflected in Matt. 27:8; Acts 1:19) where he had perished, she resolved to bring him back. She mourned and lamented, then got down to business. She descended to hell and freed her lover. Henceforth the resurrected deity reigned alongside his father as lord ("Baal") of gods and men. He, too, represented fertility, his death symbolizing fall and winter, his return signaling spring and summer.

ANOTHER CORN KING?

It is altogether natural to wonder whether perhaps the resurrection of Jesus on the third day, in the springtime, is another version of this widespread myth pattern. There are two versions of the theory. One is that there was a first-century CE historical Jesus to whom this myth was sooner or later attached. In chapter 3, "Beyond the Cross," this possibility is broached. Rudolf Bultmann and others have thought this is what happened. The other, more radical, version is that there simply was no historical Jesus and that the gospel portrait of an itinerant healer and sage is a subsequent attempt to "historicize" the mythic Jesus figure, much as Plutarch supposed that Osiris and Isis had really lived but that they were the first king and queen of Egypt. Herodotus tried to figure out when in the long scope of Greek history Hercules would have lived. But these were later attempts to rationalize. In his book *Did the Greeks Believe in Their Myths?* Paul Veyne concludes that most people did believe the gods and heroes had existed, but in a sort of twilight zone of history before recorded human history began; "Once upon a time."[1] That is perhaps what the first Christians believed about the death and resurrection of Jesus.

"Jesus" may simply have been a title or epithet of one of the older deities, and eventually it took over in popular usage, just as Vedic worshipers used to invoke Rudra by name, but they feared his terrible might and so began to call him "O Auspicious One!" And that is what "Siva" means. Eventually the epithet Siva *became* the name, replacing Rudra. In the same way, "Jesus" (Savior) may have replaced the name Osiris or Dionysus.

WHAT DID THEY KNOW
AND WHEN DID THEY KNOW IT?

Conventional Christian theologians have mounted three arguments against this theory. The first is that there is no true parallel between Jesus and these mythic saviors for the simple reason that Jesus was a historical figure, not merely a poetic embodiment of the change of seasons. But that is just the question up for debate, isn't it? Isn't the question whether Jesus may *originally* have been an ahistorical myth? And besides, as we have just seen, most adherents of these other saviors probably pictured them alive in remote history, too. On Crete they even showed tourists the tomb of Zeus.

Second, objectors affirm that there is no pre-Christian evidence of dying-and-rising gods. Thus it might be that pagans liked what they saw in the Christian gospel and decided to borrow the resurrection (and, presumably, the whole system of mystery initiation along with it?). This, it must be said, is nonsense. As we have already seen, belief in the death and resurrection of Osiris, Baal, and Tammuz is amply attested many centuries before Christianity. As for Attis, most of the surviving evidence for belief in his resurrection does happen to be later, once Christianity has begun, but not all of it. One pre-Christian vase depicts him in his classic posture of resurrection, as lord of the dance. But really none of this is necessary. All we need to know is that when the early Christian apologists argued against ancient skeptics, to whom the power of these parallels was already obvious, they resorted to the argument that Satan, knowing in advance about the coming of Jesus, planted counterfeit resurrections in the soil of paganism *ahead of time*, so as to supply ammunition for skeptics! Christian apologists never would have made such an argument if they didn't acknowledge that the pagan versions were older.

Third, we are often told that Jews would never have borrowed pagan mythemes even if they were available, since Jews were staunch monotheists. This line of reasoning assumes the same error that vitiates Alfred Edersheim's *The Life and Times of Jesus the Messiah*, the uncritical belief that Jews and Judaism in the first century were the same as they would be two and three centuries later, as if Jesus and the Pharisees alike were all Mishnaic, Rabbinic Jews. This is far from the truth, as Jewish scholars now recognize. Just as Christian apologists want to make us think that Jesus, Peter, and Paul all believed in Chalcedonian orthodoxy, traditional Rabbinic Judaism recast first-century CE Judaism in its own image. But the sources do not bear these reconstructions out.

Keep in mind that conservative apologists are also dogmatically opposed to the critical view that Israelite religion originated amid animism and polytheism. Fundamentalists prefer the traditional theological party line that Moses was already a monotheist. But critical scholarship reveals that monotheism first popped up among Jews in the time of Jeremiah and the Second Isaiah, during and after the Babylonian Exile. And even then it was a distinct minority view. It took centuries before it dominated Jewish belief. We read in 2 Maccabees 12:40 how Jewish freedom fighters against the pagan Seleucids wore amulets of the Semitic gods of Jaffa into battle!

Any reader of the Old Testament knows how attractive Baal worship was to most Israelites for hundreds of years. See Zechariah 12:11, "In that day there will be great mourning in

Jerusalem, like the mourning for Hadad-Rimmon in the plain of Megiddo." This plain is located in Israel, and the god mentioned is Baal Hadad. The mourning was the ritual of his cult. But was he a resurrected deity? Obviously he was from the simple fact that people continued to worship him as a living god, seeing in the storm clouds his mighty chariot. Ezekiel makes it equally clear that Jews worshiped the dying-and-rising Tammuz, not somewhere out in the sticks, but right in downtown Jerusalem! "Then he brought me to the entrance at the gate of Yahweh's house facing north, and behold, women were sitting there weeping for Tammuz" (8:14). In 2 Maccabees 6:7, we read that Jews were forced by the Seleucid occupiers to join in the festivities of Dionysus, but this represents the embarrassment of the later writer who cringes at the notion that any Jews should have voluntarily apostatized. One Maccabees 1:41–53 tells the truth of the matter: Many Jews gladly paganized. Some Greek writers thought Yahweh was a local version of Dionysus anyway, so these Jews may have thought little was at stake. So it is by no means evident that all first-century Jews would have recoiled in pious disgust at the worship of dying-and-rising savior deities.

THE INVISIBLE WOMAN

The case for heavy influence upon Christianity from the religions of the resurrected gods is a strong one. And the stronger that case is, the stronger also becomes the notion that a Christian goddess originally formed an important part of the myth.

This much is evident from the prominence of the goddess in

each of the pagan parallels. The savior is always resurrected *by his consort*. Baal is rescued by Anath, Osiris by Isis, Dionysus by Athena (or Semele, Persephone, or someone else in various versions), Attis by Cybele, Adonis by Aphrodite, Tammuz by Ishtar. One has to wonder if the Christian version conformed to the same pattern. Is there reason to think there might have been a consort of Jesus who saw his death, went searching for the body to anoint it, and witnessed the resurrection? Of course there is. Nor has the evidence vanished. It is hidden in plain sight.

When Luke depicts Paul preaching at the Athenian Areopagus forum, he sounds a strange and discordant note. "Some of the Epicureans and Stoic philosophers met him. And some said, 'What does he mean by this gibberish?' Others said, 'Apparently he is promoting foreign divinities.' This last because he was proclaiming Jesus and Resurrection" (Acts 17:18). Even ancient commentators on this passage understood the point of it to be that the pagans (mis?)understood Paul to be talking about a divine couple, *Jesus and Anastasis*, surely an apt choice of names, meaning Salvation and Resurrection. Luke holds the very notion up to ridicule. But where did he get the idea in the first place? He may have made it up, having Paul's opponents mistake him in a grossly literal way, so as to afford Paul the chance to set things straight for the reader's benefit. John does the same thing with the Pharisees throughout his gospel ("How can he say, 'I came down from heaven?' Where's the airplane?"). Or Luke might be repeating what was actually said on the occasion, though if he did, it would be the only instance of such reporting in the whole of Acts, where all the speeches are plainly dramatic pieces authored by Luke himself.

But what an odd thing to introduce into the narrative out

of nowhere! One cannot help wondering if this is another one of those places where Luke is bringing up a popular belief that he doesn't like in order to make it look false or silly. Similarly, he tells us that Paul was widely believed to flout the Torah and to teach Christian converts to do the same (Acts 21:21–24) and that, of course, it wasn't so! But *wasn't* it? He brushes it off as mere slander when Stephen is accused of condemning Temple worship (Acts 6:13) yet writes a speech for him (see 7:47–51) in which he *does* seem to disdain it! So we must wonder whether Luke similarly knew of Christians who placed a goddess beside their new god: Anastasis, who as her very name demands, raised her consort Jesus from the dead.

But then why do we never hear of her elsewhere, say, in the gospels? The gospels and Acts are works of the very late first to mid-second centuries. And by this time Christianity was assuming an increasingly patriarchal character. This is a common process, once a successful, socially radical sect starts relaxing back into worldly conformity and becomes a church. In such a context, it is not much of a surprise that credit for Jesus's resurrection is transferred from his consort to his Father, is it? But, just as "the Shulammite" holds the place of Ishtar Shalmith in the Song of Solomon, a familiar character holds the place of the old Christian goddess Anastasis in the gospels. She is, of course, represented by Mary Magdalene.

MAGDALENE MYTH

Even the canonical gospels tell us enough about Mary Magdalene for us to recognize her true nature and role. First, we know that she accompanied Jesus on his journeys (Luke 8:3; Mark 15:41). Second, she witnessed his death (Mark 15:40, "There were also women looking on from afar, among whom were Mary Magdalene, and Mary the mother of James the Lesser and of Joses, and Salome"). Third, she and her sisters witnessed the interment: "Mary Magdalene and Mary the mother of Joses saw where he was laid" (Mark 15:47). Fourth, they came to find and anoint the body: "And when the Sabbath was done, Mary Magdalene and Mary the mother of James, and Salome bought spices so that they might go and anoint him." As for the searching element, see John 20:13–15, "They said to her, 'Woman, why are you weeping?' She said to them, 'Because they have taken away my Lord, and I do not know where they have laid him.' Saying this, she turned around and saw Jesus, though she did not recognize that it was Jesus. Jesus said to her, 'Woman, why are you weeping? Whom do you seek?' Assuming he was the gardener, she said to him, 'Sir, if you are the one who carried him away, tell me where you have put him, and I will take him away.'"

Thus far we have a pretty complete parallel to the pattern of the myths of the resurrected gods: The women mourn for the slain divinity and seek for his body, aiming to anoint it. Meanwhile they mourn his death. Mary Magdalene, Mary of James, and Salome are obvious analogues to Isis and Nephthys, though scarcely less to Cybele, Aphrodite, Anath, and Ishtar. In one Osiris mourning chant, Isis exclaims, "Evil men have killed my lord, and I know not where they have laid him!" The similarity to the Magdalene's words in John 20:13 is striking and obvious.

Conservative apologists like to observe how women were

not allowed to give legal witness on most matters according to Jewish law. Thus, they claim, early Christians would never have made up the empty tomb stories, with their female witnesses. Surely, if they were freely fabricating, they would have had men on the scene instead. But then, we must ask, why offer the empty tomb stories at all? Doesn't the initial claim, that women weren't worthwhile witnesses, imply that the empty tomb stories/traditions *do not mean to offer them as witnesses?* The stories have an entirely different origin and function: They are scripts for the annual mourning rituals of Jesus and Anastasis/Magdalene, whose women worshipers took the role of the holy women/goddesses of the myth, just as women cultists did in the Isis and Osiris faith.

RESHUFFLED RESURRECTION

As we now read the gospels, Mary and her sisters arrive at the tomb to anoint the body but do not get the opportunity, since the tomb is open and empty. To complete the parallel with the mythic prototype, we should expect to find a Jesus version of the scene in which the Isis analogue anoints Jesus to raise him from the dead. It might be disguised, rewritten, or even omitted, in which case we would be out of luck. But we are in luck, as it happens, for the scene has found a new home earlier in the sequence. It is, of course, the famous anointing scene at Bethany. The original story here has been refracted as well as redacted through many rewritings and retellings both prior to the gospels and since. The important core element is the notion that *the woman has saved the ointment for the day of*

Jesus's burial. This is most faithfully preserved in John's version: "Let her alone! Let her keep it for the day of my burial" (John 12:7). Mark and Matthew's version, no longer in touch with the original context of meaning, has reinterpreted the words, though not quite thoroughly, since they still manage to sound a bit odd in the context. "She has done what she could: she has anointed my body beforehand for burying" (Mark 14:8). "In pouring this ointment on my body, she has done it to prepare me for burial" (Matt. 26:12).

John's wording is still close enough to our hypothetical original in which *the anointing scene would have been part of the Easter morning narrative.* Mary and her female companions approach the tomb carrying the anointing materials. Apparently male disciples, too, are on the scene. It is their carping voices we hear, jeering at the waste of an expensive commodity that might better have been cashed in for the poor. This element has survived elsewhere as the story of Judas being paid off for betraying Jesus, with the silver finally going to charity (Matt. 27:7). More importantly, it is also of a piece with the disciples' skepticism about Jesus's resurrection typical of the gospels' Easter narratives. When the woman anoints the corpse of the Lord Jesus, Judas (or whoever) complains: Since he's dead anyway, why not use the ointment to some constructive purpose, like poor relief? So little does any hint of what is to come cross his mind. But once she anoints the body, it returns to life, and Jesus himself answers the petty objection. "She has saved it for my burial."

But was it Mary Magdalene who did the anointing? No gospel says so. But what do they say, and why? There is something mighty strange about the wording of Mark and Matthew:

"Amen: I say to you, wherever this gospel is proclaimed throughout the world, what she has done will be told in memory of her" (Matt. 26:13; Mark 14:9). And yet no name is given? The whole idea of memorializing the woman demands that her name be included. Thus originally it must have been. But it has subsequently been removed as part of the redactional effort to displace and disguise the original point. For the same reason, we might suspect, the anointing has been credited instead to Mary of Bethany in John 12:1–3 and to an unnamed "sinner" in Luke's wholly rewritten version (7:36–38). Her original identity may be hinted soon after, in the beginning of the very next chapter, when Mary Magdalene is introduced in Luke 8:2. John has simply switched Marys. But it must have been Mary Magdalene, whom we are told brought ointment to the tomb to do precisely what we are saying she did on that occasion: anoint the body—and, like Isis, bring it back to life.

One more point: The concluding notice that the anointing story shall always be told as an adjunct to Christian preaching is formulaic, implying it originated as part of a ritual recital. This links it to the character of the empty tomb story as a script for the mourning ritual leading up to the retelling or even reenactment of the anointing.

Just to be clear: I am far from saying this is the way the evangelists want us to read their narratives. No, my point is that they have inherited a version (a novelized version, as per my discussion in chapter 3, "Beyond the Cross") of the story in which the older, mythic character of it has been largely effaced. But that earlier version can still be plausibly discovered and reconstructed. And when we do, we discover Mary

Magdalene as the Christian goddess of the resurrection, the Anastasis.

MAGDALENE DILEMMA

I hope to have shown, not out of any preference or any desire to advocate theological revision, that a very good case can be mounted to the effect that Mary Magdalene is a historicized version of an underlying mythic redemptrix like the Egyptian Isis. But as I hinted in the discussion of Lynn Picknett and Clive Prince's *The Templar Revelation*, we cannot very well balance this theory off against the other option for glorifying Mary Magdalene, the one considered in chapter 8, "Mary Magdalene: Female Apostle?" That is, *either* we have a historical Mary who was said to be present at the tomb of Jesus and had unique, powerful visions of the Risen Christ and, on the basis of them, built an apostolic ministry, *or* we can make her a historicized goddess and cut loose the gospel story as any kind of history at all. Dan Brown, Lee Teabing, and some of our other related authors seem to think one can have both simultaneously, but one cannot. If we decide to use, for propaganda's sake, two arguments that are logically incompatible with one another, we are being as underhanded and opportunistic as the "winners" who we say rewrote Christian history to begin with.

NOTE

1. Paul Veyne, *Did the Greeks Believe in Their Myths?* (Chicago: University of Chicago Press, 1988), p. 88.

Conclusion

THE VITRUVIAN
SON OF MAN

New Testament scholarship is a challenging and fascinating field. And if *The Da Vinci Code* has awakened your interest in these matters, then you have no option but to undertake a thorough study of them yourself. In years to come, you will look back at your old, dog-eared copy of Brown's novel with fondness, recalling that it first prompted you to take a path that is immensely satisfying.

But there is one kind of satisfaction that critical New Testament research will *not* provide. It makes it pretty much impossible for the honest student to rest content with any conventional slate of beliefs. Once one approaches the questions of the historical Jesus and Christian origins, one is sentenced forever to carry the cross of tentativeness, of indecision. Dostoyevsky's Jesus (in *The Brothers Karamazov*) came to set upon us the burden of freedom, free thought, and free choice. And it is a cross. One cannot slough off one's responsibility to weigh all theories and to favor none beyond the strength of its evidence.

CONCLUSION

Faithfulness to the truth entails a stubborn unwillingness to decide prematurely that you have it. This is the problem with conservative Christian apologists who use the tools of historical criticism cynically in order to vindicate dogmatic beliefs they hold on other, prior, grounds. They have sacrificed the sincere search for truth, ironically, in the name of Christ.

Martin Kähler, Wilhelm Herrmann, Paul Tillich, and other nineteenth- and twentieth-century theologians saw things more clearly. They knew from experience what resulted if one based one's faith squarely on ostensibly historical events. You can't afford to admit even the possibility that it might turn out to be false! Since historical judgments are based on ever-new discoveries and reevaluations of the evidence, opinions about the past must always remain tentative and provisional. But faith, the commitment that guides one's life, cannot be so tentative. Thus one is faced with two alternatives. First, like our apologists, one may secretly sacrifice the honest conscience of the impartial historian and become a mere propagandist. Second, one may keep an open mind on all historical questions and base faith elsewhere. And for this, may I recommend a striking symbol: the Vitruvian Son of Man, a crucifix displaying Leonardo's famous spread-eagled human figure that is so important in Brown's *The Da Vinci Code*. I like the way the figure simultaneously displays all the possible postures of the limbs. It speaks of the intellectual posture of the serious student of Christian origins: one must remain open to all possibilities, arms stretched wide to catch any new idea, feet nimble to cover new territory as it appears. Not a dogma, but a stance.

As Tillich said, faith will no longer be an arbitrary assent to a set of assertions held in place by sheer willpower ("I believe

Jesus did this. I believe Jesus said that. What a good Christian am I!"). It becomes instead an existential risk, the risk of choosing a worthy path to follow. One sees the Jesus figure of the gospels (and it may differ in the eyes of different beholders, as in the Preaching of John!). One weighs the sayings ascribed to Jesus. Who knows how much the portrait of Jesus one sees is historical fact? Who knows who first said these words? It hardly matters. One remains faced with the call to discipleship as surely as the characters in those old stories were. We don't know for sure who or what Jesus was, but we can get a pretty good idea of what discipleship would mean just by reading the gospels. And then it is ours to decide whether that path is for us. For my part, one aspect of that discipleship would be the unflinching courage to follow historical evidence wherever it leads. It would mean carrying that cross of chafing uncertainties when I would rather settle down with the security blanket of pleasant beliefs.

BIBLIOGRAPHY

Addison, Charles G. *The History of the Knights Templars*. Kempton, IL: Adventures Unlimited Press, 1977.

Allegro, John M. *The Dead Sea Scrolls and the Christian Myth*. Devon, UK: Westbridge, 1979.

Anderson, J. N. D. *The Evidence for the Resurrection*. Downers Grove, IL: Inter-Varsity, 1974.

Andrews, Richard, and Paul Schellenberger. *The Tomb of God: The Body of Jesus and the Solution to a 2,000-Year-Old Mystery*. London: Little, Brown, 1996.

Atwood, Richard. *Mary Magdalene in the New Testament Gospels and Early Tradition*. European University Studies Series XXIII, vol. 457. New York: Peter Lang, 1993.

Baigent, Michael, Richard Leigh, and Henry Lincoln. *Holy Blood, Holy Grail*. New York: Dell, 1982, 1983.

Barber, Malcolm. *The Trial of the Templars*. Cambridge: Cambridge University Press, 1978.

Barnes, Timothy D. *Constantine and Eusebius*. Cambridge, MA: Harvard Unversity Press, 1981.

Bauer, Walter. *Orthodoxy and Heresy in Earliest Christianity*. Edited by

Robert A. Kraft and Gerhard Krodel. Translated by Philadelphia Seminar on Christian Origins. Philadelphia: Fortress, 1971.

Baur, Ferdinand Christian. *Paul the Apostle of Jesus Christ: His Life and Works, His Epistles and Teachings.* Two volumes in one. Translated by A. Menzies. Peabody: Hendrickson, 2003.

Beegle, Dewey M. *The Inspiration of Scripture.* Philadelphia: Westminster, 1963.

Beor, R. *Philo's Use of the Categories Male and Female.* Leiden, The Netherlands: Brill, 1970.

Berger, Peter L., and Thomas Luckmann. *The Social Construction of Reality: A Treatise in the Sociology of Knowledge.* Garden City, NY: Doubleday Anchor, 1967.

Blackhirst, Rod. "Barnabas and the Gospels: Was There an Early Gospel of Barnabas?" *Journal of Higher Criticism* 7, no. 1 (Spring 2000): 1–22.

Branham, William Marrion. *An Exposition of the Seven Church Ages.* Jefferson, IN: William Marrion Branham, n.d.

Brashler, James, and Roger A. Bullard, trans. "Apocalypse of Peter." In *Nag Hammadi Library in English,* ed. James M. Robinson, 3rd ed. New York: Harper & Row, 1988, pp. 372–78.

Brooke, John L. *The Refiner's Fire: The Making of Mormon Cosmology, 1644–1844.* New York: Cambridge University Press, 1994.

Brown, Dan. *The Da Vinci Code.* New York: Doubleday, 2003.

Brown, Raymond E. *The Community of the Beloved Disciple.* New York: Paulist, 1979.

———. *The Gospel according to John,* vol. 2. Garden City, NY: Doubleday, 1970.

Bruce, F. F. *Jesus and Christian Origins outside the New Testament.* Grand Rapids, MI: Eerdmans, 1974.

Bultmann, Rudolf. *The Gospel of John: A Commentary.* Translated by G. R. Beasley-Murray, R. W. Hoare, and J. K. Riches. Philadelphia: Westminster, 1971.

———. *Theology of the New Testament*, vol. 1. Translated by Kendrik Grobel. New York: Charles Scribner's Sons, 1951.

Burton, John. *The Collection of the Qur'an*. New York: Cambridge University Press, 1977.

Campenhausen, Hans von. *The Formation of the Christian Bible*. Translated by J. A. Baker. Philadelphia: Fortress, 1972.

Carson, D. A. *Exegetical Fallacies*. Grand Rapids, MI: Baker Book House, 1984.

Couchoud, P. L. *The Creation of Christ: An Outline of the Beginnings of Christianity*. Translated by C. Bradlaugh Bonner. London: Watts, 1939.

Couliano, Ioan P. *The Tree of Gnosis: Gnostic Mythology from Early Christianity to Modern Nihilism*. San Francisco: HarperSanFrancisco, 1992.

Crossan, John Dominic. *The Cross That Spoke: The Origins of the Passion Narrative*. San Francisco: Harper & Row, 1988.

Dafoe, Stephan. *Unholy Worship? The Myth of the Baphomet, Templar, Freemason Connection*. Belleville, ON: Templar Books, 1998.

Davies, Stevan L. *The Gospel of Thomas and Christian Wisdom*. New York: Seabury, 1983.

Dawood, N. J., trans. *The Koran*, 4th rev. ed. Baltimore: Penguin, 1974.

De Rougemont, Denis. *Love in the Western World*. Translated by Montgomery Belgion. Garden City, NY: Doubleday Anchor, 1957.

diCurcio, Robert A. *Vermeer's Riddle Revealed: The Sphinx, the Jester, and the Grail Geometry: Robert A. diCurcio's Analysis of Vermeer's Pictorial Compositions*. Nantucket, MA: Aeternium, 2002.

Divine Principle. New York: Holy Spirit Association for the Unification of World Christianity, 1973.

Dodds, E. R. *Pagan and Christian in an Age of Anxiety: Some Aspects of Religious Experience from Marcus Aurelius to Constantine*. New York: W. W. Norton, 1970.

Doherty, Earl. *The Jesus Puzzle: Did Christianity Begin with a Mythical Christ?* Ottawa: Canadian Humanist Publications, 1999.

Ehrman, Bart. *The Orthodox Corruption of Scripture: The Effect of Early Christological Controversies on the Text of the New Testament.* New York: Oxford University Press, 1993.

Elliott, T. G. *The Christianity of Constantine the Great.* Scranton, PA: University of Scranton Press, 1996.

Evans, C. F. *Resurrection and the New Testament.* Studies in Biblical Theology, Second Series 12. Naperville, IL: Allenson, 1970.

Fiorenza, Elisabeth Schüssler. *In Memory of Her: A Feminist Theological Reconstruction of Christian Origins.* New York: Crossroad, 1984.

Gardner, Laurence. *Bloodline of the Holy Grail: The Hidden Lineage of Jesus Revealed.* Rockport, MA: Element, 1996.

Girard, Rene. *The Scapegoat.* Translated by Yvonne Freccero. Baltimore: Johns Hopkins University Press, 1989.

Glaue, D. Paul. "Der älteste Text der geschichtlichen Bücher des Neuen Testaments." *Zeitschrift für neutestamentliche Wissenschaft und die Kunde der älteren Kirche* 45 (1954): 103.

Goffman, Erving. *The Presentation of Self in Everyday Life.* Garden City, NY: Doubleday Anchor, 1959.

Goodspeed, Edgar Johnson. *Famous Biblical Hoaxes: Originally Entitled, Modern Apocrypha.* Twin Brooks Series. Grand Rapids, MI: Baker Book House, 1956.

Grant, Robert M. *Eusebius as Church Historian.* Oxford: Clarendon Press, 1980.

———. *A Short History of the Interpretation of the Bible.* New York: Macmillan, 1963.

Graves, Robert, and Joshua Podoro. *The Nazarene Gospel Restored.* Garden City, NY: Doubleday, 1954.

Gregg, Robert C., and Dennis E. Groh. *Early Arianism: A View of Salvation.* Philadelphia: Fortress, 1981.

Harnack, Adolf von. *Marcion: The Gospel of the Alien God.* Translated by John E. Steely and Lyle D. Bierma. Durham, NC: Labyrinth Press, 1999.

Harrison, Robert, trans. *The Song of Roland*. New York: New American Library, 1970.

Helms, Randel. *Gospel Fictions*. Amherst, NY: Prometheus Books, 1988.

Hick, John, ed. *The Myth of God Incarnate*. Philadelphia: Westminster, 1977.

Hoffmann, R. Joseph. *Marcion: On the Restitution of Christianity: An Essay on the Development of Radical Paulinist Theology in the Second Century*. AAR Academy Series 46. Chico, CA: Scholars, 1984.

James, M. R., ed. and trans. *The Apocryphal New Testament*. Oxford: Clarendon Press, 1972.

Jeremias, Joachim. *The Eucharistic Words of Jesus*. Translated by Arnold Ehrhardt. Oxford: Basil Blackwell, 1955.

Jewett, Paul K. *Man as Male and Female*. Grand Rapids, MI: Eerdmans, 1976.

Joly, Robert. *Le vocabulaire chretien de l'amour est-il original? Φιλειν et Αγαπαν dans le grec antique*. Brussels: Presses Universitaires, 1968.

Jonas, Hans. *The Gnostic Religion: The Message of the Alien God and the Beginnings of Christianity*, rev. ed. Boston: Beacon, 1963.

Käsemann, Ernst. "Paul and Early Catholicism." In Käsemann, *New Testament Questions of Today*, translated by W. J. Montague. Philadelphia: Fortress, 1979, pp. 236–51.

Kermode, Frank. "Institutional Control of Interpretation." In Kermode, *The Art of Telling: Essays on Fiction*. Cambridge, MA: Harvard University Press, 1983, pp. 168–84.

Kern, H., trans. *Saddharma-Pundarika, or Lotus of the True Law*. New York: Dover, 1963.

King, Karen L. *The Gospel of Mary of Magdala: Jesus and the First Woman Apostle*. Santa Rosa, CA: Polebridge, 2003.

BIBLIOGRAPHY

Klein, T. E. D. "Nadelman's God." In Klein, *Dark Gods*. New York: Bantam Books, 1986.

Knight, Christopher, and Robert Lomas. *The Hiram Key: Pharaohs, Freemasons and the Discovery of the Secret Scrolls of Jesus*. Rockport, MA: Element, 1997.

Knox, John. *Marcion and the New Testament: An Essay in the Early History of the Canon*. Chicago: University of Chicago Press, 1942.

Loomis, Roger Sherman. *The Grail: From Celtic Myth to Christian Symbol*. New York: Columbia University Press, 1963.

Maccoby, Hyam. *The Sacred Executioner: Human Sacrifice and the Legacy of Human Guilt*. New York: Thames & Hudson, 1982.

Mack, Burton L. *The Lost Gospel: The Book of Q and Christian Origins*. San Francisco: HarperSanFrancisco, 1993.

Madaule, Jacques. *The Albigensian Crusade: An Historical Essay*. Translated by Barbara Wall. New York: Fordham University Press, 1967.

Marxsen, Willi. *The New Testament as the Church's Book*. Translated by James E. Mignard. Philadelphia: Fortress, 1972.

———. *The Resurrection of Jesus of Nazareth*. Translated by Margaret Kohl. Philadelphia: Fortress, 1979.

Mead, G. R. S. *Did Jesus Live 100 B.C.?* New York: University Books, 1968.

Miller, Robert J., ed. *The Complete Gospels: Annotated Scholars Version*. Sonoma, CA: Polebridge Press, 1992.

Mollenkott, Virginia Ramey. *Women, Men & the Bible*. Nashville, TN: Abingdon, 1977.

Munro, Winsome. *Authority in Paul and Peter: The Identification of a Pastoral Stratum in the Pauline Corpus and I Peter*. Society for New Testament Studies Monograph Series 45. New York: Cambridge University Press, 1983.

Napier, Gordon. *The Rise and Fall of the Knights Templar: The Order of the Temple, 1118–1314, True History of Faith, Glory, Betrayal and Tragedy*. Staplehurst, UK: Spellmount, 2003.

Nicholson, Helen. *The Knights Templar: A New History*. Stroud, UK: Sutton, 2001.

Nutt, Alfred. *Studies on the Legend of the Holy Grail with Especial Reference to the Hypothesis of Celtic Origin*. New York: Cooper Square, 1965.

Pagels, Elaine. *The Gnostic Gospels*. New York: Random House, 1979.

Partner, Peter. *The Murdered Magicians: The Templars and Their Myth*. New York: Oxford University Press, 1982.

Patai, Raphael. *The Hebrew Goddess*. New York: Avon Discus, 1978.

Patterson, Stephen J. *The Gospel of Thomas and Jesus*. Sonoma, CA: Polebridge, 1993.

Perdue, Lewis. *The Da Vinci Legacy*. New York: Tor, 2004.

Perkins, Pheme. *The Gnostic Dialogue*. New York: Paulist, 1980.

Philostratus, Flavius. *The Life of Apollonius of Tyana*. Translated by F. C. Conybeare. Loeb Classical Library no. 17, vol 2.

Pick, Bernhard. *Jesus in the Talmud*. Chicago: Open Court, 1913.

Picknett, Lynn, and Clive Prince. *The Templar Revelation: Secret Guardians of the True Identity of Christ*. New York: Simon & Schuster, 1997.

Quispel, Gilles. "The Birth of the Child: Some Gnostic and Jewish Aspects." In *Eranos Lectures 3*. Dallas: Spring Publications, 1987, pp. 1–26.

Ralls, Karen. *The Templars and the Grail: Knights of the Quest*. Wheaton, IL: Theosophical Publishing House/Quest Books, 2003.

Reardon, B. P., ed. *Collected Ancient Greek Novels*. Berkeley: University of California Press, 1989.

Richardson, Robert. "The Priory of Sion Hoax." *Alpheus: Site for Esoteric History* [online]. http://www.alpheus.org/html/articles/esoteric_history/richardson1.html.

Ridley, Jasper. *The Freemasons: A History of the World's Most Powerful Secret Society*. New York: Arcade Books, 2002.

BIBLIOGRAPHY

Roberts, Alexander, and James Donaldson, eds. *Ante-Nicene Christian Library*, vol. 16: *Apocryphal Gospels, Acts, and Revelations*. Edinburgh, UK: T&T Clark, 1870.

Robinson, H. Wheeler. *The Religious Ideas of the Old Testament*, 2nd ed. London: Duckworth, 1956.

Robinson, James M., ed. *Nag Hammadi Library in English*, 3rd ed. New York: Harper & Row, 1988.

Robinson, James M., and Helmut Koester. *Trajectories through Early Christianity*. Philadelphia: Fortress, 1971.

Robinson, John J. *Dungeon, Fire and Sword: The Knights Templar in the Crusades*. New York: M. Evans, 1992.

Runciman, Steven. *The Medieval Manichee: A Study of the Christian Dualist Heresy*. New York: Viking Press, 1961.

Rylands, L. Gordon. *The Beginnings of Gnostic Christianity*. London: Watts, 1940.

Sanello, Frank, and William Travis Hanes. *The Knights Templars: God's Warriors, the Devil's Bankers*. Lanham, MD: Taylor, 2003.

Sawicki, Marianne. "Magdalenes and Tiberiennes: City Women in the Entourage of Jesus." In *Transformative Encounters: Jesus and Women Re-viewed*, ed. Ingrid Rosa Kitzberger. Leiden, The Netherlands: Brill, 2000.

Scanzoni, Letha, and Nancy Hardesty. *All We're Meant to Be*. Waco, TX: Word, 1975.

Schaberg, Jane. *The Resurrection of Mary Magdalene: Legends, Apocrypha, and the Christian Testament*. New York: Continuum, 2002.

Schmithals, Walter. *Gnosticism in Corinth*. Translated by John E. Steely. New York: Abingdon, 1971.

———. *The Office of Apostle in the Early Church*. Translated by John E. Steely. New York: Abingdon, 1969.

Scholer, David M. "Why Such Current Interest in the Ancient Gnostic 'Heresy'?" *Faith and Thought* 1, no. 2 (Summer 1983): 22–26.

———. "Women's Adornment: Some Historical and Hermeneutical Observations on the New Testament Passages." *Daughters of Sarah* 6, no. 1 (January/February 1980): 3–6.

Schonfield, Hugh J. *According to the Hebrews*. London: Duckworth, 1937.

———. *The Passover Plot: New Light on the History of Jesus*. New York: Bernard Geis, 1965.

Segal, Robert A., ed. *The Allure of Gnosticism: The Gnostic Experience in Jungian Psychology and Contemporary Culture*. Chicago: Open Court, 1995.

Smith, Morton. *Jesus the Magician*. New York: Harper & Row, 1978.

———. *The Secret Gospel: The Discovery and Interpretation of the Secret Gospel according to Mark*. New York: Harper & Row, 1973.

Strauss, David Friedrich. *The Life of Jesus Critically Examined*. Edited by Peter C. Hodgson. Translated by George Eliot. Lives of Jesus Series. Philadelphia: Fortress Press, 1972.

———. *Life of Jesus for the People*, vol. 1. London: Williams, 1879.

Talbert, Charles H. *Luke and the Gnostics*. Nashville, TN: Abingdon, 1966.

———. *What Is a Gospel? The Genre of the Canonical Gospels*. Philadelphia: Fortress, 1977.

Thiering, Barbara. "The Date and Unity of the Gospel of Philip." *Journal of Higher Criticism* 2, no. 1 (Spring 1995): 102–11.

———. *Jesus and the Riddle of the Dead Sea Scrolls: Unlocking the Secrets of His Life Story*. New York: HarperCollins, 1992.

———. *Jesus the Man: A New Interpretation from the Dead Sea Scrolls*. London: Corgi, 1993.

———. "The Unholy Grail: Notes on Laurence Gardner's *The Bloodline of the Holy Grail*" [online]. http://groups.yahoo.com/group/qumran_origin/.

Veyne, Paul. *Did the Greeks Believe in Their Myths?* Chicago: University of Chicago Press, 1988.

BIBLIOGRAPHY

Wells, G. A. *The Jesus of the Early Christians: A Study in Christian Origins.* London: Pemberton, 1971.

Wiles, Maurice. *Archetypal Heresy: Arianism through the Centuries.* Oxford University Press, 1996.

Zindler, Frank R. "Where Jesus Never Walked." *American Atheist* (Winter 1996–97): 41–42.

INDEX

SCRIPTURE INDEX

SCRIPTURE INDEX